NOW WE
ARE 40

NOW WE ARE 40

WHATEVER HAPPENED TO
GENERATION X?

TIFFANIE DARKE

HarperCollins*Publishers*

HarperCollins*Publishers*
1 London Bridge Street
London SE1 9GF

www.harpercollins.co.uk

First published by HarperCollins*Publishers* 2017
This edition 2018

A catalogue record of this book is
available from the British Library

ISBN 978-0-00-832057-7

Printed and bound in Great Britain by
CPI Group (UK) Ltd, Croydon, CR0 4YY

MIX
Paper from
responsible sources
FSC
www.fsc.org
FSC™ C007454

This book is produced from independently certified FSC paper
to ensure responsible forest management.

For more information visit: www.harpercollins.co.uk/green

The carapace of coolness is too much for Claire, also.
She breaks the silence by saying that it's not healthy
to live life as a succession of isolated little cool
moments. 'Either our lives become stories, or
there's just no way to get through them.'

Douglas Coupland, *Generation X*

Contents

Going Up, Going Down

When I edited the *Sunday Times Style* magazine, the 'Going Up, Going Down' column became something of a cult read. Readers furiously measured themselves against it: were they still wearing one of the trends we would cruelly consign to 'Going Down'? Were they already ordering the cocktail that we would crown in 'Going Up'? A shortcut to everything that is in and out of favour, like the best journalism the column was born of instinct, wit and inside knowledge. Or just how ravaging our hangovers were on a Thursday morning.

This is my version of what it's like being in your forties.

UP

Boden
Strangely good these days

Zoopla and Rightmove
Better than sex

Food
OBSESSED. When your buckwheat risotto says more about you than your vintage Prada

Witness the fitness
The Iron Man entry form is the new trophy wife; sleeveless
*   dresses the status symbol of acceptable upper-arm tone*

Paaarty!
The skills are honed

Our kids
A confetti canon of love on permanent explosion

Home economics
What you used to spend on shoes, you now spend on
*   mid-century modern furniture*

Wise, but not smug
Yep – we know stuff now. But we still want to know more

Cool
Still like it. Love it actually

DOWN

Hangovers
Crucifying. And getting worse

Luxury labels
So new money. Unless it's Gucci. Or Balenciaga. Do keep up

Having it all
Overrated

Smartphones
Remember that time when we used to go places with people
*   and do things? Walk along the street without bumping into*
*   people? No, me neither*

Botox denial
Don't get left behind, pruneface

God
Who?

Parenting
Torturous, difficult, exhausting, boring, life-limiting, endless

Money
Suddenly, irritatingly, an issue

Weight
Hmm. Getting a little harder to shift ...

Music
Rubbish now. How are you meant to find anything good in this sea of overchoice? No, I do not want another fricking app

Time
Just gone

Introduction
Don't Grow Up – It's a Trick

In the summer of 1991 I was waitressing at Pizza Hut on Bournemouth High Street. It was before I went up to university, and I was living at home, saving everything I could to go backpacking around some third world country. In the background R.E.M.'s 'Shiny Happy People' was playing, as was the KLF's 'Last Train to Trancentral'. The Soviet Union was breaking up, Operation Desert Storm had come to an end, and Sega had released *Sonic the Hedgehog*. Tim Berners-Lee announced the World Wide Web project, but not many people noticed. It was also raining rather a lot.

Those waitressing wages were not great, nor were the tips, but they were enough to fund an adventure around India, where my money would go far and my experiences would be all my own. Well, mine and all the other thousands of backpackers shacked up beside me in the Lonely Planet hostels. Once there, I would live in tie-dye trousers, wonder at the extraordinary cacophony of religions, dance at full moon parties, drink a lot of chai latte and inevitably buy some dodgy drapes.

That summer I was also reading Douglas Coupland's novel *Generation X*. Only recently published, it was already something of a hit. In the book, Coupland portrayed our generation as a listless, directionless, cynical bunch of slackers who drifted from one McJob to the next in search of a thrill. It perfectly encapsulated my life at the time, as I saw no inconsistency between serving the Four Cheese pizza to a bunch of post-pub Bournemouth lads and studying Ancient Greek at Corpus Christi College, Oxford. That was me, that was us.

So what has happened to Generation X? Have we been forgotten? If you check your emails and Facebook feeds, your Google alerts and hashtags, you will see that most conversation now is about this group of people called Millennials. Millennials, we are reminded constantly, work hard, are annoyingly entitled, love an artisanal coffee and a skinny jean, and are changing the culture, reshaping society and rewriting the rule book of living.

Or everyone goes on about Boomers. How they've got all the money and all the houses and really are only just getting started, because everyone lives for hundreds of years now, and their big, fat final-salary pensions mean they have decades of Saga holidays ahead. Not cruises – no one goes on cruises any more, that's so Pensioners from the Last Century. Boomers go wolf trekking in Eritrea and swipe right on silver Tinder. Pass the Châteauneuf, old girl!

Where are Generation X in all this? The generation also nick-named 'Middle Youth' because we were young and cool for so long, and so good at it no one could beat us at our game. No one, that is, till those pesky digital natives came along, who were suddenly so much better at the internet and stuff, and the Recession hit, which turned the tables, and quite a few of us have kids now, which makes the pursuit of cool and youth look a tiny bit tragic. And tragic is the ultimate Middle Youth crime.

But, I would argue (particularly as I am one) – Generation X are still cool! Cool not just by a hierarchy of self-expression ranked through our fashion, music, design and friend choices. The important thing about our coolness is our irony. We fully embrace irony, in as much as we see things exactly for what they are, and we stand just a little apart from them. It makes us more knowing, and we value that. We can even do it about ourselves – we laugh at our own Middle Youthness. The only slightly self-aware Millennial is Lena Dunham. But we are Caitlin Moran, Tina Fey, Sharon Horgan, Simon Pegg, Amy Poehler and Sheryl Sandberg.

(Okay, maybe not Sandberg. One doesn't imagine a whole lot of irony going down there. For those of you who have never read *Lean In* because the thought of it makes you feel tired: I am told it is a very good female tract on living and not bossy at all. I myself have ordered several copies on the internet. They are stacked, like intellectual trophies, next to my bed with all the other books I should read and don't because I'm too busy being TATT (tired all the time) or more likely, leaning in, checking my Instagram feed. By the way, it was a Millennial who invented Instagram. Kevin Systrom. He was 26 years old.)

It is not just irony that has distinguished us, but our liberalism. Britain today is a very different place to the country we inherited 25 years ago. Yes, many people have grumbled about 'political correctness' along the way, but the facts are we currently have a female prime minister and female leaders of the Scottish National Party, Plaid Cymru, the Green Party and the Democratic Unionist Party in Northern Ireland. The US voted a black president into the White House and narrowly missed voting in a woman; senior political party members, heads of business and Church are now openly gay. Race, sexuality and gender politics have come a long way, thanks to us.

We have also placed a much higher value on emotional intelligence and happiness – everyone you know might be retraining as a psychotherapist, but that has given us the tools to be better behaved to our loved ones, to know ourselves a little more.

We have advanced the idea that looking after ourselves extends not just to the emotional, but the physical too. Okay, so dancing all night wasn't quite the fitness training we wanted it to be, but we all do triathlons, bike rides and bootcamps now. We try and eat five portions of fruit and vegetables a day, we know sugar is bad, we check our breasts for lumps and men even know where their prostate is (if they haven't actually found it yet).

We were the first to make food a mainstream cultural art form, to democratise fashion, to insist on a soundtrack, to recraft our living spaces, to search meaningfully for spirituality outside the confines of the Church, to fuel the proliferation of art, television, restaurants and nightclubs. Our love of rave went on to inspire the hip hotel trend of dressing every lobby like a chillout room, while our love of travelling has fuelled a truly globalised culture in food, fashion and design.

Our social fixes are charities like Comic Relief, Greenpeace, Amnesty International, War Child, Smart Works: organisations that actively seek to redress the inequalities in the world. This is what we care about the most. Fired by youth and entitlement, in its early years of power Generation X set out to create a world that did not judge you for your colour, your nationality, who you fancied or what sex you were. It is your values, your ideas and your thoughts that distinguish you instead.

And now, that world is beginning to look a little shaky. The year 2016 brought democratic earthquakes in the shape of Brexit and Trump that look like they may be undermining much of the progress we made and fought to achieve. And we are no longer young. We are, more or less, in our forties. And being in your forties certainly makes you look in the mirror and reflect. So this seems a timely moment for something of a calibration. Where have we come from (good times!), and where are we going (uncertain ones)? It's hard to have a moment in front of the mirror these days that doesn't feel tinged with nostalgia. For instance, it is rare you go 'Look – wrinkles. What fabulous proof that I am so wise from experience and laughing so hard.' Mostly it's 'Wrinkles – you bastards. Why is the Protect and Perfect not working?' And you reach for another green juice.

The rebellion we felt in our adolescence and early youth is still there, but what are we going to do with it now? Have we really shaped society in the way we all wanted and, now we are in positions of power, how are we going to lay things down for ourselves and our children in the future?

Are we riven by midlife crisis or are we, in fact, only just coming of age? Excitingly, our best could be yet to come. As the designer Alice Temperley puts it: 'I've got to the point where I feel I've grown up. Where I realise what's wrong and what's right and what's important in life. I've worked hard to get to this point and now I feel poised to take it to the next stage.'

Danny Goffey, the musician once of Supergrass and now Vangoffey (Sample song: 'Trials of the Modern Man'), points out it was not Coupland who coined the term 'Generation X' but Billy Idol, the musician from Middlesex who used the name for his punk band in the Seventies. Idol had sourced the title from one of his mother's books, a study by two English journalists on Mod subculture in the Sixties. The interviews detailed a culture of promiscuous and anti-establishment youth, something Coupland saw as characterising the kids he was describing in his novel. Generation X is the child of the sixties, the child of punk. These movements before us evolved us, their values sit deep inside us.

Nowadays demographers commonly assign the X generation to those born between the Sixties and early Eighties; those after are known as Generation Y, or Millennials, and our kids are to be known as Generation Z, or Centennials (born after the turn of the century). Meanwhile our parents are the postwar generation, or Baby Boomers, born in the aftermath of the shattering devastation in the middle of the last century. Theirs has been a life of relative peace and prosperity, and they have benefited from enormous capital growth and social investment. The gap now between their experience and those of Millennials is perfectly illustrated in average income – despite being retired, Boomers have a higher income than the average working Millennial. Meanwhile it is the Millennials (and of course X-ers) who are paying those Boomers their income in the form of pensions.

What makes X-ers really interesting, though, is that we had the Nineties. The last decade before the internet hit, before smartphones connected us to everything, at every moment; the time when further education was free, housing was just about affordable, and, crucially, when wave after wave of youth culture crashed on our shores, each new wave a brilliant reaction to the one that went before. Oh kids, you missed out there. And Boomers – sorry you were too busy working to really enjoy them.

The Nineties were an adventure in cool. Out of grunge – a literal rejection of everything that came before it – came heroin chic (yes, drugs are cool – even the bad bits!), Britpop, logo-mania, Paul Smith, the Inspiral Carpets, John Galliano, Soho House, Alexander McQueen, Kate Moss, the Gallaghers, Quaglino's, *The Word*, Blur, Marc Jacobs, Marco Pierre White, the Turner Prize, *Loaded* magazine, pickled sharks, rave, Liam 'n' Patsy, Helmut Lang, superclubs, the Wonderbra, *The Big Breakfast*, *Trainspotting*, Chris Evans, Pulp, the Spice Girls, Tate Modern – I could go on.

In one short summer – let's take 1997 – Tony Blair was elected, the Prodigy released *The Fat of the Land*, Oasis dropped *Be Here Now* and Diana died. That was in just four months, like the arc of a single night: the build, the high, the comedown. We were crowned Cool Britannia, because right then and there, there was nowhere else in the world culturally more exciting.

There is no such roll call of cool that exists for the Noughties (Ellie Goulding, anyone?), or indeed the decade we are currently in, because instant access and transparency now conspire to make culture a pretty homogeneous mass. There are no definitive fashion trends or musical movements as everyone has access to everything everywhere and tribalism has died. Working-class culture is pretty much consigned to the scrapheap as changes to the welfare state mean there is no lifeline on which working-class artists or musicians or writers can survive and thrive. They must instead take a zero hours contract in a call centre. The Nineties, however, were the product of the disenfranchisement our generation felt during the Thatcher years, strong responses to a changing economy and society.

This was reinforced by our methods of communication: in the Nineties we physically went places to meet up, swap hairstyles and be cool, whether it was a club or a record shop or a field or a street or a store. We didn't connect on chatrooms or on WhatsApp groups. We did it face to face, in places where we met other people who expressed themselves like us, and we exchanged ideas and hung out with each other and felt our rebellion communally. Together, in self-selected communities, we practised large-scale irreverence and cynicism of everything outside of our own group, but together we were fiercely strong and loyal.

Physically showing up to something gave our communities a validity and a value that today's virtual communities cannot share. Nineties tribes were not just about how you looked – they were also about how you actually behaved, where you went, who you were with, what you did when you got there. You couldn't tell lies about that, like you can now on social media – there were no filters or hashtags. Communities were something you did together, on a dancefloor or in a pub, sharing a feeling, not alone in a bedroom, staring into a screen all on your own. As a result our communities, whether that be our friendship group or our cultural tribe, were awesomely strong and meaningful to us (while they lasted). We were the new, with the big ideas and the modern outlook and the future.

Yuppies, a job for life, Thatcherism – by the Nineties they were all over; a broken dream. The crash and Black Friday put paid to that, as did the housing market and negative equity and all those redundancies. Money was for losers, with hideous values – experience was what we valued. And government? It gave us the Poll Tax and the Criminal Justice Bill. Instead, we chose the Summer of Love and ecstasy and eco protesters and Swampy. We were Greenpeace and gay culture (not everyone was gay, not yet – it took the Millennials to progress that far, but lots of us were and the rest were our best friends), and we used marketing, PR, television and festivals to take everything that was cool and below the radar and counter-cultural and make it ours. We took it and celebrated it and commoditised it and marketed it and turned it into the mainstream – *our* mainstream.

Our idea of family was more fluid. Weddings got bigger and bigger as getting married became less about commitment and more about making a social statement and throwing a party. Sex and sexuality loosened, Europe opened up and cheap travel blossomed – no one batted an eyelid at a weekend in Prague, a night in Paris or the NY-LON (New York–London) commute. As the Nineties wore on, our liberal values became common currency. We were changing the world by the day and fashioning it in our own image.

London began, like a gravitational field, to attract everything from around it and pull it in as it accelerated into the future. Wealth creation was moving into the capital and the cultural benefits we enjoyed from Manchester, Bristol, Stoke, Glasgow, Sheffield, Cardiff and more, were hoovered up. As Alex James, the bassist from Blur, says, 'Although Britpop made us cringe and Cool Britannia made us want to self-harm, we were just so lucky to live in this tiny country with such a huge city in it. For the whole of my adult life, London has been the engine driving everything. At the beginning of the Nineties I arrived in London for my first term at Goldsmiths College. I'm getting out of my parents' car with a guitar and Graham Coxon [also a member of Blur] is getting out of his parents' car with a guitar and that was it – fasten your seat belt! It was, and still is, the place where anything can happen and dreams can come true. And they do, nightly.'

The Nineties were the launch pad for Generation X and we came out of it thinking we were pretty special. But not everything that happened turned out to be so good, and there were consequences that we are only just now beginning to realise. I'm 44, I surfed the media circus through my own career until, in 2002, I landed at the *Sunday Times Style* magazine where, as editor, I tracked the lifestyles of our generation for the next twelve years. Constantly on the lookout for a fresh trend, I was always baffled that it was our age group that continued to define the culture. I had grown up with *The Face* and *Arena*, two great channels to cool that did not survive the arrival of magazines like my own.

It was becoming increasingly difficult to find something unknown, or below the radar, as our generation was busy defining everything and selling it back to everyone. We quite categorically refused to make way for those coming up behind us, by giving them nothing to rebel against. The kiss of death, the goodbye to cool was if your mum thought it was good. Rock 'n' roll, punk, gender bender, acid house and grunge were not liked by parents at all, which conferred on them instant cool. But as eternal Peter Pans, Generation X-ers have never found anything the kids have done distasteful. We share clothes now with our daughters, get breast jobs done together, even get matching tattoos. What's the glamour in doing a line of cocaine if your dad does it? So the generation below have had to become dull, they have had no choice. They drink less, have less sex, go out less. The best they have come up with is 'normcore'.

So are we, finally, in our forties, past it now? As Millennials and tech power us even faster into the future, are we going to get left behind? Many of us are embracing it, plenty of us feel paranoid about it, and some of us are being total dicks about it. One technology executive recently wrote: 'Millennial is a nice stamp that marketers use, but it's not necessarily about age. It's more about looking at the things you have an affinity with, regardless of age. I'm 47, but I class myself as a Millennial because I have Millennial tendencies. I'm a lot more active on social media than my peers, for instance.'

God forbid we should be the sad dad trying to breakdance with the kids, but then how do we make sure our experience and the lessons we have learned meld productively with the passion, energy and excitement of the new youth? Millennials are not going to be able to pay us the sorts of pensions we are currently paying out to Boomers, so if that's the case, how are we going to find the roles in society where we can work side by side and really benefit each other? How can we ensure we are not 'bedblocking the best jobs' (as one headline had it recently) but instead creating opportunities for all, enjoying what everyone has to offer and finding real, meaningful roles for ourselves, our parents and our youngers? What can we teach Millennials from our experiences about balancing work, life and family, job satisfaction, social cohesion, emotional stamina, physical fitness and social values?

And just as importantly, how are *we* going to cope with life from here on in? What's it going to look like for us post menopause (Christ!) or when we qualify for our free bus pass? The world is in disruption – our liberalism is under attack on both sides of the Atlantic, the model for everything from fashion to news is breaking down, Christianity is in rapid decline, extremism is on the up, whole populations are on the move, happiness levels are at their lowest ever recorded – how will we emerge?

What I do know is that I will still be working to pay off my mortgage (at least I have one), with no pension to support me in my beach habit (it won't be golf). Sometimes I put on a miniskirt and (a lot of) make-up and I can go to a club where no one can see very well and I can party all night – but then it takes me a week to recover. I know the hippest place in London to order a slider and I can name Beyoncé's last single and the first one to leave One Direction (Zayn, my friends). I am on Snapchat (don't use it) and still collect rare trainers, but the truth is I am also a knackered mum who gets her kicks from surfing the specials on Ocado and shouting at the neighbours to keep the noise down.

Occasionally I'll book a weekend away, but I'll look forward to it not for the sex, but the sleep. I still go to Ibiza but these days it's the yoga teacher's number I have on Favourites. I have Mary Beard and Madonna's unauthorised biography on my bedside table. (Mary Beard is filed under Sheryl Sandberg. Madonna's biog is well thumbed.) I have even begun to order soup for starters.

I live life in between young and old. I am neither Boomer nor Millennial. I am still an absolutely cynical witch who likes to do naughty things and wants to burn down the establishment – except, I *am* the establishment now. From government ministers to CEOs, the family GP to my kids' headmistress – they are all my age. Once the rulebreakers, now *we* are the rulemakers. Like a zombie, I teach my kids to be good and recite their times tables and respect their teachers and work hard so they can go to university and get a good job. For what? – as I might have asked 25 years ago.

So are we just a bunch of directionless cynics who have now hit middle age and feel a bit sad and conformist? Do we know what we're doing next, or are we not sure, as all the exciting stuff seems to have migrated to either side of us? How have we retained our rulebreaking and innovation, how have we changed the world and how are going to go on changing it? Did we free ourselves from the daily grind as we always hoped we would, or just create a new cage to live in? And do appearances – the threads, the 'do, the language, the who, the what and the where – really still matter?

Here's my evidence. You decide.*

* Rule Number 1 of a features journalist: it takes three examples to make a trend. And once you've got a trend, you've got a feature. Features journalism is based entirely on subjectivity and three randomly encountered examples. For the purposes of this book I have interviewed slightly more than three people, but I am claiming equal subjectivity – mine, and theirs. Any time you get distracted, just turn to the Appendix where you can learn fun things about the handful of people I talked to. It's nice, easy reading – what we features journalists would call a 'sidebar'.

1

I Was Eight in the Eighties

I was eight when the Eighties began. Too young to live them, but old enough to be knocked around by what was going on. I got my info from John Craven on *Newsround*, Bruce Parker on *South Today* and *Smash Hits* magazine. I remember the Falklands War and the sinking of the *Belgrano*, probably around the time Wham! entered my orbit. Of course, Thatcher was a consistent backdrop (my parents, traumatised by the economics of the Seventies and being utterly broke, were breathless for her and would not hear a word against her in the house). The miners' strike was a thing, but it was a long way away from Bournemouth, where my dad had taken up a job as a vascular surgeon. He was a big believer in the NHS being run by passion and vocation, and the importance of public services, but Maggie's privatisation schemes were all good – and private medical practice served my dad pretty well.

Being an adolescent in Bournemouth was actually really fun: there were beaches in the summertime and boys with boats, there was a Wimpy bar that served Knickerbocker Glories and a cinema or two (I saw *Desperately Seeking Susan* on my first date), and there was an ice rink where my friends would have birthday parties. We'd hang out on bikes in the park – I had a Gresham Flyer, which was denim blue. My brother's BMX had a much comfier seat but the handlebars were a bit weird.

Then a roller disco opened and that felt pretty edgy – a daytime nightclub and sexy women skating round in miniskirts and legwarmers. One was a steward named Hayley, with long, blonde hair and a pneumatic body. She had a red pleated mini-skirt like the women in Bucks Fizz wore in 'Making Your Mind Up' and she was the prettiest girl in the rink. Ask any boy from Bournemouth what he likes best about his hometown and he'll tell you it's the girls.

But mostly I remember *Top of the Pops*, and me and my friend Lizzie religiously learning all the words to the songs like they were lines in a play. I would record the Top 40 on Sunday night on a cassette tape so I could go through it all the next week copying the lyrics down into an exercise book – 'Hey Mickey' by Tony Basil, Howard Jones, the Thompson Twins. I had a picture of Wham! on my wall – my party trick then (and now) was to recite all the words to the 'Wham Rap'. I properly fancied Andrew Ridgeley. He was my first crush. *Smash Hits* did a pullout centrespread of him and George that I tacked on to my Laura Ashley wallpaper. Then Mum had another baby and we got an au pair who had this really weird short haircut with a side parting and she loved the Human League. And so began my fascination with cool: something remote I didn't quite under-stand but absolutely wanted to be part of.

This was a world with no internet, no mobile phones and just three TV stations. Everyone sat down together and watched *Saturday Swap Shop* and *Tiswas*, shows that would foreshadow *The Big Breakfast* and *The Word*. You couldn't stream *Dallas* and *Dynasty* in bulk episodes, you had to wait until Saturday night, and watch them episodically week by week. They depicted Reagan's America, an off-the-wall land of excess, where ranch-ers drank whisky and drilled for oil, women inhaled champagne and sported massive shoulder pads, and everyone was a total bitch to each other. The whole thing looked incredible. My parents wouldn't let my brother and me watch either of them to begin with, but they were quite often out on a Saturday night, so we used to pour the babysitter enormous gin and tonics (my dad thought it was very important we knew how to pour a gin and tonic; it made us useful around the house) then sneak downstairs and watch them over her shoulder through the crack in the door.

The nation's station was Radio 1: Bruno Brookes, Dave Lee Travis, Mike Reid and Simon Bates's Our Tune. We did things together as a nation, communally, and we went places to meet each other face to face. Girlfriends would phone in the evening to chat on the phone and my dad would be furious to discover me still on the line 40 minutes later – not only was he footing the bill but he was also on-call to the hospital and there was no other way for emergency care to get hold of him. No Skype or mobiles back then.

Eventually I was allowed to take the bus into town on my own and watch the high street change around me. Bournemouth was a town that had been known as God's Waiting Room when we arrived. It was full of retirement flats and blue rinses, but it started to thrive under Thatcher's economy, and the average age of the population plummeted. I began to rebel against my mum's choice of wardrobe for me – she loved all those Eighties bright colours. There was a big C&A at the top of the town that peddled this stuff, along with a Chelsea Girl, an Etam, Tammy Girl and Dorothy Perkins. The high street was not cool back then, not by a long way. It was cheap clothes in nasty fabrics with lairy designs.

Mum eventually relented and gave me a clothes allowance, and I got a pair of pixie boots and a trilby hat on a trip to London to Kensington Market. Then the Body Shop opened in Bournemouth and every Saturday I'd go there to buy peppermint foot lotion and cocoa butter. The Body Shop felt cool: it had all these messages about not being tested on animals, and there was talk of the tribal heartlands where the ingredients were sourced.

Social consciousness began to register. Sting brought an Amazonian warrior onto *Wogan*, Greenpeace set up shop on the high street, and my mum and I used to cry over the whaling footage on the six o' clock news. We both signed up to Greenpeace and would cheer on the *Rainbow Warrior*. As the TV presenter and entrepreneur Richard Reed says: 'Greenpeace were the great disruptors and agitators. They were really high profile when we were growing up – they approached everything in a way you couldn't help have empathy with.'

Reed, who went on to make millions out of his company Innocent Smoothies when he sold it to Coca-Cola, still supports Greenpeace as publicly as he can. 'It's a charity that gets up people's noses and creates problems and difficulties. And I say Yes, that is exactly its role. I went on a trip with them to the Amazon to look at the light they shine on deforestation. Multinational companies that ship the world's grains and seeds, actively involved in illegal deforestation – how can they get away with that?'

The environmental movement was just being born: suddenly everyone was talking about the ozone layer, the CFC scandal kickstarting a boom in roll-on deodorants. Environmental protests against road-building at Newbury, Twyford Down and Fairmile, Devon – which made a hero of the hapless 'Swampy' – saw protestors tie themselves to trees and digging tunnels.

Nelson Mandela was also still in jail and, against a backdrop of sanctions and anti-apartheid campaigning, racism seemed the most illogical injustice the human race was capable of committing. I was old enough to go to Wembley for the Free Nelson Mandela concert, and lap up all the books and films – from *Cry Freedom* to *Disgrace* – that dominated our cultural youth. Over in the States NWA were fighting prejudice on different fronts, and rap and hip hop culture, threaded with political protest, was booming. The Rodney King riots were to burn all that home to me.

And then came the graphic pictures of starving Africans crawling across their drought-ridden plains, their bellies swollen, flies feasting on their saucer-shaped, tear-filled eyes. It was a new frontier in television reporting, prompting a scruffy rock star to leap onto news studio sofas and catalyse the rescue package. Band Aid, Live Aid: we were very aware as we were growing up that there was plenty to fix in the world, and it was going to be up to us to fix it.

Spiritually, questions were beginning to come up. I went to church a bit as a girl, and opted to get confirmed when I was around 13. Ironically, it was this process – even if I did in the end take my confirmation, and still do receive communion when I take my kids to church – that prompted me to question a faith that until then I had accepted readily at the hands of teachers and my parents. Slowly, I became aware of other faiths that were beginning to blossom around me. A trip to India several years later, during which I volunteered at a Christian orphanage, finally put paid to my sense of belonging to the Anglican Church. The orphans were brought in to the orphanage from a wide area in and around northern India: Buddhists from Tibet and Ladakh, Muslims from Kashmir and Hindus from Himachal Pradesh. All were whitewashed with Christianity. There was no tolerance or liberalism towards their native faiths. Spiritually dislocated, I eventually ended up doing what many of my generation did – turned to yoga and healers.

Meanwhile my girlfriends and I were reading Jilly Cooper novels. Our parents didn't really talk to us about sex – why should they? It wasn't in their culture to do so – no one had ever talked to them about it. My mum muttered something to me about getting myself down to the 'FPC' (I think she meant the Family Planning Clinic) when I left home and that was that. School gave us a clinical biology lesson but no one, *no one* talked about it honestly. For that, we had Jilly.

We – I – owe a lot to Jilly Cooper. Books passed around like contraband at schools were so much more informative than biology. And since when did the facts of sexual reproduction prepare you for the world of dating, dumping, mating and marriage? Romping in haystacks, undignified rolls in the back of horse vans and jodhpur-clad bottom-slapping removed much of the glamour around bedroom antics and allowed us to experience a more realistic view of life between the sheets. As Jilly herself said:

'I remember my editor saying: "Darling, do you think you should have this bit about sperm trickling down the thigh?" I mean, it's not nice. But we were in this little pocket – from the Sixties to the mid-Eighties – where people weren't worried about sex. We had contraception, it was before AIDS; it was joyful and exploratory.'

For glamour, we had Rupert Campbell-Black ('Greek nose, high cheekbones and long, denim-blue eyes'), just the sort of cad/hero a girl wanted to drop her knickers for (or play nude tennis with). Cooper's sex scenes were wondrously frank, from blowjobs to extramaritals, sexual dysfunction to orgies, and the heroines completely hapless. But Rupert and all Jilly's cads were incredibly seductive. Cooper girls were up for it, and either knew how to enjoy themselves or were desperate to learn. Crucially, they were also often utter failures and total embarrassments to themselves. Oh, how we identified.

Those girls that graduated to Jackie Collins (under the duvet, with a torch) were given instructional manuals in how to practise fellatio; meanwhile Shirley Conran legendarily told you something about a goldfish that went on to become female folklore (*Lace*, page 292, but then X-er girls probably know that already). And then there was Erica Jong's zipless fuck, Judith Krantz's *Scruples*, even Barbara Taylor Bradford had a useful message or two – just the sort of sex education to prepare a woman for the world. Way better than the diet of internet porn around today. The most we saw of porn before we came of age was a glimpse of our brother's *Razzle* under his sticky bed.

Cooper, Collins, Conran and their crew were women's women – their writing took care to focus on the female orgasm, allowing what, to our mothers, had partly seemed a myth to be put in the spotlight of our own pleasure. When Pagan works out in her unsatisfactory marriage to Robert in *Lace* that she can bring herself to orgasm in five minutes (she measures it with an egg timer), there were no longer any excuses.

Fast forward to now, and Mickey, in Judd Apatow's Netflix series *Love*, is masturbating in her hipster dungarees on her bed in front of the cat. Who is distracting her by licking its own pussy. Those Eighties bonkbusters – several hundred well-thumbed pages of sex, sin and scandal – produced a generation of women primed to take charge of their own sexuality. It's hard to stress how new this was – although the Sixties had supposedly been about free love, it was only really happening down the Kings Road with the Rolling Stones. Most Boomers did not behave like this – they married young and that was that (until they had an affair or divorced, and many of them did).

Then along came AIDS. Just as we reached the age of consent, the playing field became fraught with danger. Although terrifying for the gay community and heterosexual men, I wonder if it wasn't actually weirdly liberating for women. Suddenly there was a jolly good reason to insist on a condom – every public health announcement and piece of sex education insisted we ask, removing much of the stigma. Following AIDS, there was no longer any inhibition or shame in asking him to put something on. Women were licensed to take charge.

And if we were in any doubt about our ability to ask for what we wanted, or explore a little further, there was Madonna. Cavorting around on stage with her male dancers and her Jean Paul Gaultier conical bras, she showed us all what we could ask for, and how we could ask for it. And for reference, she published *Sex*, a high-fashion, high-gloss tome packed with beautiful black and white photographs shot by Steven Meisel. Now everything from bondage to role-play was on the menu. She might have been scandalous, and confrontational to the Catholic Church, but for her fans Madonna was two steps ahead of the path we were on. If Madonna could have it every which way, then why couldn't we?

And so we asked for it. If the Eighties were all about swinging your man around the boardroom by his tie (doing it his way, in other words), the Nineties became about girlie sex. What did *we* want? Could we reinvent sex as something sexy, rather than as a sport? Could sex finally be about us, and what we wanted?

But that's not to say the pleasure wasn't hard won. Tell me a good 'losing my virginity' story and I'll show you a satisfied nun. The problem with untutored sex and early relationships is no one has a clue what they are doing. The emotions are disproportionate; the sex is pretty unmemorable, although I did have one boyfriend who insisted on playing Prince every time we made out. That was cool.

But we were lucky, so much luckier then than now, as the playing fields were relatively safe. Leaving aside AIDS, there was less sexual disease, condoms were de rigueur (you could buy them in the Body Shop) and there was no internet porn teaching kids that a shaved pubis, boulder breasts, hair extensions and a repertoire of groans and grinds was normal. Or that anal was normal, or threesomes, or goats, or gang rape or abuse or whatever else gets passed around in the playground these days. I think, when it came to sex, our timing was very fortunate indeed.

So from the Eighties we had economic prosperity, but we saw the pain of its cost in the strikes, the decline of manufacturing and the polarisation of the working class. We had social consciousness in Band Aid, Greenpeace and the anti-apartheid movement. We knew what it was to come together as a society in great national moments, either via the TV, or Live Aid, or politics, or pop music. The progress of sexual equality in the Eighties was teeing us up nicely – I was educated to have a career, unlike my mum and many of her friends, who were educated to get married and be good at sewing on buttons.

Sex was an adventure that was ours for the asking. Life seemed positive, progressive, relatively peaceful. The wrongs in the world were being put right. Famine, prejudice and environmental destruction were being held to account. Life was not unmanageable, things were not moving too fast. So what would Generation X do next? What, as they came of age, would change? What did we have to give?

As the Eighties drew to a close, up in London a whole new scene was happening – a cultural cutting edge that was about to explode into the mainstream and change what we all thought forever. But that was still a long way away from me in Bournemouth, in 1989, aged sweet sixteen.

2
Four Go to Ibiza

In the summer of 1987 London's nightlife scene was fractured. The Leigh Bowery performance art scene at the Blitz was burning itself out and the music of soul boys, hip hop, rare groove and pop was progressing independently of each other. Four friends who worked the scene as DJs and promoters decided to celebrate a birthday with a trip to Ibiza. The birthday was Paul Oakenfold's, and his friends were Danny Rampling, Nicky Holloway and Johnny Walker.

They had been to Ibiza before but had never experienced the 'after hours' scene that people were beginning to talk about – the places people went to after the clubs had shut. They had heard of a place called Amnesia, an old farmhouse out in the countryside that was an outdoor club for those in the know. It opened at 3 am and went on till noon the following day. They had also heard about this new drug, ecstasy. None of them felt inclined to take it until they got there – but under the stars, in the warm summer air, 'hearing this amazing mix that DJ Alfredo was playing', and finding themselves in the middle of a scene not even they could have anticipated, everything changed. 'I was really anti-drugs in those days,' says Nicky Holloway. 'I used to chuck people out of my clubs for having a puff. But everyone round us was doing it, and it looked like so much fun. I was like, alright then.'

'There were no laws: people were making love on the dance floor, drinking and dancing, taking litres of liquid ecstasy between them,' reported one of the barmen at Amnesia, a German by the name of Ulises Braun. 'It looked like a Federico Fellini movie; every personality was different. Everyone was dressed up. I dressed like d'Artagnan, in high boots.'

In the middle of the dancefloor was a mirrored pyramid, around the edges were bars and chill-out areas with cushions and plants. It was like being in a tropical garden.

'It was a complete revelation to all four of us,' says Danny Rampling, 'out there in the open air, on that dance floor on that Mediterranean island. It was all about music and hedonism, but what was so unique were the people – they were really cosmopolitan. Even the DJ, Alfredo, was a maverick on the run from the junta in Argentina. He had fled to Ibiza as a political refugee.'

'We would never have gone to a place with 40- or 50-year-olds back in London,' says Holloway, 'but Amnesia didn't have any barrier – of age, colour or country. There were people from Switzerland, Holland, Singapore, Germany, Brazil. And the music was completely different, too. It was Balearic, which means it would go up and down. There was house music, but then Alfredo would play Carly Simon or Kate Bush – things we would turn our noses up at, at home. But on ecstasy, in that euphoric club, the whole thing made sense. At 7 am, in the morning light, Alfredo put on U2's "I Still Haven't Found What I'm Looking For". It opened our ears and our eyes. Everything fell into place.'

'All four of us changed that night,' says Rampling. 'In Ibiza I got my brief to do what I wanted – I wanted to play to my own crowd of people.'

'We came back like salesmen,' says Holloway.

Within five months of their return to London Paul Oakenfold started Spectrum, Danny Rampling started Shoom and Nicky

Holloway started Trip. 'At that point the London club scene was based in the past – funk and soul and things,' says Rampling. 'When house music came along it completely changed everything. It was revolutionary. It brought with it a wave of empathy and unity, fuelled by one thing and another. Ecstasy, yes, but also the political and economic situation in the mid Eighties. At that time Great Britain was very depressed – there was high unemployment. A lot was changing around the world: the apartheid regime in South Africa was imploding, the Wall was coming down in Berlin – there was change going on and we all were experiencing it.'

Shoom became a legendary success. There were 50 people on the first night and twelve weeks later 2,000 people were queuing down the street. Spectrum and Trip were similarly groundbreaking. 'It just caught a wave,' says Holloway. 'It couldn't have happened without E – let's not pretend – but overnight it went whoosh! We were doing Tripping the Sin at Centrepoint, and everyone would empty out of the club in the morning and start dancing in the fountain, singing songs and hugging each other. The police just stood there – they didn't know what to make of it.'

Without the internet – with only word of mouth, flyers and some helpful PR from the tabloids – the scene still went national. 'I remember the *Sun* doing a story on evil acid house and how bad it was,' laughs Holloway. 'They had pictures from a rave at an airfield – but by putting it on the front page they were unwittingly advertising it to everyone. Everyone was thinking, "That looks fun. I'll have some of that!"'

Every kid who dropped one of those tablets – Doves, Rhubarb and Custard, Pink Cadillacs, Mitsubishi; they were given cutesie names to describe the experience they gave – felt the 'shoom' as the rush tore through their body, and the transitory, almost hallucinatory feeling that they had found the secret key to a better world, one where everyone could come together and live in sweet harmony.

'There was a lot of spirituality in the music. Songs of hope, like Joe Smooth's "Promised Land", were gospel-driven records. All these records out of Chicago and New York were made by former disco producers who were really into gospel and great songwriting, and that fuelled all this optimism and hope and unity – and change. With everything that was going on, this was quite overwhelming to some people.'

There were a lot of sweaty hugs and 'I really love you, man' uttered in the early hours of the morning on heaving dance floors, often just to the stranger standing next to you – whoever they were. 'You'd go out with one set of friends and come home with another,' says Holloway. 'It smashed down the walls,' says Rampling. It helped everyone feel everyone else's importance, it put us all on an equal footing.

There was one apocryphal moment in Shoom when a punter opened a page in the Bible and insisted that Daniel – Jesus' disciple – was in fact Danny Rampling. 'This is you! This is you! This is what's happening now!' he insisted. 'These people were using a lot of LSD,' grins Rampling.

Parts of the country that did not have access to nightclubs were just as involved – in the form of illegal raves conducted outside in fields or inside in disused warehouses. They were staged by the traveller community, do-it-yourself DJs, sound systems and party collectives, as the craze spread like wildfire through the towns and country.

'I was living in the Somerset countryside at the time,' says the fashion designer Alice Temperley. 'It was like discovering this underground culture. The whole thing started with the music and that sense of liberation, that you felt like you were able to express yourself. It was like being swept up in a cult-like movement, you felt you were part of something, part of a pack. I was about fifteen or sixteen, and in some sense it was just kids wanting to misbehave – getting into a car and ending up in a convoy in some field and partying until sunrise – but it was very seductive.'

A couple who straddled both scenes, fields and clubs, were Pearl Lowe and Danny Goffey. Pearl was a fixture on the London club scene, Danny was a schoolkid in Oxford. Both went on to form successful bands and become part of the tapestry of Nineties culture, but this was where it started.

'I was expelled from Wheatley Park Comp in Oxford just at the start of the illegal rave thing,' says Danny. 'The sound system Spiral Tribe was going all round Oxfordshire. I didn't tell my parents I'd been chucked out of school. Instead I signed on and started to hang out at travellers' sites, going off in convoys to Gloucestershire or wherever the next rave was happening. I went to stay in a caravan with some travellers called Chris and Julie. I used to smoke dope with them and listen to techno. They had an Alsatian dog called Skewer. It was a bit like a second home for a while. I started a band called the Jennifers. Chris played guitar; he was in a band called White Lightning after the acid. We used to sit up and play really mad music, lots of Hawkwind and rave. He was into thrash metal – that was the crossover of those two scenes – sort of crusty dance.'

'I was putting on nights in Chelsea with two friends,' says Pearl. 'The three of us hosted these raves for this dodgy guy. We would go up the Kings Road with flyers, and he would make loads of money – there were queues down the road. We'd go to Subterrania on Friday nights and my friend Jasmine Lewis, who was quite a big model, and I would dance on the stage. Joe Corré, Steve Strange, Jeanette Calliva were all there. Then there was the Limelight that everyone went to, Boy George and Rusty Egan and Philip Salon. Es had just come out, so we would end up at Ministry of Sound at 5 am.'

'In London things were trending quite quickly,' says Danny. 'Where I was, there were no clubs, or one in Oxford. So when that all kicked in it was a scene like punk – everyone who was my age got really into it. Everyone who could drive would go off on these two-day adventures. Then the band started kicking off, and Oxford seemed quite small, and I wanted to move to London. We got signed and then I met Pearl and went to live in her house.' The tribes started to move together.

Before it became polluted by gangs and bad drugs, marketing and commoditisation, the house music scene had a very positive effect on society. It quelled the football terraces, brought down class, sex and race barriers, and imbued an entire generation with the belief they could go out and express themselves, do something they believed in. 'It was a Do It Yourself culture,' says Rampling. 'We created our own industry and scene, which allowed people to create their own jobs and follow their dreams, whereas punk, which certainly had great energy, had been all about anarchy – leave your job and stick two fingers up. It was very destructive. Acid house, by contrast, was all about positivity, hope, optimism and bringing people together.'

The DIY nature of the movement – that it was happening despite government and law – was profoundly influential. Why trust and accept the structures around you, if they don't trust or accept you?

The size of the scene eventually became too much to ignore, and led to the Criminal Justice Bill. Bizarrely wide-ranging, the bill sought to criminalise offences previously termed as 'civil', giving police and the courts greater powers to prosecute. It included everything from extending the definition of rape to include 'anal', to the criminalisation of the use of cells from embryos and foetuses. However it drew the biggest objection for its response to the free parties put on by the traveller community, whose occupation of common ground was causing middle England some distress.

Plenty of Gen X youth were extending their summers of love at these parties, the most famous of which was a week-long festival at Castlemorton in Worcestershire. In May 1992 tens of thousands of travellers had already amassed in the area for the Avon Free Festival, which the police cancelled, fearing a noisy party that would get out of hand. All the groups ended up settling on Castlemorton Common. As the sound systems cranked up, the police were left powerless to act, marooned helplessly at the bottom of the hill. The media swarmed around the event, which had now become something of a spectacle, but their headlines and front-page coverage only served to swell the numbers.

These free parties were quite something when you consider they were all organised in the pre-internet and pre-mobile world. Living in Oxford at the time, I also got caught up in this scene, and it was thrilling to be a part of it. Word would get out to meet at service stations on B roads, sketchy directions would be distributed by Chinese whispers, shouted through car windows at traffic lights – as an overloaded Vauxhall Astra playing house music off a mix tape on a tinny stereo would pull up beside you, clouds of spliff smoke pouring out of the windows. We would sometimes just literally head off into the dark, following the tail lights of the car in front, listening out for the distant thumping of a sound system.

Finally, when it didn't look like we could get any closer, we would abandon the car and head across fields towards the noise, blood pumping through our bodies in expectation of the revelry ahead. There was such an illicit thrill to the whole thing – the idea that there was this self-created network, unchecked by the authorities, creating a scene beyond their control, connecting people and beliefs through 'ley lines' and 'energy centres'. We were another, alternative lifestyle, a different community; this was our new world, beginning under the moonlight, in fields, warehouses and squats all over the country. As the sun came up, our new best friends from the night before would still be dancing on the top of cars, grinning from ear to ear with the innocent joy of discovery, drugs and the sense of being part of something new. It was huge, and it was beautiful.

It reached its apotheosis in that May of 1992 as the police looked on at the ravers, crusties and their dogs bouncing around on the top of Castlemorton Common. All the sound systems amassed together that week – Spiral Tribe, Bedlam, Circus Warp and DiY. Me too, although my memory is, funnily enough, patchy. I do remember the generator running out of power at one point and some dreadlocked dudes doing a whip round with a bucket. Some time later I saw the same dudes chasing a guy down the hill before beating him up viciously with fists and sticks. I think he had tried to nick the bucket of money. That bit definitely wasn't beautiful.

The public–police stand-off at Castlemorton provoked the Criminal Justice Bill – in particular Section 63, which banned 'sounds wholly or predominantly characterised by the emission of a succession of repetitive beats'. This lit up the music industry. The band Autechre released a three-track EP labelled 'Warning: "Lost" and "Djarum" contain repetitive beats'. Orbital released a mix of its track 'Are We Here?' that it titled 'Criminal Justice Bill?' and which consisted of four minutes of silence. The Prodigy included a track 'Their Law' on their album *Music for a Jilted Generation*, which was introduced in the sleeve notes with: 'How can the government stop young people having a good time? Fight this bollocks.' Meanwhile Dreadzone released the single 'Fight the Power', which sampled Noam Chomsky urging people to think about 'taking control of your lives', and advocating political resistance. The ruling party was as culturally divorced from its youth as it was possible to be.

The bill didn't just target ravers – the legislation also attacked hunt saboteurs, squatters and football fans. Essentially it amounted to a judgement on people's lifestyles – which enraged us. It repealed the councils' duty to provide permanent sites for travellers; police would have new powers of stop and search; the right to silence would be affected; and the criminalisation of 'disruptive trespass' had consequences for squatters, travellers and protesters alike. Uniting in protest, formerly unrelated movements began to come together in coalitions: students, trade unions, sound systems, traveller communities and direct action groups.

Three marches were planned in central London, the first two of which passed peacefully, with Tony Benn standing on a box in Trafalgar Square. Raves in London squats and on Wanstead Common took them into the night. The third ended in a riot. Tear gas was deployed, civilians were beaten up by police, dogs died, and any impression the groups had given the establishment that they were a civilised bunch with a civilised point of view was seriously damaged.

Once the bill came into effect, the free party scene withered. Instead, the right to party went overground and became a thriving industry. Nightclubs, DJs and festivals were the ultimate winners. Festivals still loosely embed political and socially conscious messaging into their line-ups, in a nod to the DNA of the scene that birthed them, but actually they are more about having fun and taking a break from normal life than raging against the machine. Your alternative lifestyle in one three-day £150 ticket. Sponsored by Vodafone. If you go to a festival now you are part of an entertainment culture, with nice bathroom facilities, wrist bands, glamping and fancy cocktails. It's a long way from those crusty sound systems and cans of Strongbow. Those sound systems headed into Europe, making way for Paul Oakenfold, Carl Cox and their progeny – Calvin Harris, David Guetta, Tiesto – to embrace a life of money and fame.

Ibiza went on to flourish. Surviving the scandal of *Ibiza Uncovered*, the television series that exposed the messy 'Brits on tour' years, it has remained a hedonist's destination. It continues to supply a 24/7 smorgasbord of distraction, and when the low-cost airlines opened it up to weekend clubbers, no one ever caught their flight home. It was like a super, sunny, brown-limbed version of Castlemorton, with glamour, glitter and sand.

These days Ibiza is mostly off limits except to the super rich. It has risen above the raving riff-raff by hiking prices, and much of the partying takes places in expensively built private villas rather than the clubs. Many who built and bought those villas passed through the raving nineties – Ibiza's hippie values and dance music culture suit their millions very well, even if they have built their own private nightclubs underneath their tennis courts. They no longer smile at strangers as the sun comes up, but at each other on board a yacht back from Formentera where they have just blown a grand on a rosé-soaked lunch at the see-and-be-seen beachside restaurant.

For the rest of us, there is 'glamping'. Evolving the notion of abandoning yourself to the countryside for a night of hedonism, Generation X has consciously curated the experience – applying all the signifiers of cool to the original idea of striking out and leaving societies and communities behind. Being out in the open, ignoring the rules around night and day, creating your own environment to suit you, somehow morphed into £400 bell tents and Cath Kidston bunting. 'Wild' camping converged with the 'free' party experience, and we styled it up with duvets, double-lilo blow-up beds, tealight chandeliers and yurt hotels to make it as luxurious as possible. If your urban experience traps you Monday to Friday, you can load up the car on a Friday night and head off with your mates (and kids) for a weekend of (relatively) comfortable escape. Someone can always bring a sound system.

Some of the activist momentum was retained, however. 'I remember being in Shepherd's Bush when Reclaim the Streets took over the roundabout,' says Martha Lane Fox. 'Which I guess was to do with politics loosely, but it might just have been a massive rave. I'm not sure we had a sense of social purpose. We didn't want to change the health service or change governments. We were just like, Fuck Thatcher, here's a new way of being.' However anti-establishment and vaguely political the movement felt, it was more a feeling that we were different from the world we had been born into, and that we were going to express ourselves differently. 'We were culturally ambitious, but not politically,' says Martha. 'We went because it was a laugh, not because everyone was really up in arms.'

The Criminal Justice Bill succeeded then – despite the protest. It forced music and dance culture to be legalised, regulated and commodified, so it could be moderated and taxed. But it didn't kill the music. Far from it – the Nineties were a period of incredible musical creativity, producing wave after wave of new music culture, from rave to Britpop to house to trip hop, to acid jazz to trance and drum 'n' bass.

Much of that was to do with the growing multiculturalism of British society, and all the glorious influences that brought with it, in music, politics, fashion and community. Britain's second generation of immigrant culture was just coming of age, and the social take of what those kids were offering up was absolutely the height of cool. As June Sarpong, a Ghanaian who grew up in Walthamstow, says, 'Being in London during that time was so interesting. We were immigrants who had grown up and integrated with white people in a way that our parents just hadn't. I was hanging out with Jazzie B and the Soul II Soul crowd at that time, and I found myself at the heart of this shift in the thinking of the city, the birth of a culture.'

Second-generation immigration culture was nowhere near the

ruling elite economically or politically – but culturally they were absolutely centre. Economically, there was displacement, and violence and drugs. 'I had a terrible car accident in 1989 that took me out of action for two years,' says June. 'I was hospital-ised, stuck in a bed unable to move. Those big, formative teenage years were wiped out. All my friends grew up in social housing, they were doing drugs and getting wasted, things you do at that age. The accident was like a crazy intervention from the universe because I missed out on all of that. That's the reason I don't drink, or smoke, or do anything now, not because I'm judgmen-tal but because the time I would've started I was ill. By the time I got better, I'd spent a lot of time on my own thinking in a way that would keep me from going mad. I had had to grow up.'

When June came out of hospital, Soul II Soul took her under their wing and got her a job at Kiss FM. 'It was when Kiss had just become legal and they had all of the cool DJs from the illegal days – Trevor Nelson, Judge Jules, all those guys. I started working with them, going to Ibiza and Manumission. It was crazy, I used to go out dancing Thursday, Friday, Saturday, Sunday, out till 4 am and still manage to get to work on Monday!'

Kiss was the platform for all the new music coming through, breaking acts like Jamiroquai and providing a platform for labels like Acid Jazz (set up by Gilles Peterson to promote the music he found to play in the back room in Paul Oakenfold's club). 'The tide had changed,' says June. 'Kiss was a legal radio station playing the kinds of music our generation wanted to listen to. It went on to completely change the content of Radio One, and that brought cool into the mainstream.'

Scenes were taking off in Manchester and Liverpool too. Down in Bristol the Wild Bunch sound system birthed Massive Attack, Tricky and Bristol's trip hop scene. Nellee Hooper moved to London and became a producer for Madonna and U2.

Meanwhile Bristol University was bringing in a bunch of white kids from privileged backgrounds and mixing it all up. Ben Elliot, the Etonian who went on to found the luxury concierge company Quintessentially, got his first taste of clubbing in Bristol. Before he went up, he was working at the *Independent*; Massive Attack had just released *Blue Lines* and a copy had come in for review.

'The *Independent* was brilliant at that point. Their Saturday Review magazine was running all these great, edgy black and white photos, reflecting a lot of what was going on. When *Blue Lines* came in I remember thinking, "That looks cool," and nicking it and thinking it was incredible. Then I arrived in Bristol. Even though I went there with no friends, because of this scene I suddenly met masses of different people. I met a huge Pakistani guy from Somerset who sells furniture now. Another guy was a mature student who was really in with 3D and Tricky. I began to put on club nights and we'd get Daddy G [of Massive Attack] to come and DJ. I think at one stage I even had a pair of silver trousers. There were shops on Park Street in Bristol where everyone would go to get kitted up for Friday or Saturday night.'

It didn't take long to spread north. 'When I was 16 and growing up in Wakefield I remember going out to the local club, where they played terrible music – Stock Aitken Waterman,' says Richard Reed. 'Everyone got really drunk and I remember seeing this guy getting a glass smashed in his face. Later that night I saw the same guy in a kebab shop, still with the blood running down his face. It was dripping into his kebab, and he was eating it. No one was having any fun, it was all drunken aggression. A year later I went out again and the music had changed, everything had changed. Everyone was happy – smiles on their faces, hands in the air. House music had ushered in some kind of difference.'

The son of a nurse and a bus conductor, Reed was surprised when his school suggested he apply for Cambridge University. 'I wanted to go to Nottingham because that was where all the best clubs and DJs were. I thought Cambridge was going to be full of posh people talking about rugby. I got to Cambridge and guess what? It was full of rugby blokes singing rugby songs, listening to terrible music. Everything I feared. I thought, we need a bit of house music here. I met Adam, from London, who loved the acid jazz scene, and this guy John and us started to put on house music nights. We realised we were having more fun organising them than the people who were queuing and paying to come in – at that point we realised we've got something here, this is what we should do.' The three of them still work together today.

This time in our lives taught us influence can lie with the individual rather than the organisation. It empowered us, made us question the establishment. 'The Criminal Justice Bill and the Poll Tax riots made everyone realise you can't keep on telling us what to do,' says Reed. 'We can be subversive, question the status quo, do things differently from the way they have been done before. The Nineties roughed things up a bit – you couldn't go out and dance all night in strict fashion, you needed to be comfortable in trainers. There was a bit of darkness going on with the political unrest and that helped people question things and reject the choice architecture.'

Cool, which we got from music, fed into fashion, film and everything else that sprang out of that scene. Cool was our possession, we loved it, nurtured it, crafted it. 'Contrived it, yes, but that's because we actually considered it,' says June. 'We cared. It didn't matter what music scene it was, whether it was Indie, Blur or acid jazz, all of them were cool. You just wanted to be part of them, didn't you? I wanted to be friends with Oasis and Meg and all that lot, they were just so fricking cool. Still are!

'I think the legacy of that cool is, our generation will be forever young. My mother was late thirties, forties, at that time, which was like an old woman. Whereas we will be like this for another 20 years. I don't think that's the same for the younger ones. I think we're going to catch up. When we're 60 and they're 40, I don't think there'll be much difference at all!

'Also we monetised cool, exploited it, which is a good thing because for so many years interesting artists have been broke. Thank goodness the Damien Hirsts and Tracy Emins made loads of money. Great, why not? But at the same time, it meant that we lost some of the really important changes. And one of them for sure is making politics interesting for a disengaged group.'

With cool comes irony, and in the end irony is a great dehabilitator of progress. Irony eventually means you believe in nothing – it leads to nihilism. Maybe the reason we dropped the ball politically is because we couldn't take anything seriously – even ourselves – in the end. The political denouement to all of this was starkly illustrated in the Brexit vote. The inclusive, liberal, multicultural society we thought we had built was rejected by just over half the country. Brexit was a shout from those whom this society did not benefit – or who did not understand its benefits. Those for whom multiculturalism was not a benevolent positive force; for whom the metropolitan acceleration was too fast and too self-oriented; whose sense of nostalgia and nationalism extended back to before this time. There's a job to do now, to bring those two halves together, and a lesson for Generation X that when cool becomes too exclusive, it writes itself out of the system.

But politics aside, we had learned a lot from the dance music revolution – it was time to make a living out of what we had learned.

3

Just Be Good to Me: How Business Became Sexy

Like many X-ers I had no vocation. In 1993, when I left university, I had no clue what I was going to do. The idea that you dedicated your life to a company or institution then retired on a nice, big, final salary pension was being knocked out of the park – my friends' parents were being laid off all over and there were chilling tales of suicides in the papers. The professions were unattractive to me – law looked boring, medicine was what my dad did. As I drifted about, I thought that probably the most suitable ambition was to try as many things as I could in order to build up as rich an experience of life as possible. Experience, after all, was far more interesting than money.

I wasn't afraid of work – I had a Saturday job in a sweet shop from the age of 14, I waitressed all the way through my university days to pay my debts, I thought nothing of double shifts to save up for a holiday. X-ers are not shirkers – in fact I often curse myself for such a Protestant work ethic; it is uncomfortably at odds with a life of travel and a fondness for high-octane leisure.

A team of contemporaries noticed our generation's demand for a high-quality lifestyle, but also that the world's demand that we work for it was at odds with the life itself. They set up *The Idler*, a media brand in praise of intellectual pursuits and creating the time and place for reflection. They threw very good parties and its founder, Tom Hodgkinson, has tried to monetise it in the form of workshops, classes and a magazine (man and woman, it turns out, cannot live on poetry and fishing alone).

'In essence it was about freedom,' says Tom. 'I felt stuck in a job I hated, in contrast to the experience I'd had at university, school and my first job working in a record shop. There I'd had lots of free time to play in bands, work on magazines, listen to music and engage in cultural pursuits and philosophy. I wanted to find ways to re-engage with that side of life.'

Following a hiatus in which Tom moved to the country and had children, the brand is now back, and enjoying something of a revival, particularly through its Idler Academy, a school where you take courses in everything from learning Latin to playing the ukelele. 'We've narrowed it down to three fs now – freedom, fun and fulfilment,' says Tom.

But at this rather junior point in my life, I was happy to accept that work was a means to enjoying a lifestyle, not building long-term wealth. Double shifts in Pizza Hut meant I could go travelling around India and Central America. In Douglas Coupland's *Generation X* he called these 'McJobs': 'A low-pay, low-prestige, low-benefit, no future job in the service sector. Frequently considered a satisfying career choice by people who had never held one.'

This way of working – of taking shift work to save up for a period of extended leave – has definitely stayed with Generation X. My colleague Anthony, now deep in his forties, turned up for work recently with a backpack on his back. After he finished his shift as a sub-editor he was off to New Zealand with his girlfriend for five weeks. She had a slot to show her art film at a festival out there, and they knew some friends of friends who said they could come and stay – and that was enough.

Thinking that my kids at home and my staff job afford me no such freedoms I felt uncomfortable pangs of envy before checking in with Douglas again: 'Poverty Jet Set: A group of people given to chronic travelling at the expense of long-term job stability or a permanent residence. Tend to have doomed and extremely expensive phone-call relationships with people named Serge or Ilyana. Tend to discuss frequent-flyer programmes at parties.' Note: written before the age of Skype.

But after university I did want to get ahead, get on with things. I wasn't sure what I wanted to do – I took a secretarial job in a PR firm as that was all I could get. This was 1993 and the recession had jammed everything up. But the job was in London and I could afford to move there with my friend Lara because back then housing was within our reach. The job paid about £13,000 p.a., which was not bad, and we rented a studio flat in Notting Hill off the boyfriend of a friend of ours. The rent was about £350 a month, which was just about do-able when we split it between us, especially when we nicked the toilet roll and teabags from work and had egg banjos for dinner most nights. We saved our money for Cosmopolitans and trips to Hyper Hyper. Obviously.

It wasn't as if PR was my dream career, but clearly it was just the beginning of an exciting professional adventure that lay before us. The media was booming – glamorously, and what's more it looked like the young and cool were in charge. Very few of my peers wanted to go into public service or the charity sector. 'I think people were ambitious,' says Martha Lane Fox. 'They may not have been money ambitious but they were ambitious. But a lot of it was about ambition for yourself as opposed to that wider sense of the world. How that's changed now.'

For Generation X the dream career was finding a job in one of the cool bits of youth culture that were exploding. Serena Rees, who founded the erotic fashion brand Agent Provocateur with Joe Corré, says her party and her work life were entirely intertwined. 'Going out was dancing, wearing crazy outfits. But

I worked really bloody hard too, in advertising, and had a lot of fun.'

For Rees, the clubs were her university of life. 'I left school when I was 16 so I didn't ever have that grown-up education where you're hanging out with people and sharing your ideas. We did our sharing of ideas in clubs and bars. In the early Nineties I met Joe and started working with his mum, Vivienne Westwood. Everyone was grafting – even the people that were running the clubs.'

The work ethic, she thinks, came from Thatcherism. 'There's got to have been some good in the bad with Thatcher. That work ethic to get yourself out of the shit gave everybody the push to go and do it. We were also given the opportunity because we were in a recession and it was like, right, you're brave and you fight and you're not scared of failure. Just go and do it.

'When we opened that first Agent Provocateur on Broadwick Street in Soho, Katie Grand, Stella McCartney, Giles Deacon – all that lot used to come and hang out. Isabella Blow and Philip Treacy would pop in for a cup of tea. All the people I'd known from my club years, all the kids at St Martin's round the corner in Charing Cross, would come and sit on the steps and share what they were working on. Back then there was only a handful of places to go, whereas now I suppose it's less congregational. Kids these days don't have places where they go and hang out, because they are all on their devices. No one does an actual physical shop because you can do a shop online.'

For Rees, the path to retail goddess was organic. 'Joe was trying to run his mum's shop, but he was struggling so I went to help him. Everything is pretty fundamental about any business, I think – you've just got to roll up your sleeves and get on. Joe and I wanted to do our own thing, so we started researching this idea in our spare time. My first job was working for this company that produced all the books for the top models in New

York, Paris and Milan, so I knew every photographer, stylist and model from all around the world. Every day I was seeing the best photography. Then working in the advertising agency, I learned about getting a photographer or an illustrator or graphics person, bringing an idea to life and making something. I'd had a good training. All the campaigns we did for Agent Provocateur, all the fly posters and shoots – I knew how to do all of that.

'The difference between now and then, is back then we didn't care about being successful or making money, that wasn't what it was about. It was nice when it worked and there was a queue of people. But what was exciting was sharing what you think is great, and finding out everyone else thinks it's great too.'

The brand grew, eventually to over 100 shops in 13 countries. Its success lay in the careful shepherding of its balance between sex and fashion – crotchless panties may have sounded tacky, but when they were shot on Kate Moss by Ellen von Unwerth, they were the acme of desire. Joe and Serena surrounded themselves with the coolest models, artists, film directors and celebrities, which powered the brand into the high end fashion arena, even though it was selling a bedroom fantasy. Where Joe brought the raunch, Serena brought the taste, with an uncompromising demand for quality fabrics and design. This brand was more Prada than Ann Summers, and in 2007, 13 years after they opened that first shop, a private equity firm bought an 80 per cent stake for £60m.

'Kids now think you can be successful quickly – there's too much Dragon's Den giving them this false hope,' says Serena. 'It's not going to happen unless you work your arse off and you've got a good idea.' She now invests in and advises new businesses, and doesn't like what she sees. 'People are doing it because they want to be famous, to make loads of money. That's their drive, rather than it being real.'

As Agent Provocateur proved, first you need a good product (and post Gerald Ratner everyone now knew that) and second you need to tell a good story around it. 'The marketing guy used to be the least important person in the business,' says Richard Reed. 'But in the Nineties you saw the rise in priority of telling a story about your product. It's got more and more important, to the point now where the marketing guy's actually on the board. It's product and story: the whole company has got to really care about what you are producing and serving up.' Marketing became a creative art.

The pursuit of money, or going into business, on the other hand, was not perceived in any way as creative at that time. It was for people in suits who carried briefcases and wanted to hang out with dreary bank managers. Besides it was all about money – and money, post Eighties, was vulgar. Business was Arthur Daley or Harry Enfield's Loadsamoney – only for the greedy and the brash. Post Eighties, we all know where that ended: Black Monday, a property crash, the collapse of the economy. Thatcherism was deeply unfashionable. Nevertheless, the idea anyone could now have a go – could propel themselves up the social and economic ladder – should they so wish, was embedded in Generation X. The subliminal message of Thatcherism struck deep. It was to supercharge the entrepreneurialism of the next decade.

'It's always been quite trendy to Thatcher bash, but for me the idea about freeing up the ability to do your thing was a really important part of my psyche,' says the fitness trainer Matt Roberts. 'As a 15-year-old, I had the idea for doing the business I now have. I grew up in the leafy county of Cheshire, a white, middle-class area. But my parents came from South Wales, my dad was from the Valleys, and only got out because he played football. First for Arsenal, then Wrexham, which was how we ended up in Cheshire. He had this great opportunity for leaving the Labour heartlands of the Valleys. My grandmother had a council house on an estate in Swansea but when my dad retired from football – and in those days you didn't have anything like the cash you have now – my mum made the money by setting up a clothes shop. For my friends, that wasn't the case. They're from classic Labour-supporting families and didn't believe they could go and do anything different. They settled for being in the same four-room box house.'

But the idea of what a business was and could be was about to change. There were already two trailblazers offering a different type of model: Anita Roddick and Richard Branson. The latter started out by setting up a record label (obviously cool) and the former was militant in using her business to promote a new kind of ethics: not testing products on animals. These two voices may have been alone in the idea that business could be a force for good, but they were also very loud and influential. It was not to be until the time of the Millennials – when business, aided by the digital revolution, became the new rock 'n' roll – that the idea that business should help shape society took hold. Innocent was about to show how it could be done, how business could marry our values and social consciousness, and be interesting and fun at the same time.

Founded in 1998 by three student friends who met through their shared love of house music, it mixed up the cool of nineties advertising and marketing messages with the health of a generation on a hangover. Their cute, colourful bottles of mango and passion fruit, strawberries and banana and kiwi, and apple and lime juices, spoke directly to the customer, promising 'to help you and heal you', advising you to 'shake before opening not after' and even flirting with you: strawberries were included because they 'go very nicely with your lipstick' ('wackaging' or wacky packaging, as it came to be known). At the time, this challenged all the ideas of what big companies thought of as business. Innocent started with the consumer first. What do they want? What language do they speak? When they think of Innocent do they want to think of a boardroom of suits or someone like them?

Richard is now a handsome fortysomething who is still sporting scruffy hair, T-shirt and skinny jeans, exactly the same outfit that so disrupted the business community back in the Nineties.

'Innocent was always just a little bit subversive,' he says. 'Other businesses were obsessed with supply chains and the bottom line, whereas Innocent was about thinking about the individual first. We are a very individual generation. In the Nineties we saw everything had started to change, that you could reinvent what it is that you want. You can say, Do you want a blue sweater or a red one? Or you can say that you don't have to have either. Reinvent the choice architecture.'

What they did was pledge to donate 10 per cent of all their profits to charity. They also invested their staff in their company, gave everyone beer on a Friday and handed out £1,000 scholarships. Headquarters was 'Fruit Towers' in Notting Hill, a colourful building with astroturf, table-tennis tables and beanbags, and they drove around in funny-looking trucks covered in grass or painted in cow print. (This was just as Silicon Valley culture was beginning to make hoodies and office table-tennis tables a thing. Now of course, they are a total cliche.) Innocent caught our attention – partly because no one had been sold a fruit drink promising 'ground-up cats' before, and partly because the City and the business pages had never met 'businessmen' like this before. 'If you're going to turn up to a meeting in a T-shirt, you've got to be even more on top of your game than a guy in a suit, so people take you seriously,' smiles Reed.

Being nice to people was the company culture too. It wasn't solely about feathering your own managerial nest and hitting your profit targets, it was about having a nice time. After all,

Reed and his partners, Adam Balon and Jon Wright, had started out in business putting on club nights together. 'At Innocent we had ten babies out of it – everyone was copping off with each other!' Business started to take on a new kind of shape. 'Hippies with calculators', is how one newspaper article described them, which Reed likes a lot. The father of hippie capitalism.

As their traction grew, so did the interest of the big corporates, and in 2009, pre sugar crisis, Coca-Cola invested in the company – going on to buy it out three years later for £100m. 'When we cashed in I ended up with a big number in my bank account – and believe you me it was about 30 per cent bigger than the number we thought we could ever achieve in our wildest dreams. But far better than that was the fact that everybody in that building also had a number in their bank account that day,' says Reed.

'We made several millionaires, and that for me was the benefit of what we did. That was where I felt good about what we had done, and was worth far more to me than the 10 per cent profit difference in my own actual number. Do you need that extra 10 per cent or are you going to get more spiritual value for sharing that out amongst the people that got you there? I still don't understand even today why other businesses don't do that.'

The truth is, many new businesses now do build in an ownership or partnership structure. As the dotcom queen Martha Lane Fox says, 'Everything I've started now is not for profit, but I like to think that the world has so dramatically shifted that unless you embed some wider social purpose right from the beginning, your brand would not be so robust. If I was starting my travel business Lastminute.com again, I think people would now expect that extra dimension of "Okay, so you're doing all this travel, where's the carbon offsetting? Why don't you have more holidays to help clean up beaches?" You'd have to invent that right at the beginning, but it didn't occur to us when we started that social purpose was something.'

It wasn't just marketing and social purpose that Generation X brought to business, it was also design. Products and services needed to be cool if they were going to be at all desirable (whereas now in our world of frenetic speed, practicality is enough. Just ask Amazon – the ugliest and most successful service in the world).

Matt Roberts was single-minded in his pursuit of design and lifestyle cues when he was setting up his fitness brand. 'I was fascinated by the cool stuff, about how you lived your life. I spent a lot of time going round anywhere that was cool to try and get bits of what they did. I got my hair cut in Nicky Clarke by Nicky because he was then *the* stylist. I used to go and stay at the Wilton Hotel in New York because that was the cool place to go – it was dark and moody. I'd eat at Quaglino's, and when Conran opened the restaurant Mezzo, that was a big deal. I picked up things from magazines like *The Face* and *Arena*. That was a really formative time to be in London. It was the start of what happens now. This hotel here, this is the net result of all of those different things.'

Matt is sitting in the Mondrian, one of London's latest 'design' hotels, in a modern lobby designed by Tom Dixon (X-er), drinking expensive coffee on tasteful yet slightly challenging furniture. Roberts is right at home. His tightly disciplined body is neatly clothed in Boss and Prada, while the scent of Tom Ford hangs about his neck. Initially, Roberts trained to be a sprinter, with his sights set on the Olympics. He dropped out when he realised his friend and training partner – Darren Campbell – was going to be a whole lot better than him. Roberts didn't want to be second best, so instead he turned to business and for inspiration looked to America, which in the Eighties and early Nineties was way ahead of London both in lifestyle and business.

'The first time I went to New York, in the mid Nineties, I thought it was the coolest place on the planet,' he says. 'I started doing courses there and I'd come back fired up. But then London would drag you down slightly. It didn't have quite the same drive. What the US did was package things well, the front sell was really good. Behind it, the substance wasn't that amazing, but it looked incredible.'

What was happening in America wasn't that exposed over here – there was much less media to tell you about it, which gave New York cool hunters an opportunity in Europe. What Roberts saw in New York was a swelling fitness industry – better standards in terms of what was on offer in gyms, and greater engagement in the population. If getting fit could be made to look a little more attractive, and it could fit in with people's lifestyles rather than the other way round, maybe it might just catch on. So he launched a bespoke training service in Mayfair, made his gyms high design and hi tech, and started attracting aspirational clients like Geri Halliwell and Elle Macpherson.

Roberts had his opportunity. Celebrities began to take on personal trainers, and paparazzi pictures of LA gym bunnies like Madonna, Jennifer Aniston and Gwyneth in their sportswear ramped up the idea fitness could actually be a fashion choice. With no cool gyms to go to, people turned to books, which served Roberts well: 'In my prime, we'd sell 40,000 copies of a book a month. One of my books was selling in 26 countries, doing phenomenal things.'

The marketing plan was working.

4

When Noel Gallagher
Went to Number 10

Marketing, advertising, PR, and any of the media that relied on those things, from magazines to TV stations, were proliferating. Digital wasn't happening yet (we weren't even using email – imagine that), nor were mobile phones much of a thing. But media was growing – mass media as it began to be known. Media studies courses became absurdly popular, because media looked like it wasn't just about making money, it was about being creative and having a good time.

'I remember after uni some people were going off to get jobs in management consultancy,' says Richard Reed. 'What was management consultancy? They said they were going to get jobs in the City and I was like, "What? London?" I didn't even know the "City" existed. I went for an interview with P&G to be a sales person, and I thought, "Really? Drive round shops selling shampoos? No thanks." I went into advertising because it sounded fun.'

For those then that couldn't sing or dance or write or act or draw or paint or take photographs or design or make – there was advertising. The advertising industry would like to think of itself as one of the cornerstones of Britain's creative industries, but Britain's creative industries would be horrified to include it in their midst. 'I remember making this ad for a car brand,' says Reed. 'It was pictures of ordinary people holding placards with surprising things written on them. A picture of a guy in a suit holding a sign saying "By night I'm Melinda" – that kind of thing. At the time the artist Gillian Wearing had done exactly that and won the Turner Prize. The advertising creative had totally ripped it off.'

The advertising industry regards itself with astonishing self-importance. They hand out awards for bravery. Bravery, in advertising. When I started in the advertising business a few years ago, my *Sunday Times* colleague Marie Colvin had just lost her life in Syria reporting on the atrocities. I found it very hard to swallow someone being awarded a gong and a cash prize for their 'bravery' in rebranding an estate car.

But advertising can make a positive contribution to culture. You always remember the great ads – You've been Tango'd, Budweiser's Wassup? and Marky Mark's Calvins were Nineties classics. Nowadays the John Lewis Christmas TV spot, Nike's sponsorship of young creative collectives and General Electric's reporting on scientific innovation are all just as influential. But the advertising world is now largely swamped by digital: irritating pop-up ads and low-grade, interruptive creative that is actually prompting us to install ad blockers.

Those that commission advertising are being seduced by the online world of cheaply made content, prioritising the scale and frequency of distribution over what you are actually distributing. Just shout – shouting anything will do. The Nineties world of ad men and women would never have let a client get away with spending less than six figures on a creative. An advertising spread in a magazine requires care: thought, craft and budget. And how much memorable it is than some annoying bit of programmatic clickbait.

The halcyon years of the Nineties yielded so much creativity, and so much creative media to transmit and report on it. This boom in youth culture was a gift of the recession. As Noel

Gallagher once said, 'In the Eighties and Nineties it was really easy to start a band. We've got to thank Thatcher for all the disused warehouses we could rehearse in.'

Jamie East, founder of gossip website Holy Moly and now a radio presenter, started out as a singer in the indie band the Beekeepers. 'We got a record deal in the mid Nineties, because we had been able to support our rehearsing on the dole. The dole was the lifeblood of the music industry, as it actively nurtured creative talent,' he says. 'You could sign on and be creative – artist, musician, designer – it gave you the luxury of time to do that. When they introduced Job Seeker's Allowance, all of a sudden you couldn't claim housing benefit and get your £37 dole. I remember we were front page of the *Derby Evening Telegraph* on the same day I was having to go and lie about having to sign on. The headline was "Derby band heroes go off on 4-week tour", and I was down the dole office having to say I was actively looking for a job. It stifled everything.' In the end East left the band and went off to work at Sky TV.

Media went from three TV stations to the national launch of another two terrestrials (Channel 4, Channel 5), then came satellite and cable, the launch of commercial radio stations (Kiss, Virgin), and the expansion of magazine publishing houses (Arena, Frank, Esquire, Q, Red and Elle Deco) and more national newspapers (the *Correspondent*, *Today*, the *Independent*).

TV was exciting – there was *The Big Breakfast* and *The Word*, anarchic, youth-oriented shows where the kids were in charge, and there were no rules. Paula Yates could seduce Michael Hutchence in bed live, bands could swear at Terry Christian, Amanda de Cadenet got a speaking part. Of course it wasn't all creative, and someone had to pay for it. Canny types saw the opportunity to marry up brands with this new sexy media. Brands had the money, Britain was brimming with creativity. One of the most canny was Matthew Freud, whose PR agency brought the two together. His agency could place a packet of crisps on a TV show, or a toothpaste tube on a magazine cover; celebrities could be bought and sold; a soft drink could sponsor a film premiere. It gave PRs and brands the illusion they were in control, and gradually, they were.

Kris Thykier, Freud's right-hand man, remembers Planet 24's Christmas parties as 'legendary'. The year Planet 24 launched *The Big Breakfast*, its other show *The Word* was in full flight. Two of the most anarchic TV programmes that had ever been made – produced and presented by young people, for young people. This wasn't any longer middle-aged men in expensive suits in Madison Avenue and Soho telling young people what was cool. The kids were doing it for themselves.

'We took over the Ark in Hammersmith, which had just been opened and was the building of the moment. We threw a party on the top floor and it was the first moment where you sensed there were young people in charge. It was the year the Groucho was up and running. I was 20 years old and already representing the programmes, the presenters and the production company, talking to all the newspapers. It was mad. But the media were encouraging it and we were storming it,' he says. 'That party that year was the meeting of the teams that made *The Word* and *The Big Breakfast*. Two shows, one first thing in the morning and one last thing at night, talking to a generation that hadn't really been talked to by television before.'

The same thing was happening in the print world. Newspapers began to expand to accommodate all the new advertising streams, with features and lifestyle and fashion sections starting to appear. These sections naturally invited in more staff, many of them young and female. This was where my career took off: I went from being an unpaid work experience on the listings section of the *Observer* (a job I had blagged through a friend of a friend of a friend), to a paid

researcher on their *Life* magazine supplement. From there I
went to the *Telegraph* as a commissioning editor in charge of
food (where my patrician, silver-haired boss called me 'The
Infant Tiffanie' as I was, as far as he was concerned, outrageously
young to be in the job).

Courted by PRs, riding the London cocktail circuit of launch
parties and openings, it was the ideal spot to watch the Nineties
unfold. Like Thykier, I went to some legendary parties and
witnessed some great moments. I remember attending one party
in Cannes at the film festival, hosted by MTV in Pierre Cardin's
space-age villa, a collection of pink Teletubby pods built into the
edge of a cliff on the Cote d'Azur. Ostensibly the week-long
festival in Cannes was a showcase of the film world's upcoming
releases – and they were so exciting, as directors like Quentin
Tarantino and Guy Ritchie were bringing a rock 'n' roll edge to
Hollywood.

In 1998 *Lock, Stock and Two Smoking Barrels* was released,
giving London an international film voice – and making it very
attractive to brands looking to cash in. There were probably
about a thousand people at the MTV party that year, every
named DJ in the land playing, and endless test tubes of Absolut
Vodka going round. Everyone was cool, young and fashionable.
At three in the morning they closed the party down and emptied
out the villa – and at four they started it up again, for those that
remained. We danced on the terrace as the sun came up over the
Mediterranean and there was nowhere cooler or more at the
centre of things on earth than that terrace right then – we were
all exactly where we wanted to be.

As such a source of economic prosperity, the thriving creative
industries, which had previously been dismissed as a bit ridiculous and inconsequential, were now being embraced by the
establishment. They were part of Brand Britain – something we
could sell on to the world to drive our economy and elevate our

national pride. Taking his cue from America, which was so good at marketing itself, the newly elected Tony Blair held an event in 1997 that was to become the pivotal moment of the Nineties. He celebrated his election with a series of parties at 10 Downing Street, and all these artists who had set themselves up as anti-establishment, disruptive voices, were invited to Number 10, the heart of the government.

Blair was Cool Britannia – he had rebranded politics and reinvented it for our generation. For a generation so expert on and obsessed by cool, Blair's relative youth and embracing of the creative industries was intoxicating. He must be a good thing. One of the first things he did in government was celebrate British design and creativity with a party – a party! Suddenly the emblems of what had previously been considered fringe culture were invited in to be celebrated by the establishment itself. Thatcher had had little time for culture. After 18 years of Tory rule, there were clear changes afoot.

'It was an exciting time, to have so many people from all these different industries included,' says June Sarpong. 'Architecture, design, he had them all. It wasn't just the obvious musicians and fashion and art.' Geri Halliwell had just brought the Union Jack in from the cold, Blur and Oasis were fighting it out for cool points, the cast of *The Full Monty* were on set, the 'Sensation' exhibition was about to open at the Royal Academy, *Loaded* was in full swing. Tony Robinson, Vivienne Westwood, Ben Elton, Chris Evans and Kevin Spacey all trooped up the street to that famous front door. Blair hit cool paydirt when he got the photograph of the decade – chortling over a glass of champagne with Noel.

'The fact that a guy who'd been in a band, owned an electric guitar and has probably had a spliff was prime minister really meant something,' said Gallagher later. 'He might be one of us.' And Blair knew how to handle himself. When Gallagher asked him how he had managed to stay up all night on the night of the election, he quipped, 'Probably not the same way you did.'

'That government, because they were all so young themselves, understood how important shaping British culture was, not just for Britain but as a message to the rest of the world,' says June. 'They understood the importance of selling that image so that the world wanted to be part of the UK. It was quite American thinking.' Politics, then, began to use marketing too: the age of spin was born. Blair's PR man was Peter Mandelson, a silver-tongued figure hated by the media for his slippery talking, whose responsibility was to cast the New Labour project as the bright dawn of liberal thinking. The danger was that the shiny sheen Mandelson applied to the policies and personalities left them open to suspicion.

Momentarily, Blair brought that disengaged group in from the outside. Ultimately, though, politics did not benefit from its embrace of marketing – in the end its reliance on spin just earned it distrust. By the time Cameron came along with his lookey-likey 'Cool Britannia' party (Eliza Doolittle and Ronnie Corbett: the guest list didn't have quite the same cachet), the cultural zeitgeist had moved on. He would have done better to invite Millennial vloggers and the Silicon roundabout digipreneurs, but of course that just isn't as sexy or cool. Cameron was a posh boy who went to Eton (nobody likes privilege) whereas Blair presented himself as classless. He may have come from a relatively affluent background and even gone to public school, but Blair was socially much harder to place – the level playing field we all wanted so much.

It was to be some time before the scales were to fall from our eyes. As *Private Eye* had it so perfectly, Tony Blair was our saviour. Working on a national newspaper, I was not only party to all the cultural changes happening around me, but was on the inside track of the political ones too. I felt like I was living right in the middle of it – and physically I was. I had moved in with a boyfriend (TV producer for one of the myriad new satellite channels) who lived in Primrose Hill, not far from Islington and the street where Blair lived up till the election. I used to visit one of my writers who lived near the Blairs' old home, and pass the door Cherie Blair famously answered in her nightie on the morning of the election.

Creation Records opened their HQ in Primrose Hill village, and for a while the genteel street that was then lined with green-grocers, tearooms and bookshops also housed pop stars, paparazzi and music industry types. The ancient bohemian ladies of Primrose Hill, who dined at Odette's in their hatpins, beehives and endless necklaces, were rather a pleasing backdrop to the northern swagger of the Britpop scene. Everything, it seemed, was being overrun by the noisy clash of modernity.

Round the corner was The Steele's, a pub where Kate Moss and Bobby Gillespie of Primal Scream would drink; The Queen's played host to Chris Evans and Oasis; David Baddiel, Rob Newman, Sadie Frost and David Walliams all lived nearby and would pass in the street. It felt as if I had landed in the heart of everything, that I was part of this new world. By now I had moved on from the *Telegraph* to the *Express* features desk, where we could be reactive to the news unfolding around us. Racism in the police, the care of the elderly, the shenanigans at Westminster were all fair cop, although my finest hour was probably 'Too posh to push' – the truth behind Victoria Beckham's caesarean.

I definitely gravitated towards the more fluffy side of news: my boyfriend at the time was producing a TV series with the comedian Leigh Francis (who now portrays the comedian Keith Lemon), and a pilot on video gaming with Dexter Fletcher. I was literally living next door to Liam 'n' Patsy and I think I was rather blinded by the glitz and the excitement. While tabloid culture is a clever mix of both hard and soft news, it wasn't clear to me at the time how we were shaping the future. How Saviour Blair was, or was not, paying it forward. How distracting and eventually corrosive celebrity culture would become. How Blair's 'New Deal' – a cornerstone of his welfare reform in his first term, which withdrew benefits from those 'who refused reasonable employment' in exchange for training and subsidised employment, and the introduction of tuition fees that withdrew free arts education, stifling social mobility – was to have such far-reaching consequences for talent and creative culture.

The recent death of the actor Alan Rickman brought this into sharp focus: could a comprehensive boy who had grown up in a council house make it to the summit of the acting profession now? Twenty-five years ago, if you had no money you could live in a squat and draw dole to fund your rehearsal time, and you could beg, borrow or steal cheap studio space.

'We rented a whole floor of an old disused mill for band practice back in Derby,' says Jamie East. 'It cost us £40 a month that we made back by sub-letting it out to other bands.' These days 'disused studio space' has been turned into loft-style apartments. Bands can afford no such luxury, but it was a luxury afforded to Generation X talent: the YBAs, Kaiser Chiefs, Oasis, Jarvis Cocker et al. Where are the Alan Rickmans of today? Is it any wonder Eddie Redmayne, Dominic West, Tom Hiddleston and Damian Lewis all went to Eton?

Or that the best pop can offer is a new hierarchy of talent decided by shows like *The X Factor*?

5

Clinton's Cigar

With greater transparency comes greater accountability. As the media exploded, and the traditional respect for privacy and restrictions around reporting on authority began to melt, power fell victim to the truth. Celebrities, once revered beasts of glamour, found themselves exposed as the humans they actually were. Tom Cruise was a cult Scientologist, David Beckham was a suspected adulterer, Jude Law was a wife-swapper, Jennifer Aniston's marriage was on the rocks. But it wasn't just the A-listers who were morphing into tragic soap stars in front of our eyes – it was the highest levels of government and those who had once been utterly untouchable, the Royals.

The Monica Lewinsky affair in the States seems incredible even now in the excruciating level of its detail. It was perhaps the last deliberately careless act of an American presidency that relied on secrecy. Back in 1998 Bill Clinton underestimated the growing power of the internet, the scrutiny of an ever more powerful press, the advance of technology in collecting DNA evidence. It was also the moment popular culture took on politics. Clinton's affair struck at just the moment when technology, science, the press and popular culture came together.

Rumours of the Lewinsky affair first surfaced on the Drudge Report, at that time a fairly insignificant politics blog. Picked up by the *Washington Post*, it was enough for Clinton to utter the eleven words that were later to bring him down: 'I did not have sexual relations with that woman, Miss Lewinsky.' An investigation was set up on the popular satirical sketch show *Saturday Night Live*. The internet hummed with rumour and speculation. The presidency of the United States was now reduced to a conversation around blowjobs and cigar dildos. And then investigators found DNA evidence on a blue dress. There was to be no cover-up this time. An independent investigator was appointed to ascertain whether the president had lied. Eleven months and acres of media coverage later, both parties were left shamed and broken.

Over here in the UK, we had already witnessed the unravelling of Charles and Diana's marriage in similarly glorious detail. Charles found himself the victim of a leak of phone tapes, caught red-handed talking to his mistress and expressing a naïve (aristocratic? who knows!) desire to be her tampon. Pretty hard to command future kingly respect following that one. Diana played her hand as the wronged siren, finding lovers in surgical operating theatres and on yachts with the sons of Middle Eastern billionaires, turning up at openings in drop-dead gorgeous designer gear. Charles sought to rescue his credibility with TV confessionals but he was no match for his wife, who was much more in tune with the times.

It was the endgame, as we now know, and as the final acts of both events played out to a watching world, they ended in spectacular tragedy: impeachment for the president and the self-proclaimed prophecy of death for Diana. Diana's ride around the Med on Dodi Fayed's gin palaces ended in horror as the paparazzi chased her to her death on a midnight flit from the Ritz in Paris. The gradual erosion of authority that had kicked off the decade had ended it with shame for the British Royal Family and the American political establishment. Nobody believed anything any more about our inherited structures. The old ways were broken. But what did that leave us?

'We are the first generation for whom the level of media scrutiny has made it impossible for anyone to make a move into political life,' says Kris Thykier. 'Until the election of Donald Trump last year, we have only had people in government who have been in politics all their lives – because unless you're in politics all your life, you haven't run a life that will allow you to be in politics. It may have been possible in the Sixties and Seventies, even the Eighties. But it stopped being possible in the Nineties.' The life of JFK was no less colourful than Clinton's – but that was no impediment, far from it. 'When Clinton came to power in 1993, the "I didn't inhale" line was a fudge, an indication of what was to come.'

What followed was two decades of scrutiny on our politicians that has possibly manacled some of the free-wheeling entrepreneurialism and colour that kept the political populous and discourse lively and diverse. While Generation X was busy ushering in a period of intense cultural change, the establishment failed to find an alternative route. The year 2016, however, saw all that turned on its head. Fed up with the status quo, fed up with a government that effects incremental change that seems only to be in the best interest of the elitist few, the British electorate voted themselves out of the European Union, and the American electorate voted in a man who was the antithesis of what we thought was acceptable in a politician. Dismissing liberalisation and globalisation in a great sweep, America now waits to see what kind of change a Trump presidency will bring. And Britain faces years of legal wrangling and paper-pushing as it attempts to disentangle itself from membership of the EU. Where change should and could happen is through politics – perhaps as we head into the latter years of this decade this is where we will begin to see it again. Because for a long time our attention was diverted from the political to the personal – it was, after all, much more fun. After the Clintons came the Osbournes. MTV's reality series of life at home with a bonkers rock star began the era of 'Reality'. Svengali of the series was Ozzy's wife Sharon; portrayed as the long-suffering partner of a drug-addled, unfaithful star, it soon turned out that truth was stranger than fiction when tales of her defecating into a box and leaving it on people's desks turned out to be leaked by none other than Sharon herself. She was manipulating a willing audience into believing her pantomime family was as off the scale as it appeared.

Hardly anyone who watched *The Osbournes* could name a single Ozzy song, but it didn't matter. This lunatic rock musician, famous mostly for biting the head off a bat, now turned out to have a domestic life that was fascinating in its gross absurdity and yet also its mundanity. Celebrity rockers have marriage problems just like the rest of us, and they also have untidy houses and stroppy teenage children. It was a revelation.

'The Kardashians have got nothing on the Osbournes,' says Jamie East, founder of gossip site Holy Moly. '*The Osbournes* made us realise we didn't like the gloss of the celebrity world. What we liked instead was watching Sharon call her husband a bastard and crying about his drugs or the time he threatened to shoot her. People could watch *The Osbournes* and think, "I had a similar argument with my husband. Okay, he didn't earn a million quid and he's not on cocaine but he spent our last 50 quid in the bookies and the kids didn't have sandwiches in school for a week!" All of a sudden we realised celebrities left skid marks in the bowl just like the rest of us.'

East at this time was a lowly mole working at Sky TV. Celebrities and tasty morsels of gossip used to pass by his desk, and he needed somewhere to pass them on. That place was Popbitch. Starting out as an email newsletter of crude and rudi-

mentary – yet dehabilitatingly hilarious – stories, it rode the
wave of media from print to digital.

East saw the opportunity to set up a rival website, Holy Moly.
'We were riding this wave of snark. Nick Denton was doing it
overseas with Gawker, but our remit at Holy Moly was that we
would always go where no one else would go – we were blunt.'

The industry that had sprung up around the celebrity class
had plenty of leaks, and the really bad behaviour and filthiest
secrets needed a platform – Holy Moly would publish where
Popbitch wouldn't dare. 'It was the make-up artist dobbing in
the presenter that asked them for a hand job, it was the runner
that got the sack because a famous footballer didn't like the way
he spoke to them,' says East. 'It wasn't about selling the stories,
it was about setting the world to rights. The tagline of Holy
Moly was "Being a celebrity is a ridiculous way to make a living
and it is our job to point that out". We had entered an era where
Kerry Katona was making half a million off Iceland adverts,
which is just nonsense. It was the backlash to that reality class
– them trying to dress themselves up as having a right to be
there. And us knocking them down a peg or two. It was punk.'

With such a willing and broad network of sources, Holy
Moly soon had all the best stories. 'We had a great story about
[famous Hollywood actor who everyone knows is gay],' relates
East. 'He used to go and pull men at Pacha in Ibiza when he was
out there filming. He got his special-effects men to make him
this mask, and he would go and pull men wearing them. But he
got too brave, and started fucking this man in a foam party and
all the latex started melting. So this guy turns round and sees
over his shoulder this melted face, rips the mask off, reveals
[famous actor], and he's like WTF!' Needless to say, the story
found its way back.

Holy Moly also broke the Madonna divorce story. 'An
ex-neighbour was sat in a beer garden on a table next to a confi-

dant of Guy Ritchie. This guy was a bit pissed and shooting his mouth off,' says East, illustrating perfectly how the internet had become the digital version of the neighbour's garden fence. 'So that night I went back, and hit the button. Everybody called me out on it – the *Sun*, the *News of the World*, the *Mirror*, Madonna's record company, Warners, her PR who threatened to have my business closed down. I just dug my heels in and turned my phone off, and within a week they'd announced it. That was Holy Moly's crowning glory.'

What had happened to us, that this was now everything we wanted to hear? The dirtier and more disgusting the better, it seemed. 'The dotcom boom had just gone bust, people were skint and miserable and wanted to be made to feel better,' says East. 'In previous decades we enjoyed rags to riches stories – a period where you revelled in other people's success. Faye Dunaway, Marilyn Monroe, *Lawrence of Arabia* – you wanted to be soaked up in their majesty, you wanted Omar Sharif to be a multi-millionaire and a masterful lover and you went to bed dreaming of that and that was your escape. The thing that changed was that people thought, "Fuck you – what gives you the right to be actually a terrible actor, on the front page of all those magazines, and earn all that money? You're no better than me!"'

As the role of celebrities went from aspiration to identification to victimisation, intrusion began. We didn't want glamour any more, we wanted flaws. *Heat* magazine shamed girls' bodies for post-pregnancy weight, dramatic weight loss or cellulite. In came *Big Brother*, where members of the public were put under a microscope in a live televised experiment of what would happen if you locked unhinged people up in a house for a month. These unknowns became celebrities as the *Sun*, *Mirror* and weekly magazines found a new source of stories and everything evolved again.

'It was now achievable. Celebrity was something that anyone could achieve and somehow being a celebrity was a goal in itself,' continues Thykier. 'That fame as a commodity could be monetised, definitely knocked things forward. The notion of fame was fame.'

'It changed really quickly – and then it became a bit of a firefight,' says East. 'Where I come from in Derby, people in pubs call people a "cunt". So we launched "Cunts Corner", and in 48 hours it just took off. It got up to 10,000 submissions a day at one point, of people calling famous people a cunt: "Richard Madeley's a cunt. That Ali G impression? What a cunt!" They ranged from naff, inarticulate entries to diatribes that were sort of Partridge-esque: "Nick Owen from Central TV opened our school fete in 1982 and knocked my ice cream out of my hand. You cunt!" It was a free for all – "Paul McCartney is a cunt because he once told my mum to get out of his way," or "Jeremy Clarkson is a cunt because he cut me off on the A38 in 1987"; "The guy from the Bostik advert, he's a cunt." We were the spleen for the UK to vent, and there was no holds barred. The celebrity gossip was great but it was very cliquey, it brought very small numbers in. Cunts Corner was for everyone.'

It was, if you like, the beginning of trolling. Now your next-door neighbour could have their say, the guy in the park could make his voice heard, the checkout girl had a public platform. Soon there would be pictures and video, blogs and vlogs – soon the bloggers and vloggers would become the celebrities themselves. But before that, we had to level the playing field. Our celebrities, who had started out as inaccessible, fantastical depictions of talent and glamour, could not survive the scrutiny of the pulsing, heaving, growing media. Cigars, tampons and cellulite had them down.

6

Let's Get Digital

Do you remember what it was like before we had the internet? Go on, think, and really think. Think back to a world of delayed gratification, where you had to wait to find out the answer to something, go somewhere to do things, meet people to make things happen. A world where cats were not famous, where you had no social media feeds to check the moment you woke up, where you spoke in full sentences, and made spelling mistakes, and had to describe how you felt with actual words rather than emojis.

If we wanted to get somewhere, we had to actually look it up in an atlas, and then write out the directions. We got lost, and asked actual people the way, rather than Siri. We used dictionaries and encyclopaedias, we watched TV programmes when they were actually on TV – and missed our favourite programmes. We knew our friends' phone numbers off by heart, we had to wait for our photographs to be developed before we could see them, we had arguments with people at dinner and no one could settle the result by Google. Worst of all, we had to deal with CDs, the most infuriating medium for music ever invented.

The internet crept up on us, slowly, and then all of a sudden it was here and *everything* was different. 'I remember being about 19 or 20, and going to California with a girlfriend,' remembers Ben Elliot, the nightclub entrepreneur who went on to found the luxury lifestyle concierge, Quintessentially. 'She had some friends who tried to explain to me what the internet was. I was sitting with this guy in LA and he showed me that I could find out anything I wanted about *Star Wars*. It was incredible. All I'd known up to that point was going to PC World in Southampton to buy a Toshiba laptop. Computers were basically just something I used to write essays on.'

'My friends thought I was nuts for going to do anything with technology,' says Martha Lane Fox. 'I only got into it because of going to work for a consulting company that was focusing on media and telecoms. I actually thought it was a TV production company, but luckily realised in the interview it wasn't. If I hadn't by chance met the guy who was starting this business, I probably would've done something completely different. It was serendipity.' Spotting her opportunity, Martha ended up becoming the poster girl for the first dotcom boom when she founded, and famously floated, lastminute.com, a digital business that sourced low-cost travel deals.

'I thought the idea was good because I thought more exploration is good,' she says. 'I remember working late one night in a horrible building where we had our first office, a really disgusting skyscraper where I kept getting arrested by the security guard because I burnt the toast. One evening I wrote the strapline: something like "We want to help people live their dreams at unbeatable prices". The idea was to help people be more romantic, more spontaneous. Obviously there was a commercial element too, but I remember thinking this was good, this is encouraging more fun and people to have a good time and explore the world and see things and be outward looking.'

It was the perfect idea for a generation that had formalised backpacking and gap years, who were already exploring the world and now wanted to cash in on the Easyjet life of weekends in Prague. 'I remember this absolutely insane trip I took with a girlfriend in 1993 from the middle of Mongolia, we didn't know what the hell we were doing. We hitchhiked all across Kyrgyzstan, Kazakhstan, and Uzbekistan down into China, Pakistan and India for four months. What were we thinking? I remember ringing my mum from the Mongolia–China border and she hadn't heard from us for five weeks, and she wasn't going to hear from me for another five weeks. Can you imagine that now?'

All that travel in far-flung places must have helped influence the more liberal outlook of our generation. At the very least, 'We've all got a lot of rugs,' points out Martha. But it definitely gave us a taste for more. 'It influences you on the edges. You are a different person having travelled. This girl I travelled to Mongolia with now coordinates the relief effort for UNHCR into Syria from Jordan. Another works for a charity based in Africa. In another time, it would've been hard for women particularly to have had that breadth and depth of travel experience.'

My university college had a relationship with a children's charity in India; in the summer of my second year I was given a holiday job there. The previous year I had saved up to travel around Central America with a girlfriend; meanwhile other friends were travelling to Romania to work in their pitifully funded orphanages, or driving aid trucks to Kosovo. The world was a much smaller and more accessible place for us than it was for our parents. I think my mum and dad thought foreign holidays were a bit 'nouveau' in the Eighties. And my dad certainly had a particularly robust view of travelling for the sake of it: in his mind, it was 'self-indulgence'.

Lastminute was of course only one of thousands of businesses that set up in the first internet gold rush, all promising better ways for us to live and serve our lives. The way Uber, Airbnb and Deliveroo have transformed our lives now was foreshadowed by the generation of digital services led by Lastminute. Everyone could see the potential, (perhaps not quite the extent of it – but then it was unimaginable at the time) and venture capitalists poured money into the sector indiscriminately.

'Four doors down from where we set up Quintessentially in Soho was this fashion e-commerce company called boo.com,' says Ben Elliot. 'Every day, new people were being hired. Their offices got deliveries of Coke machines and pool tables. They were like the advertising agencies of their day. They burnt through £300 million in the end. On the day they launched I wanted to become a customer and buy my trainers online, but because I didn't have Flash on my PC, I couldn't see the trainers.'

There was a time when everyone you met was either going to work for an internet company or was setting one up themselves. 'We all drank the Kool-Aid,' says Ben, 'which is that everything would change. And it did change. But it didn't change the basic business principle that it's not just about eyeballs; you actually have to qualify your model with revenue.' That should have rung alarm bells, but everyone was too blind and buzzed to see it.

Something else happened during this time as well. Women went from an equal-opportunities world, to being alarmingly excluded. And we hardly even noticed. 'It's just breathtaking,' says Martha. 'And the consequence is that nowadays women are just absent from the creation and running of the internet.'

Google, Facebook, Amazon, Apple – the four big horsemen of the digital apocalypse are run and staffed mainly by men. Notable exceptions are Apple chief executive Angela Ahrendts, and Facebook's Sheryl Sandberg, but they are the exceptions. As men have become the dominant workforce, women have started to complain about sexist behaviour. A high-profile case amongst the founders of the dating site Tinder illustrates the problem: a woman pushed out by her three male colleagues filed a lawsuit accusing them of sexual harassment. She said she was asked to leave 'as having a 24-year-old girl as a founder was an embarrassment'.

But it didn't start out like this. 'Women were actually the first software engineers, although it was not quite software,' explains Martha. 'It was the late Sixties, early Seventies, and it was happening because it was women who were controlling the machines that were doing the automation design. For example, the Lyons tea factory was one of the first places that had a computer. It was the women's bureaucratic jobs that were being made slightly less bureaucratic, so it was women who were trained on the machines. An amazing woman called Dame Stephanie Shirley had a company in the late Sixties employing only women, all working from home, about 3,000 at one point, programming software for things like the Polaris submarine and Concorde – really hardcore stuff.'

But what came next was disastrous. 'In the Eighties computing became professionalised. Big corporates moved in and installed male managers as there were just more men. As Stephanie Shirley might say, men got wind this was going to be a big and profitable industry and something happened.'

You might expect it from the Eighties, but how did we, our generation, with all our equal opportunities and liberalism, allow the internet to become such a powerful force controlled by so few people, who are mostly men?

'By the late nineties, there were still a few women knocking around,' says Martha. 'But the internet became commercialised through a series of strange steps from, as always, some brilliant, crazy entrepreneurs and some strange people. It grew quickly through platform-based businesses – businesses that have 20 employees and 200 million people using them. Very quickly, you end up with a monoculture.'

Which is ironic, as the promise of the internet was always that it was going to be a big democratising force. The communality of hackers and developers who shared their work with everyone in order to progress it was true to this principle – that the internet, as its inventor Tim Berners-Lee declared, was by everyone and for everyone. But then along came Google and Facebook, and in a very short space of time they came to dominate everything.

'These businesses just went whoosh and created a completely different web, a kind of walled-garden web.' As organisations, individuals and even governments have found to their cost, you can do little online without collaborating with one of these giants. 'Nowadays you couldn't possibly get your internet business going without a relationship with Google, it would be impossible. But when lastminute started, there wasn't a Google. We did lots of individual deals with Yahoo and other companies, all of which have now disappeared.' Eaten up by Google.

It wasn't just that these businesses grew quickly – another factor was, as Martha puts it, 'the absolute religiousness of software development and design'. Software development was dominated by classic nerds in bedrooms, a culture that women just weren't a part of – which is not to say they are no good at it.

'Do women like solving problems and creating and building new things? Of course they do. We use different language and we do it in a different way, but building brilliant software is all about collaboration and women are good at that. It's just that there's a particular male culture that is creating it at the minute. And when that culture suddenly got incredibly rich because they were building Google, women were not in the door. If you have someone at the head of a company, however well meaning the company, however well meaning the boss, that culture is still that culture. Larry and Sergey started Google, Mark Zuckerberg started Facebook, another man started LinkedIn, another man started Instagram – all these businesses use such a small group of people. And they have all gone whoosh in a way that's certainly taken my breath away.'

Blinded by all the clear benefits that the internet has brought us, from cheap taxis to grocery home delivery, fitness trackers to social networks, I wonder if the wider world realises quite how impactful this 'slip-up' has been.

'It's bad,' says Martha. 'I reckon about 4 per cent of the code that is the internet has been created by women, if that. So in 20 years we've gone from one industrial establishment, run by white men to another, which is all white men, with a few Indian and Chinese. Excuse me? What the hell?'

Now the way technology is being developed is almost entirely without recourse to or thought for women. Take the Apple health app. When it was released, it contained no information or tracking abilities on periods, the menopause, fertility, pregnancy or birth. Because it had all been designed by men.

And then there's the culture. 'Too many tech conferences are full of supermodels and champagne corks and fast cars – that's what success looks like? You just think, so retrograde.'

Martha's latest venture, Doteveryone, is, according to its mission statement, 'a new kind of digital organisation that's here to show what's possible: tech that does good, at scale, for the future. We work out what will make people's lives better. We listen to people. We build prototypes, and make them work for the people who are actually going to use them. For everyone, by everyone.'

With Martha at the helm, it is staffed entirely by women. 'One of our projects is looking to build a service for end-of-life care for the NHS. The team that's doing it are all women – a female designer, female technical lead, and two women doing the coding. I didn't say it had to be like that but it's like that because when you have a woman leading, they know more women and then the networks are just built up.'

There's another, equally pernicious problem with digital: access to opportunity. 'Look at the dynamics of it,' says Martha. 'I'm on the board of Marks & Spencer and we have 83,000 employees and we turn over about £10 billion and make £650 million or so in profit. Facebook has 23,000 employees, has revenues of £200 billion and profits of nearly £4 billion. Anybody that argues tech isn't taking jobs is wrong. It is.

'Just a few people control the entire newsfeed for Facebook across the entire billion people that it serves. In defence, I don't think Facebook thought they would grow as quickly as they did. In those early days I think Mark Zuckerberg must've been pretty surprised it grew so fast and I know people at Google say a lot of it is quite chaotic because they're still trying to work through the fact that in ten years, they've become one of the most powerful companies in the world.'

Media, meanwhile, has been savaged. £7.2 billion is now spent on digital advertising, which equates to 40 per cent of all advertising spend in the UK. Of this, Google and Facebook take 65 per cent between them, leaving plenty of non-digital businesses out of pocket. It's worth noting that neither Google nor Facebook are publishers – they don't make anything. One is a search engine and the other is a social network. So all that money is being used to do little other than make more money. Google has dropped its founding principle – 'Don't Be Evil'. Just as the end of the Industrial Revolution laid waste to so much of the country and workforce in the final decades of the last century, the last fifteen years have seen the publishing, music and TV industries in total disruption. Now it is technology, not the creative arts, that dominates the playing fields.

There's also the issue of tax, as these big companies, who take so much money out of the countries they inhabit, are paying a

pittance in corporation tax. By cynically housing their headquarters in Dublin, or the Caymans, and claiming that is where
the large part of their business happens, they benefit from much
lower tax rates. 'And that,' says businessman Richard Reed, 'is
just plain shonky.'

'In the end they're commercial organisations and that's how
they operate,' says Martha. 'We need global tax regimes now, for
sure. The gender thing is depressing, the data piece as well, arguably. Data that has been looked after by all these companies has
been pillaged and raped. The other aspect is about now they've
got so much cash and are so powerful that every small start-up
gets bought by one of these enormous platforms. Everything
gets sucked back up to the US.'

The big tech companies are now so rich they are able to buy
up not only all the world's most exciting businesses, but all the
world's brain power too – Harvard economists and their like are
all being sucked up by Google as no one else can compete with
their starting salaries of £200,000 a year.

Depressing indeed. It's hard to frame technology as a creative
revolution when so many companies, creative-content-making
companies, are falling victim to their hegemony and greed. But
then I would say that, as the industry I work in, newspapers, is
struggling to survive. Quality journalism needs investment, but
the once profitable organisations that used to fund it through a
combination of advertising and circulation sales are seeing
dwindling revenues in both areas.

One thing is for sure: we will miss quality journalism when it
is gone. But there are plenty of reasons to celebrate too, and not
just because your Uber is on time. Digital gave everyone a fast
track to entrepreneurship and in the aftermath of 2008, it saved
the Millennial generation. Tools like Shopify allowed every stay-
at-home mum to start a retail business (hand-knitted Cornish
tea cosy, anyone?). Suddenly there was an app for everything

and marketing and advertising a start-up could be targeted, cheap and effective.

But it wasn't just the internet that let women down. There were other factors at play.

7

Three Lions

There was a moment in the Nineties when on the lower ranks of the career ladder your progress as a woman was accelerated. Businesses realised that they needed more female employees, more women as managers. The penetration of the female workforce was still in adjustment phase. In the newspaper industry, where I worked, there was a crunching realisation that half its readers were women, and yet 70, 80 per cent of its editors were male. Lifestyle sections sprang up to cater for the readership, and they needed female editors. Patronising to say that women could only edit these sections, but the knock-on effect was almost immediate – once you had a female features editor sitting in news conference, why couldn't you have a female politics editor? Or comment editor?

These 'shrill' voices began to be heard in conference meetings, expressing valid and interesting points of view. Suddenly we had our first female national newspaper editor – Rosie Boycott, at the *Independent* (1996). The founder of *Spare Rib*, the ultra-radical feminist magazine of the Seventies, was now editing one of our national newspapers. The *Independent* was a success, and Rosie was poached to take the helm at the *Express* in 1998, a middle-market tabloid that was losing out to the *Mail*.

It was thrilling. At the time I was on the features desk at the *Express*, and as Rosie promoted those above me I became features editor. I was 28. The foreign editor was a woman, the features editor was a woman, the news editor was a woman, even the night editor was a woman. Rosie looked about one day and, clocking all her female cohorts, said, 'We need a photograph of this.' I have it still – eleven of us, in the middle of the newsroom, making a paper that was bought by over a million people nationwide. I asked Rosie recently if the female-heavy leadership was by accident or design. 'Design,' she answered, without missing a beat.

Unfortunately the project didn't last – Rosie's liberal values were not an easy sell to a constituency of readers who were historically much more right wing. We did not stem the tide of readers to the *Mail*. But it didn't matter – Rosie was infectious in her enthusiasm and energy and it did really feel like we were trying to change things, to move the dial. The *Express* was sold by United News and Media two years into Rosie's reign to Richard Desmond, the media baron who had made his fortune out of porn titles such as *Penthouse* and *Asian Babes*. Ironic, huh? Two steps forward, three steps back.

Desmond turned up in our building one day, took over the corner office and brought his butler, a man whose chores included bringing him a banana on a silver platter every morning. You can imagine the vast amount of common ground Desmond and Rosie had to cover. Rosie left, and I went to work on the News Review desk at the *Sunday Times*.

Has the newspaper industry been feminised? Janet Street-Porter briefly edited the *Independent on Sunday*, Sarah Sands now edits the *Evening Standard*, Rebekah Brooks edited both the *News of the World* and the *Sun* (and is now CEO of News UK), and both *The Times* and *Sunday Times* have women as deputies, foreign editors and executive editors. But if you look carefully in the comment pages of newspapers you will not see an equal gender balance of male and female columnists. Indeed, there are hardly any women in the Westminster political lobby. Most political editors are male (the BBC's Laura Kuenssberg is a wonderful exception), and you will also find that most news and business editors are men too.

'The world is still seen through a pale, male and stale lens,' says Eleanor Mills, editorial director of the *Sunday Times* and chair of Women in Journalism. 'Sure, there's tokenism, but like all organisations, if publications feel they have one high-profile woman, then they have ticked the equality box.' A study by Women in Journalism in 2012 revealed that male bylines and sexist stereotypes still dominate Britain's national newspapers. In a study of nine UK national newspapers, it found that 78 per cent of all front-page articles were written by men compared with 22 per cent by women. The WiJ report also looked at the lead pictures on the front page and found that the Duchess of Cambridge and her sister Pippa Middleton, along with victim Madeleine McCann, were the most regularly pictured females.

'There's a severe lack of women with agency featured in newspapers,' says Eleanor. 'Too often the women we do see are victims or arm candy. There aren't enough women featured for being successful or doing things in their own right. Hopefully, with Theresa May running Britain that may start to change.' What a shame we so narrowly missed having a woman president of the United States as well.

Despite what happened subsequently, at this point in the late Nineties and early Noughties, women felt empowered. We felt valued in the workplace, our contribution to the culture was everywhere: from the female YBAs to the queens of pop, TV, film and the chick lit of the fiction world, women had a loud and strong voice. We felt so empowered, in fact, that we felt we could reclaim sexuality for ourselves. 'Hello Boys' didn't feel like an affront – Eva Herzigová in that Wonderbra campaign actually made us feel good.

(Imagine if that Wonderbra picture were to be released now – the outcry! A recent poster campaign for the diet brand Protein World depicting a beautiful girl in a bikini that asked 'Are you beach body ready?' generated a petition that 51,000 people signed in protest. Best, though, was Protein World's own response during the attack: an unrepentant Twitter feed that basically told everyone to suck it up if they didn't like it. Sales rocketed.)

But, Millennial girls, our bad. All this is our fault. Generation X women took our eye off the ball just at the moment when we thought the battle was won. We thought it was okay to admire push-up bra posters, regard pole dancing as a sport, cast Page 3 girls like Katie Price as figures to be admired and emblems of freedom. It was even briefly fashionable to have a diamanté thong hanging out the back of your jeans (yes, massively sorry about that one).

We celebrated this new 'raunch culture', as it came to be called, and its poster girls, the WAGs, or 'wives and girlfriends' – women famous for being married to someone talented and interesting. So – not talented in themselves, just married to it. I'm not sure we spotted the irony of this at the time. The WAGs eventually met their demise in a flurry of hair extensions, designer sun goggles and shopping bags when they were held responsible for England crashing out of the World Cup in Baden-Baden in 2006. Millennial girls, meanwhile, have not been okay with the hand they have been dealt. They do not like the way women are portrayed in the media, the way they are trolled online, or the pay gap, or the number of women on boards, or the disparity between men and women in almost every important institution around the world. For this, we now have the third wave of feminism. So, Generation X, how could we have taken our eye off the ball so completely?

For the answer, you need to scroll back ten years to 1996, when England hosted the European Championships. This was the height of lad culture, epitomised by the comedy duo Baddiel and Skinner, who teamed up with Britpop's the Lightning Seeds to release the single 'Three Lions' – a call to English football to bring the trophy home. Baddiel and Skinner were hosts of TV's popular *Fantasy Football League*. Laddism celebrated working-class culture as a middle-class pursuit – leading to the famous comment that prawn sandwiches were the food of choice in corporate boxes at Manchester United's Old Trafford ground. Ecstasy might have broken down the class system, and Hillsborough might have put an end to the terraces with fixed seating, but the price of a ticket to a match was rapidly going up. Still, football was now officially cool, and as Nineties music culture embraced it, what was there not to like?

'The whole laddie football thing brought people together,' says Ben Elliot. 'It was a common language. People from all backgrounds could say they supported this team or they were into this music. I remember people throwing milk bottles at me as a 13-year-old posh boy in Portsmouth. It was really scary when I first started going to football matches, but in the end the terror was taken out. They put seats in and it became a different atmosphere. Rave culture definitely had something to do with it – there was a mentality of going to a football game, having a couple of lagers and then going out dancing all night.'

Working-class culture, of which football was a constituent part, became aspirational – 'mockney' or fake cockney accents emerged as nice middle-class boys like Damon Albarn and Guy Ritchie dropped their aitches for credibility. 'I think that's what laddism was – people who were middle class trying to be a bit working class because it was cooler,' says the musician Danny Goffey. 'All that Seventies music we liked, like the Clash, the Jam, the Sex Pistols, those bands were quite working class. Middle-class people didn't want to come across as spoilt. Now class is a bit more squished together and there isn't such a thing about it.'

'There was such an inverted snobbery in the music industry, especially around the *NME*,' says Danny's wife Pearl. 'If you were posh they would go crazy. The girls in those bands at the time – Sleeper, Salad, Justine from Elastica, they were all quite posh. Justine had a £2 million house in Notting Hill. My dad is a bouncer from Bethnal Green, who tells stories about his days with the Krays. For me, I tried very hard not to be working class.'

Amongst women, it became fashionable to support football. Whether this was because girls were genuinely into football, or whether it was because girls were trying to be more like boys, is arguable. In 1996 I was living in north London surrounded by Arsenal supporters, and like the ladettes around me – Zoe Ball, Sara Cox and Denise van Outen – I was swept up in the hysteria. Football was celebrated, cool and fun, why not enjoy it? (As it turned out, it was never that enjoyable.)

As girls, we felt safe and secure – feminism was for unsexy girls in horrible dungarees who 'burnt their bras'. Ugh, so unattractive. But nor did we yet feel threatened by this new form of masculinity. Laddism felt cool and celebratory – and why shouldn't we celebrate boys? We felt we had busted through sexism and had come sufficiently far out the other side that we could do this now. Besides, laddism was a cool, modern way to be masculine, a way out of the hunter-gatherer fields and the woods and through the hunting grounds of offices and mortgages. Mostly it was characterised by football, birds, white-collar boxing, Britpop (and there were some great female Britpop acts too: Elastica, the Cranberries, Powder) and, um, lager ... ('Lager, lager, lager, shouting ...').

At the centre of it sat *Loaded* magazine. It launched in 1994, with Gary Oldman on the cover. It was targeted at 'men who should know better'. Following covers included Reeves and

Mortimer, Gazza, the Simpsons, Neil Morrissey from *Men Behaving Badly*, Ross Kemp, who along with Steve McFadden, portrayed the Mitchell brothers in *EastEnders* – classic East End hard men who struggled with women, lager and violence, but were employed in the manly pursuits of garage mechanic and pub landlord.

Kris Thykier, in his role at Freud Communications, was minder to many of these celebrities. 'I walked through airports with massive movie stars and with Ross Kemp, and I can tell you that there was a point in the mid-Nineties where if you walked through an airport with Ross Kemp, there was no one more famous,' he says. 'There was also no one with less distance, because everyone thought they knew him. Celebrity and public were colliding – everyone thought they owned him and had a direct relationship with him.' That divide between celebrity and the public was made thinner by Kemp's marriage to Rebekah Brooks – then editor of the *Sun*, whose circulation was thriving on this new culture of lads and ladettes.

In short, there were plenty of male heroes around to encapsulate the new male ideal. It was a reaction to the 'New Man', a previous ideal of manhood that was meant to take in men's increasing involvement in domestic life and fatherhood. A rather limp character, he was not exactly sexy, but at least he was modernising. Lads on the other hand – well, everyone wanted to sleep with them.

Danny Goffey stood at the nexus of the two groups. Just as Supergrass hit the Britpop mainstream he became a father. He was happy to play New Man to his wife, at the same time as being a Britpop superhero.

'Pearl has always been quite controlling about everything, but I never had a problem with it. There were always strong women around me. My mum was a freelancer who worked really hard – I always saw women as working harder than men anyway, self-sufficient and making decisions. But I did go away on tour, so I was away from the family a lot too.

'I took to fatherhood quite well. When Alfie came out he looked just like me and I used to love it, pushing him around. I remember the *NME* got a picture of us pushing the pram and they were taking the piss about the "New Dad" thing – a man pushing a buggy. I had a Mohican when Alfie was born, as I'd just been on tour with the Prodigy and they'd influenced us a bit, but I remember a couple of times people said, "Is that your child?"'

Imitators took the *Loaded* recipe and dumbed it down for a bigger audience, dialling up the sex. Mike Soutar, the editor of *FHM* (which by the mid Nineties was the biggest-selling UK magazine ever, selling over 900,000 copies a month), had noticed a change in the sexual preferences of young men. He might have been editing a glossy magazine, but his readers were a long way from the Hollywood Hills. It wasn't Julia Roberts and Sandra Bullock they wanted pictures of, but actually the likes of Kelly Brook, Gail Porter and Rachel Stevens.

'The separation between public and celebrities was diminishing in terms of sexual attraction for young men,' says Thykier. 'Mike discovered that actually readers were much more attracted to someone who was like the girl next door because she was in the realm of the possible. It began with film stars, then it became TV stars, then soap stars and the gradual reduction of distance between the celebrated and the celebrators found its nadir in reality. Turns out, actually all that people really wanted was other people to gawp at.' *Loaded* and its definition of lad culture eventually descended to the depths of *Zoo* and *Nuts* – weekly all-but-porn magazines that eventually lost out to the porn that was readily available on the internet.

In the midst of the current feminist mindset, laddism survives in the form of The LAD Bible – a digital channel that has cornered the young male market. Interestingly it is as funny and sharp as *Loaded* in its heyday, but swerves away from any content that is derogatory towards women. So in many ways, laddism proved a success, if ladettes landed us all in the shit. There's a lot of talk now about 'lost' men, fuelled by the fact that 75 per cent of suicides are amongst men under the age of 45. Interestingly, I asked all the Generation X men I spoke to for this book if they felt there was an identity crisis in masculinity, and they all insisted absolutely not.

And yet. As the chef Thomasina Miers says: 'Where is all this trolling of women coming from – the ill-educated ones? Men literally don't know what their place looks like in society today.' Throw into this a cultural clash of immigrant societies with no history of equality and a readily available diet of internet porn, and you end with the toxic mess of the Rotherham child abuse scandals.

The artist and TV presenter Grayson Perry quips that what makes a man now is not some kind of Bear Grylls survival skill set but the ability to find an affordable flat in Finsbury Park and get your kid into a decent school. The casualties are everywhere – not least the ones who never came down off the rave. Bobby (not really his name) was a DJ who used to play at parties I went to. He was a great guy, cool and funny with excellent music. He found a beautiful girlfriend, an ethereal type who made jewellery; she was grounded and yogic. But for Bobby the party never stopped. And when it did, there was the next one. His girlfriend could see he was beginning to lose control, and she moved them both to the countryside to downscale the situation. But Bobby still found the parties – he was a DJ after all. That was his living.

His drug consumption went up, his finances went down. They couldn't afford the heating any more, and eventually the rent. His girlfriend left him. He crashed on sofas and stayed with friends, but his friends noticed that things were going missing from their houses – valuable things that could be sold on. Finally

Bobby went missing. No one could find him. Several weeks passed. Missing posters and Facebook feeds yielded nothing.

Eventually Bobby was found. He had taken his own life. He was 43.

There were many reasons why this happened but Bobby was depressed. He had a diminishing professional output, no familial role and physically there was nothing around him to help him with his identity. He also had no children, something that makes many men move on to the next stage on their lives, as they take on a more responsible role of bread winner and provider. But our generation has put off marriage and children for as long as it could – responsibility and money were not high on our list of priorities. That approach has claimed its casualties.

So where have women been in all of this?

8

Sex: The Consequences

Samantha, Carrie, Miranda and Charlotte. All of us girls were one or another of these characters, the perfect articulation of Noughties woman. The devil-may-care sex maniac, the blue-stocking lovely, the career-focused lawyer, and the dreamy, self-examining fashion girl. Drinking cocktails, dressing up, mooning over men, buying shoes, cashing wage checks, getting Brazilians, OD-ing on chocolate cake, hanging with friends and living in girl palaces.

And weren't our homes a type? Stripped pine floorboards, white muslin curtains and twinkly chandeliers, piles of sparkly fuschia Indian scatter cushions, cashmere throws and the best cotton sheets we could afford. Orchids were our flowers, lighting was scented candles and fairy lights, and like Carrie, we would occasionally use our ovens for extra clothes storage. No one cooked, everyone brunched, and if you opened the fridge there would be a jar of out-of-date pesto and a half-empty bottle of vodka. The single girl's diet. We wore our gay friends like accessories and the girls' night out was the acme of living. The independent woman was finally setting herself up in exactly the way she wanted. (I'm afraid independent women these days don't have it so good. They live with their parents.)

Sex and the City was Noughties woman: single or dating, earning her own money, not particularly interested in marriage and kids (where was the fun in that?), spilling Cosmopolitans and hunting down high-class fuck-me shoes. It was a time of maximum credit: if you couldn't afford the Mulberry Bayswater, you could just whack it on a card and live the consequences later. Vodka cocktails made us forget and, besides, we were having a ball.

Sex and the City writ it large and glamorous, a fantasy version of our lives where we all wore fabulous clothes, had unbelievably successful careers and careered around New York hopping from bed to bar to store. It depicted a life where girls could have what they wanted, when they wanted with few consequences. They could be submissive and girlie, dominant and unruly. They could spend, spend, spend because they were earning. (Carrie quite often references her finances but it's never so bad she can't buy a pair of Manolos. In a final reckoning near the end of the show she realises she can't buy her flat because her deposit has been converted into boxes and boxes of designer shoes.)

Sex and the City broke down the single-girl experience and made it stylish – allergic to the settled, boring life and in celebration of its gospel of freewheeling, rootless fabulosity.

And then there was the sex. Now it does not seem such a big deal, but at the end of the Nineties this unashamed, guilt-free depiction of getting, having and enjoying sex, whatever which way, was thrilling. Thrilling like Lena Dunham's sex is in *Girls*, for featuring real life and real bodies, *SATC*'s was women in control in the bedroom for the first time. It reflected what was actually happening – that women were sleeping with whom they pleased, how they pleased, when they pleased. And it was them on top. If they couldn't find a man, well, as Miranda says:

'Men are going to be obsolete in fifty years' time. You don't need them to have kids with any more, and you don't even need them to have sex with any more, as I've very pleasantly just discovered.'

'Uh oh, sounds like somebody just got her first vibrator,' says Samantha.

'Not first. Ultimate. And I think I'm in love,' replies Miranda. Miranda had just invested in a Rabbit.

My flatmate of the time was a television producer with a string of interesting conquests. She dabbled with artists and music industry types and journalists and marketeers – let's just say her easy-going nature, good humour and ability to be the last one standing at a party won her no shortage of admirers. But over take-away curry nights, she eventually admitted she had never had an orgasm. Not once in her probably around 15 years of sex life. It was time for The Rabbit. My flatmate gave it a go, over a period of several weeks. Until one morning, shrieking with joy, she emerged: the soundtrack of a woman who had finally got there.

I wonder how many Boomer women never got there? This was the generation that claimed the contraceptive pill as the most liberating tool for women of the last hundred years. For our generation, there are those who would claim the BlackBerry (RIP – but pre-smartphones the BlackBerry was the first device that allowed you to blend work and life, parenting and career; for that, it will always have a special place in my heart). My friend, however, would vote for The Rabbit.

This high-fashion, highly sexed environment women now found themselves in, produced a series of vibrator launches designed with women in mind – vibrators that went way beyond the traditional dildo. I had bought my first vibrator years ago in a seedy sex shop in Oxford – I had to sneak in, head down, negotiating rows of greasy men pawing over magazines, to find the wall of sex toys at the back. And what a sea of revolting pink plastic fake penises I found. Eventually I settled on one which I thought was just about tasteful: it was ribbed, and coloured black and gold. But as customer demand increased, so did the choice of what was available. The early Noughties erotic lingerie brand Myla even commissioned the furniture designers Tom Dixon and Marc Newson to make theirs (no such thing as a notable female product designer yet).

But The Rabbit changed everything. A vibrating, rotating sex toy that featured the usual phallic tower, The Rabbit had a double-eared clitoral stimulator designed in along the shaft. Hence the name. Instead of pink, it came in a variety of colours on the Fisher-Price spectrum, which was perfect, because of course that is what it was – a toy. Not a replacement penis. Its efficiency and brilliance changed the expectation of the female orgasm for all of us. It proved multiple orgasms did exist. Delayed orgasms exist. G-spot orgasms exist. Great, minute-long shuddering orgasms exist. It was so goddamn good, that, as Charlotte says when she purchases one and takes it home, she is afraid that if she carries on using it, she may never have sex with an actual man again: 'I think I broke my vagina!'

For girls living the single life, with periods of no regular boyfriend on tap, it was more than just a solution. It made sexual prowess not just a fantasy but an immediate, on tap reality.

Sex is not always a celebration, however. Sometimes it goes wrong, terribly wrong. The heartache came when you did something you regretted – frequently that meant *someone* you regretted. There is a consequence to casual sex, and any girl who thinks she can sleep with as many men as she likes and not beat herself up is lying. Sex always has been a precious gift, and no social or historical circumstance changes that. Which is why sex in a loving relationship, where there is trust and care, is the best sex of all.

There is also crazy sex and crazy love, and those are the most intense experiences, but, as wise ones know, they are draining and depleting and eventually unsustainable. They will tip you over the edge, make you mad and deranged until your friends don't want to know you and your life turns upside down. When they eventually burn out – and they always do – you will be left broken, a cinder. Good luck with the recovery. It's a long haul.

And there always have been and always will be men who take more than is offered, who fail to decode the semantics of when no means no (and, you know what, it is complicated). Generation X's new sexual mores gave rise to the term 'date rape' as men, women and the law tried to figure out what this meant.

Many women have experienced date rape, many never report it or even acknowledge it to anyone other than themselves or close friends. Date rape is sex that may have started somewhere down the path as consensual – maybe simply in accepting an invitation to go out. But there is a misunderstanding as to where and when that consensus ends. Someone goes further than the other person wants them to, allowing something to happen that is unwelcome at the very least. We are lucky now that date rape is even recognised: who knows how many previous incidents went unreported, injured parties left to suffer in silence. The fact that rape claims have gone up can be put down to a greater transparency around the legality of unconsensual sex, but the question is, have boys been educated enough about this? Have women?

Either party, and it is normally the woman as she is usually the physical inferior, cannot always be in full control of a physical experience, and if either of you is under the influence of alcohol or drugs your ability to make the right judgement is depleted further. Equally your ability to be tough about your negative experiences, and chalk them up to education rather than traumatic, life- and mood-changing events, is not always a sure thing.

By this stage in our lives, most Generation X women have figured out the sexual landscape; they know how to conduct themselves in it in a way that is safe, pleasurable and exploratory. Affairs and Tinder may complicate things, but at least we have experience and confidence on our side. Just as well, as the landscape that has opened up in our wake is far from safe.

While we came of age in a post-AIDS world that was delightfully laced with Jilly Cooper and friends, Millennial girls have had to wrestle a generation of men bred on internet porn. Whereas X-ers enjoyed an unfettered approach to the joy of sex, Millennials have only had E. L. James and the *Fifty Shades* canon to counter the brutality of that which is widely shared on the Net.

'When we were first dating, we wore flat shoes, baggy trousers and raving kit,' says Eleanor Mills, 45, who as a journalist has campaigned against the wide availability of online porn. 'What we wore and how we presented ourselves was for the large part non-sexualised. We were raised to understand that when you fell into bed with a man, he was just unbelievably grateful to have you there. Nowadays women dress in skinny jeans and tottering heels, wear bucketloads of make-up and shave off all their pubic hair – they are much more sexualised in the way they feel they have to present themselves. I can't help but put that down to the prevailing porn culture – about what you have to look like to be attractive to a man.

'What's really scary, though, is there's a whole generation of girls having sex now, who are not enjoying it for how it feels but instead worrying about how it looks – do I look like a porn star, do I look like I'm enjoying this?

'It's gone from being something internal and cerebral and the boy being excited about being in bed with you, to everyone feeling intimidated by all these images of what they think sex should look like. Not to mention the smorgasbord of horror that's really affecting the kind of sex teenagers think they should be having.'

For Eleanor, raunch culture was a dangerous cultural trend that paved the way for internet porn. 'Misogyny doesn't go away, it mutates,' she says. 'Raunch culture encouraged men to view women objectively. If you're dressing like a slut and doing a pole dance in stripper heels, whether its simply to please yourself or because you're being "ironic", you are nonetheless still dressing to please men and feed their desires. The result of raunch culture has been a horrible internet backlash, where the vast majority of images show women being humiliated or hurt. Imagery of women having their heads stuck down loos and multiple cocks thrust in their mouths is now just one click away. It's been utterly normalised. Now we have a whole generation of young men raised on porn that denigrates women. A weird twist in the culture has sent everything careering backwards for women again.'

As the misogyny has surfaced, the response has been movements like Everyday Sexism, a digital petition highlighting examples of chauvinism, however tame and however severe, with the message that none of it is okay. It records casual sexism, instances where men thought they were being complimentary or acting in a way they thought was acceptable, but which women were no longer willing to let pass ('Calm down, dear'). At its best, Everyday Sexism has for sure exposed society's latent chauvinism, but there is a sense that it has also rather joylessly stripped the fun out of the interplay between men and women. If you are that sexually empowered, can't you take a compliment? Or issue a retort? Perhaps it is our fault, X-ers, for letting the ladettes and the raunch culture go too far. The result has been a backlash of reverted sexism, where girls insist on safe spaces where they can exist man-free, as they feel so threatened by the potential violation any man might wreak.

I wouldn't want to change anything I did now. But I say that from the safety of eventually having found a loving relationship that has born marriage and children. I will not advocate anything less than a spirit of adventure to my daughter, and also to my sons. But I know she will cry and she will hurt as much as she will shudder and she will thrill. And the boys will make their mistakes too – they will hurt others and they will hurt themselves. That's the jeopardy. There were many tearful moments, broken hearts and instances of regret that made up my and my friends' dating careers. We went through more relationships than our parents did, simply because we married later, but also because we thought we could.

Sex is a lifelong adventure, one you have to take care to nurture. Long-term-relationship (or married) sex is an enduring emotional journey, often a barometer of the relationship itself. Sex as parents is a skill – one at which you can be brilliantly efficient (The kids have woken up! Quick, we've got 40 seconds!) and laugh over (Daddy, what exactly are you doing with Mummy?) but also agonise over, as too much of the time one of you is too tired to care for the other. When was the last time you, as a married couple, stayed up all night drinking wine, making love and smoking in bed? There are those who, Michelle Obama-style, like to schedule sex into their weekly diary – it's Thursday, time to get your pants off, darling! – but enthusiasm is something that has to be conjured, not timetabled.

The French (and others) have a cure for this, and as long as no one tells anyone else, it's a given that at some point, and maybe even several points, husbands and wives will have an affair. When my friend Anthony got divorced at 40 and found himself back on the dating scene, he was taken aback by how voracious women had become – particularly married women.

'I got together with my wife when I was 22, and divorced when I was 40 so it had been a long time since I had been out in the field. Wow, has it changed. Women now know exactly what they want from sex and how to get it – the sex happens almost immediately, and unprotected too. But what really shocked and amazed me was how many married women were propositioning me – I thought if you had a ring on your finger that was it. But all these women were sleeping with me, having unprotected sex and then going back to their husbands. How did that happen?'

Plenty of marriages survive affairs, and it's something of a fortysomething quandary whether it can quite be justified. Anthony claims in his defence that each of the married women he slept with ('and there were only three') stayed with their husbands, saying their little fling had helped them regain confidence and feel desired again. But there are other routes: I have a friend who bought her husband a tantric love course for their tenth wedding anniversary, and another who embarked on a ten-week Better Lovemaking course with a group of singletons. She smiled all year. But these are unusual exceptions – sex therapy is still regarded as somewhat alternative. Let's change that.

Marriage has not turned out to be quite the non-stop party we were used to in our youth. I was quite shocked after I got married to wake up the next morning to discover I was facing the first day of the rest of my life. I had not thought beyond the princess fantasy of knight, white horse and castle. What do the knight and the princess do after they've rolled around in the castle for a few months? The thrill of passion has to make way for reality, for mundanity and comfort, for the inevitable certainties and predictability of middle age. Not quite slippers, but certainly mid-week suppers for two, joint bank accounts and getting the plumber in. Bor-ing.

Generation X may be the divorce generation – many of us are the product of acrimonious Boomer splits or relationships that ground on despite mutual resentment and hostility – and so, just as we reinvented youth and work for ourselves, we have the same intentions with long-term relationships. (Note that this is a safer term to use than 'marriage': many of us have chosen to cohabit rather than marry, as we feel the very impermanence of what we are choosing to embark on.) We want our relationships/marriages to be meaningful, experiential, important, truth-telling, adventurous and fun. We don't want to settle for less. We work hard at realising these ambitions, are certainly more honest with each other about them and are more likely to meet each other on a more level playing field as both of us are more likely to be working and earning.

We are equally ambitious for ourselves as individuals within the marriage, whereas the traditional model was that the wife would be the homemaker, and be rewarded with jewellery, holidays and a domestic allowance, while the husband was free to pursue his career goals. Our newfound equality has changed this relationship power balance. We don't expect different things from each other – we expect the same.

My friend Ruby was offered a job in Ibiza for nine months (pretty much her dream job), but her husband Simon, whom she had married in her twenties, had just been offered a promotion in London. Neither of them wanted to compromise, so they arranged a year-long marriage sabbatical. Both were free to pursue their professional dreams, and they gave their relationship a break to see if it was strong enough to survive.

A year later, Ruby returned to London, 'so happy to come back to Simon', and a few months later rearranged her professional ambitions so she could accompany Simon to New York where his company were relocating him. Of their 'summer off' Ruby now says, 'It gave us both a chance, seven years into what had been a whirlwind romance [they met and moved in together within six months], to touch base with ourselves as individuals. To remember who we both are outside of our partnership. It set a precedent in some ways. We've now been together almost eighteen years, and I think retaining our independence has been one of the secrets to what is a very happy marriage.'

Equally, the friendship networks we built up in our twenties and thirties help us sustain a more communal approach to life – those experiences that used to be confined to just family, like Christmases, holidays and Sunday lunch, now tend to take in an extended network of family and friends. Sharing this helps us negotiate our coupledom and lifestyle and alleviate some of the loneliness, suffocation and frustration that long-term relationships can incubate.

Many of us have had different experiences that have led us to this point. We also need to consider that marriage and children are not the only option. 'I feel like a strange outlier because I don't have children, and that has been a massive difference between me and my female friends,' said Martha Lane Fox. 'Because of my accident, I was forced to rethink my working life, because physically I just can't do the things that I did before.'

Shortly after Martha sold lastminute.com in 2005 she was injured in a car crash and only just survived. 'I was 31 when I had the accident, which is an important age in lots of ways. During the period of time I was in hospital, which was two years, 31 to 33, most of my friends had their children or settled down or shifted gear. When I had the crash I'd just met [her partner] Chris, and I probably thought I'd have some kids.' In fact Martha and Chris did go on to have kids, and are now the parents of newborn twins, ten years later than many of their peers. Meanwhile she and Chris have chosen not to marry.

'My parents each have been married three times, and although they were together until I was 16 it wasn't a terrible broken home,' explains Martha. 'I don't think I'd ever had that notion that relationship equals the next stage of life. My dad's an academic who always challenged me. He would take away that apologetic bit at the front of my sentences. I feel lucky that I was always challenged to go and do something, to have a career and think about it.'

'My mum, on the other hand, didn't go to university and was never encouraged to get a job, and is one of the smartest people I know. She was married at 20 and had me when she was 22. Her take on us lot would be: you have this unbelievable longevity and depth of friendship we didn't have. Our generation had the whole of our twenties, and more, living with friends. Our family was created in our friendship group who got married much later.'

Relationships are clearly an ongoing project at this stage in our lives, and Generation X are using the tools at hand and experience to date to navigate them. Many of us regularly see marriage guidance counsellors, or couple therapists, something previous generations saw only as a final resort and the ultimate humiliation.

'You go and see a therapist to get over your lingering issues from your parents' divorce, so why not see one to fix your marriage?' says my friend Charlotte, a fortysomething who works in public policy. 'Jim and I go once a week and it's the best money I spend. It helps us work out a lot of the issues we have and keep our lines of communication open and healthy.' Jim earns considerably less than Charlotte, which requires a framework for making the relationship work that few of us have inherited. In fact it is one our generation has had to invent.

'Our generation of men are the most confused, because they're not sure what their place is,' says June Sarpong. Generation X women have proved they don't need men to support them economically, socially or culturally – but they haven't yet worked out where they do need them. 'We feel weird letting a man pay for dinner or open a door for us – we are also the first generation of women who may earn more than our husbands. As a result, you have a lot of dissatisfied women and a lot of emasculated men.'

While the alpha-female, beta-male marriage is fine on paper – she earns, he lets her earn – it rarely feels comfortable. 'Men are really confused about their role,' agrees hairdresser John Vial. 'Friends of mine have just separated after 20 years of marriage. It was amicable – she was very successful, he sat at home, cooked and looked after their son. It was an absolute role reversal. He got half her money – by which she's done the right thing. So what's his part in life now? He's depressed, a 50-year-old man with no point of view or career history.'

Young men don't like the look of this. They don't like the prospect of a world where they have been written out of the script, and it is this fear that is unnerving so many and contributing to the hatred that is allowed to bubble away anonymously online.

But if there is one thing we have taken a bullet for, Millennial sisters, it's the lesson of timing your fertility. Bridget Jones and all the millions of women who 'left it too late'; 'concentrated on their career'; 'were too picky'; who found themselves at the back end of their thirties and early forties desperately trying to find a mate, juggle the IVF injections or do it all on their own, either via a sperm bank, a friend or adoption. Let us be a lesson to you.

Maybe science will step in for Millennial women who don't meet the right man in time for their baby-making window, maybe they will be smarter about sorting out parenthood sooner. The signs are not good, though – Millennial women are even slower than us both to get married and to have children, even though they are well aware of our struggle to mate and conceive. Of course they have noticed the number of single fortysomething female households, the women who have had children on their own (doubled in the last five years), and the egg freezing lie (only between 2 and 12 per cent of eggs are viable). You would need to have been asleep for the last 20 years not to have heard the clamour about IVF and women who are now involuntarily 'childless' – the expense, the emotional pain, and in some cases the challenge to your relationship such pressures can bring about. Likewise they hear the statistics about older mothers, they see many of them about, they know it's possible, just not always. Maybe they think they will be one of the lucky ones, maybe they will find the right partner in time.

'I can see younger women now thinking, "Okay, 25, I want to start thinking about a family, take some time out and then go back into my career,"' says June Sarpong. 'I think our generation's mistake was career, career, career – and then oops, I haven't had children. We're not honest. We live in this delusion that there isn't such a thing as a biological clock, when there just is. You can't pretend.'

Like many women, June is approaching 40 and is looking around for a decent match – but it's slim pickings in the man pool. Those that are available are also much more likely to be attracted to a younger woman than a late thirtysomething with her life all set up and compromise not top of her agenda.

'Our generation of women are not truly comfortable with men,' says June. 'There's a mistrust, a disconnect, and it was something our mothers managed to navigate. Even if they weren't happy with their men, our mothers still knew what a man was for. I don't think we know what a man is for. We know we fancy them and it's nice having them around, but we're the first lot that can do everything ourselves and we just haven't figured out where men fit in. The younger lot are much more comfortable with that – it's fine if the woman earns more. They just see each other as equals, even if boys have different interests and roles from girls. Whereas Generation X, we all wanted to be the same. It's sad, and that's part of the reason some of our generation of men prefer younger women because it's clearer in those relationships. Less complicated.'

Men see successful women having babies on their own, either through insemination, via a sperm bank, friends or adoption. What do these women have to offer mid-life men? Thirty, fortysomething women bring demands and baggage to a relationship. They are probably used to an independent life – it's much harder for them to accept the compromises needed to share a life and a relationship. In fact, compromise feels wrong to a woman who has worked hard to have it exactly the way she wants it. She has her own home, career, set of friends, lifestyle. A twentysomething woman, on the other hand, has clear features, advantages and benefits.

'We're confused when a guy brings a 25-year-old home,' says Sarpong. 'We're thinking, "It's just because he wants a younger woman." No, it's not – it's about how that man feels when he's around that 25-year-old. Of course it's not just about looks – we know that eventually that's bullshit in terms of actual living with someone day in and day out. It's how do they make him feel? They make him feel like a man. A lot of our generation are quite good at making men not feel like men!'

We are not honest enough about these issues. Currently women have to fit in university, a career, marriage and children in less than 20 years. It is a tight schedule, and it takes strategic planning and sacrifice. Likewise if they have kids younger and delay university and career, women face the problem of paying for the education and the childcare to get back into the workplace.

Anne-Marie Slaughter wrote the most high-profile essay on this matter (and also one of the most widely shared pieces of journalism on the internet). In 'Why Women Still Can't Have it All' she explained why she walked away from one of the most senior posts in government to spend more time with her teenage son, who was struggling at school. She admitted: 'I can't do both.'

Slaughter's compromise didn't sound so bad at all – she didn't stop working just to stay at home and bake cakes (not that there is anything wrong with that); instead she got a job teaching at

Yale. Still, voices accused her of setting women back 40 years. 'Actually,' points out June, 'she was making a smart practical choice to help shape a valuable human being, her son no less, that's going to be of benefit to society.'

Another honest conversation we need to have is around our respect for other women's choices. The working mum versus the stay-at-home mum; the mother versus the woman who chooses not to have children; the woman who conceives naturally versus the woman who uses IVF; natural birth versus caesarean; bottle versus breast. Women find it so hard not to judge each other's choices. That judgement, often unspoken, is always there, and sometimes it bubbles over with damaging results.

The Tory MP Andrea Leadsom's doomed campaign to be prime minister hit the rocks when she insinuated she had a stronger vested interest in our future than Theresa May because she had children (collectively, the women of Britain winced). This judgement, spoken or unspoken, makes us all insecure in our choices. We are constantly looking around, searching for clues that help us validate our own choices, furiously calibrating our lives against those of other women. When we are losing it with the stress of work and kids, it's strangely comforting to pick a weeping friend up off the floor who feels empty and lost without a job, and is terrified of putting herself back in the workplace after years of school runs and cake sales. Likewise, there are many women who feel agony over leaving their kids in the morning to go to work – but it is almost impossible to run a household these days on a single income, a big change from the Boomer years.

My kids go to a local school where there is a mix of all types of parents who have made all types of choices. The mothers who are there for their kids after school keep an eye on the kids who are looked after by nannies, au pairs and play centres. They help out with the fetching and carrying, the emergencies and the

PTA, and they keep the social cogs turning. Without them the school and my kids' lives would be a poorer place. These women do not earn a wage for their role. As most of us need to earn actual money, we have to go out to work – indeed most of us expect and want to work. So women need to help each other whenever they can at this point in our lives. It's simply too difficult otherwise. Judgement and jealousy just make everyone more uncomfortable.

Around me I see many women juggling hard. I see pain behind their eyes, deep circles beneath them and a kind of panic-induced desperation as they scan from one woman to the next, searching for someone who might have something the rest of us missed. Was this what we wished upon ourselves when we worked hard at school, set out on our career paths, dreamed of the ways we were going to make our lives meaningful, experiential and fun?

These women, us middle youth 'powerhouse mums', are now machines, honed through necessity to become super-efficient engines of productivity whose contribution to the economy (listen up, Government) and society (listen up, schools and care homes) are paramount to everyone's survival – but really, at what cost?

Nearly every day in my life there is a moment where it feels like the whole edifice is hanging by a gossamer thread. One slip and the whole structure might come tumbling to the ground. Natalie Massenet, the 'superwoman' behind the Net-a-Porter empire, once told me that it wasn't building a global fashion empire that broke her, nor her divorce, nor her trying to raise her two daughters alongside her full-on job, but the acquisition of a puppy. She would come home from a long day in the office to tuck her daughters into bed, a global mega-deal teetering precariously on the edge – and the labradoodle would have pooped all over the carpet. 'The dog was an amazing catalyst for me to get some help,' she admitted.

And for 'powerhouse mums' it's usually the little things that push you over the edge. It's the white shirt that went through the tumble dryer when it shouldn't have, the extra bicep reps in the fitness class, that time you opened the fridge and there was no milk. This is a time of life when the demands that surround us make us very fragile. Too much of the time we are running on empty, careering towards the next holiday in the diary, eyes shut tight, breath held. We swap intel on anti-anxiety pills (Shall I? Should I?) and doctors sometimes smile kindly on us.

Sleepless nights have become the norm ever since our babies wouldn't learn to sleep – I find I can sometimes go through a whole night now with barely half an hour snatched before dawn. I have trained myself to ignore the devilish ghosts that haunt the insomniac's night, and try to use the time usefully to think through the things I need to think through. After all, why get worked up about not getting enough sleep? Once you have proved you can do a full day's work on no sleep, well, you can do it again.

'Work, where does it stop?' asks the chef and activist Thomasina Miers. 'At the moment it's completely normal for me if I can't sleep to get up and do an hour and a half's work. Then I go back to bed. Completely normal.'

Tommi has two young children at primary school and a third on the way, but in the same vein as all busy women she is the sort who takes more and more on. On one of her 'maternity leaves', she organised a social protest around permissible food waste. As well as running the fast-food chain Wahaca, she also writes recipe books and a newspaper column, and is running a project at her local school to repurpose spare land as a vegetable garden for the children. She says she gets away with her workload because so much of it is about passion and what she believes in. And cooking – time alone over a stove – is her 'mindfulness':

'Cooking is very meditative; it feels spiritually good. But then the other side of it is just crazy, relentless working, and I wonder where that stuff's going – at some stage it is going to send everyone bonkers.'

Do today's career jugglers acknowledge their vulnerability? No way! We've spent too long convincing men on the way up that it's all possible, even though none of us have a wife at home to cook supper, look after the kids and get the window cleaner in (like you know many of your male bosses do). We take on more because we see others around us supposedly managing it all – sailing calmly over the waters of parenthood, career, charity project, creative sideline.

'I think we all just want to prove we could throw all the balls in the air and keep on juggling,' says Tommi. 'But I don't think it will be the future.' I hope it's not – I can't imagine that the human race has evolved to punish itself so severely.

It's not just the women suffering – of course the men do too. These days they are doing so much more of the parenting and the chores, their share of early starts and midnight feeds. They take the bins out and mow the lawn and pay the gas bill, they bunk off for sports day and to take the kids to the doctor. We are still a long way from equality, however, as Tom Hodgkinson points out,

'When I go and pick up my son from primary school, I'm the only male there.' It's still not quite as acceptable for men to tell their boss that they've got the school carol service so they won't be making the meeting. But hopefully when they are the boss – well, then they will understand for those men coming up underneath. The importance of paying our understanding forward is not something Boomers have done for us. It reminds me of an older, famous fashion editor who complains bitterly whenever any of her staff take maternity leave – she never did in her day, so why should women be allowed such generous parenting allowances now? In the name of progress, that's why.

But we muddle through. Silvia Ann Hewlett, the great American career guru, advises about constructing on-ramps and off-ramps in your career. If you are forced to take a career break because you cannot afford the childcare, or indeed are lucky enough to be able to choose one because you can negotiate part-time, or flexible hours, or can afford it, then you need to be equally smart in rebuilding it when you step back on the tread-mill. Many retrain into a kinder industry or profession, or make lifestyle choices in moving to a less expensive part of the country to allow themselves a better life. What we all worry about all the time is not what this is doing to us, but what it is doing to our children. Are the kids alright? As long as we are setting a good example then we can excuse anything.

What is clear is that it is our generation, Generation X, who are working out the blueprint for those to come. Let us make the mistakes, so you don't have to. You can take a long, hard look and see if we came up with the answers – if, aged 60, we are smugly rubbing our hands with delight at our brilliant fortunes and careers, then well, you can suck it up knowing it's going to pay off for you in the long term. But if our children don't recognise us in the street and we are all in mental asylums with stress disorders, then, er, you may want to think again.

There is a saying – it's the cracks that let the light in. That to suffer is to be interesting and beautiful. June Sarpong thinks this. As a woman of Ghanaian descent born and raised in Walthamstow, she has felt the struggle. 'I'm so grateful, as a woman, and particularly as a woman of colour, to have been born when I was born. The things that I have been able to do, particularly in this country, I wouldn't have been able to do at another time. My mother would not have had the opportunity, and younger women haven't had the same struggle. It's a lovely balance: you have the opportunity, but you also really value it. There's an extra layer you get from struggle. It's like people who are considered attractive by society tend not to be that interesting. That's because of not having to struggle. Having some kind of struggle in your life makes you a more rounded and interesting person.'

So comfort yourselves, sisters, it may be hard work, but at least we can value our riches. Millennials, June feels, take too much for granted. 'I don't think they appreciate their freedoms. They're a little bit more reckless because they can be. I think we need to be better at passing that down to them.' Maybe so, but I often catch Millennials looking at women like us with something of a sideways glance. Hmm, they think, what are you doing to yourselves? They often question us about children and work and you can see them making the sorts of calculations I wished I had made 15, 20 years ago. Let's see how it works out for them. Honestly, girls, there's got to be an easier way than this.

It may be that for some the answer lies is not having children. Instead be an auntie or a godmother. Nurture yourself, your partner or your career instead. Or build yourself a way of life that can accommodate children comfortably, and with meaning. There are many women who stopped working at kids – at marriage, even – whose education, even up to a university degree, now lies redundant, a waste of investment and opportunity. For those happy with a life of school runs, tennis mornings and book clubs, congratulations. You won out. For those who feel an emptiness, or live with a husband killing himself to bring home a big enough wage to support you, we all feel your pain.

Girls of our generation have become aware of the breadth of choices available, and we have learned through experience that we need to be strategic about making them. Generation Y see what we our currently coping with and it scares them. I think we have been hijacked by it – I don't think we saw it coming. We grew up designing exactly the kind of life we wanted, the kind of work we wanted, the kind of fun we wanted and the kind of politics we wanted, and as a result marriage and parenting have come as something of an inconvenient truth. We are not afraid of hard work, which is why we plough on, but that doesn't make us happy with it.

In her book *Out of Time*, the journalist Miranda Sawyer mourns the fact that her two young children, born in her forties, have limited her days of gigging, clubbing and travelling. 'I find small children and the routine that's involved with them really hard to deal with,' she admits to me. 'Getting up at the same time every day, taking the kids to school every day completely does my head in. I do it because I'm not a git and I want to look after my kids and I don't want to be fined £700 for taking them out of school, but for somebody who's used to living a freelance life where no day is the same, I find it stultifying. And it makes the days go really fast.'

'Our generation felt we always had time,' says June. 'At 30, I wasn't even thinking about starting a family, it wasn't a consideration. I think it's because we felt young, we thought our insides were young in the same way.'

We are the Peter Pan generation, and Peter Pan never married Wendy. He continued to play on the high seas with his friends, always the boy, never the man. He became incredibly adept at fighting pirates and building camps, but he never had to deal with school parent evenings, a part-time wage, homesick au pairs – and in the end, Wendy left him in Neverland. Our dream has ended, and pitched battles on the high seas are now something of a reality.

9

Meet You in the Gastropub

You may remember, if you are a child of the Nineties, the birth of the term 'gastropub'. It was the moment when collectively we rejected the Harvester restaurant school of frozen scampi as an acceptable form of lunch. But the gastropub was not wholly a good thing – like prawn sandwiches, it represented the march of middle-class culture. Gastropubs edged out the traditional boozer and working men's club, and were something of a monoculture ripping through what were once thriving – and now failing – local pub communities. The working men's club I knew was The Cobden in west London, which had been co-opted by Notting Hill record industry types and turned into a party venue. It was achingly hip (a very Nineties phrase), often playing host to the latest DJs and their media-type fans.

The gastropub recipe was simple. Buy up the lease on a failing boozer in a hip part of town, install a chef and a blackboard, and start churning out red onion and goat's cheese tarts with wine by the glass. The pickled eggs in a jar were replaced by bowls of pistachio nuts (the pickled eggs are back, firstly with irony, now with feeling) and make sure the menu includes at least a salade niçoise, gourmet sausages with onion gravy and a lemon tart with crème fraîche. They were a cliché, gastropubs, but at least they rescued pubs from being turned into 'luxury' flats. How food and drink rescued us as a nation is another story of our generation.

In 1996 I joined the *Daily Telegraph* as their commissioning editor for food. One of my ideas was a partwork series from Britain's then new hot chef, Gordon Ramsay. He had just opened a restaurant in Chelsea called Aubergine, and the critics were raving about it. Chefs were starting to become famous, rock stars in and of themselves. They were getting TV shows and live gigs and book deals and newspaper and magazine columns.

The biggest rock star of them all was Marco Pierre White – a rough, handsome, half-Italian brute from Leeds, who would throw diners out of his restaurant if they dared complain. He married a supermodel then dumped her 18 days later (supposedly because he didn't like her wedding dress); he was dangerous, passionate, irresistible. Ramsay had trained under Marco, but had broken away to open Aubergine – and was beginning to steal some of Marco's limelight. A reservations book went missing from Aubergine, which in those days detailed all customer details and reservations (remember, no computers in the Nineties!) and Ramsay publicly blamed White. The feud took off and we all booked front-row seats.

Ramsay himself, an ex-footballer from Glasgow with a face creviced by scars and frown lines, was very civilised to me, crafting his foam-flecked, truffle-infused works of art into the kind of recipes *Telegraph* readers might like to talk about at dinner parties. (Nobody was actually cooking this stuff yet.) This kind of food was a long way away from what we were actually eating (in the gastropubs), but it was a bit like Yves Saint Laurent to 'Designers at Debenhams'. We loved to aspire to it and know about it, but for our actual lives, we obviously just popped down the high street.

It seemed to me a complete anomaly that this huge, muscle-bound, foul-mouthed disciplinarian should be the master of such a beautiful and delicate craft. After a while working on the supplement together, I asked him why he called his restaurant Aubergine. There were no aubergines on his menu and none in his recipes. 'After the size and shape of my dick, Tiffanie.'

It was too good a story not to share, and I wrote a potboiler novel called *Marrow*, about two London chefs vying for supremacy, one of whom calls his restaurant Marrow after the size and shape of …

Ramsay got wind of this just before publication and rang up the *Sunday Times* newsdesk (where I was recently employed) to claim we had had a torrid affair and I had written the book as a kiss and tell. All completely untrue, but genius media manipulation on his part. I had to grovel on the floor to my new boss and beg him not to splash it over page 3. Marco adored the book (he came off rather better) and took me out to lunch several times to tell me so.

But those two were just the beginning of it. Tom Aikens, a red-headed firebrand from Norfolk, became the youngest person ever to receive two Michelin stars in 1996, when he became head chef of another posh London eaterie Pied à Terre. 'Gordon and I went head to head when that came out,' says Tom. 'We both got the two stars at the same time, but because I was the youngest, my name was all over the press and he got just a little caption. We became enemies overnight – serious rivalry. All that fuelled the rock 'n' roll side of what goes on in the kitchen and what chefs are really like.'

These men – and then chefs *were* all men – spent years training in hot subterranean kitchens, working long hours, chucking knives and fire around, shouting at each other. Suddenly they were thrust into the limelight, giving interviews to magazines and talking to camera. They were still unfinished brutes, fresh from years of being bullied as kitchen apprentices, and inheriting the role of bully as chef. They were in fierce competition with each other, and the rivalry – driven by the famous Michelin grading, was intense.

'There was a lifestyle of working hard and partying hard, chefs doing lines of cocaine to stay awake,' says Tom. 'Anyone that was a head chef in the Nineties knows it was a much harder game then than it is now. There was no HR, just an endless line of chefs wanting to come and work because cheffing was becoming cool. But there were far fewer restaurants back then, so people had to take less money and do the hours.'

Three years later Tom walked out of Pied à Terre mid service, after losing his temper in the heat of the kitchen. He was accused of branding a young teenage chef with a hot knife.

'I was this young, wild animal, with no man-management skills,' he says. 'I was working 18, 20 hours a day, six days a week. I was getting up at 3 am to go to Covent Garden market, after sleeping two hours and then coming in to work. My whole world was saturated in being the best, making the restaurant the best. When you're in that zone, you don't step back – it's suffocating to everyone around you. An insane control freak, I was having anxiety attacks worrying about whether I had done something, waking up drenched in sweat.'

By now restaurants were opening up all over the capital – led by Terence Conran. First came Bibendum, then Bluebird Garage, then Orrery, Quaglino's, Mezzo, Le Pont de la Tour, the Blueprint Café and Butlers Wharf Chop House. 'Everyone thought this guy's crazy, who's going to come to these restaurants?' says Tom. 'But he was absolutely right. Before Conran there weren't quality casual eating restaurants – eating out was Pizza Express and Bella Pasta. He made that big market for himself.' The design and creativity that laced the Nineties had now settled on food.

TV was quick to cash in: *Ready Steady Cook* brought cooking to daytime, *The Naked Chef* made his first appearance, *Two Fat Ladies* were launched, *Masterchef* turned cooking into a national talent contest, *Come Dine with Me* took over the airwaves. Rick Stein built a Cornish empire dubbed Padstein, Nobu above the Met bar became more famous for having Boris Becker shagging in the broom cupboard than its sushi, Fergus Henderson introduced nose-to-tail eating and The River Cafe, run by Rose Gray and Ruth Rogers, became the New Labour canteen.

It's no coincidence that the pact Gordon Brown and Tony Blair reached about the leadership of the Labour party was brokered in a modern Italian – Granita, in Islington. Matthew Freud recognised eating out was not about the food but where was cool, who had the best design credentials, who was going – and he opened Pharmacy in Notting Hill with Damien Hirst, who was then in full flight as the ringmaster of the YBA circus.

'If you look at the TV chefs pre Jamie or Nigella, the Pru Leiths and Delias – who we love, so no offence – but they didn't make cooking cool,' says June Sarpong. 'It was still very much middle England housewife in the kitchen cooking for her family, doing the dutiful thing. Whereas our generation of chefs made it interesting to know about food, and to entertain. They made food a source of connection and exploration.'

In the same way that second-generation immigrants brought their music onto the scene in the early Nineties, so multiculturalism brought cuisine too – and the second generation fused it with British values and made it interesting. Ken Hom taught us about Chinese, Peter Gordon about the Pacific Rim, The Cinnamon Club and The Red Fort about modern Indian. Generation X did to food what had been done to music.

Food was becoming a lifestyle indicator – what you ate, bought and cooked became a label of who you were. It began to be photographed in a pornographic manner to make it as gorgeous as possible. Marks & Spencer and Waitrose were to rise to the top of the grocery tree by appealing to this ultra-aspirational food ethic. Farmers' markets were to settle on street corners and squares, and even our homes were going to change as the kitchen became the centre of everything, triggering a tsunami of 'knock-throughs', 'side returns' and 'open plans'.

Our interest was to morph into obsession, giving rise to subcultures of macrobiotic, gluten-free, dairy-free. Eating out was to take over from going out, and nightclubs were to give way to hipster eateries, tapas bars and supperclubs.

'You were starting to get places that were cool and great to be seen in, where the food was secondary,' says Tom. 'Chris Corbin and Jeremy King had The Ivy, Le Caprice and The Wolseley where they created the culture of a club, somewhere a select few people would go, and if you were in that club you were cool.'

We thought they were restaurants, but shortly after Richard Caring, the retail millionaire and friend of Philip Green, bought them, we realised they were actually now a brand, as branches of The Ivy opened up in Kensington, Chelsea and abroad. Restaurants became preferable to nightclubs – which is how we ended up with today's celebrity-packed Chiltern Firehouse. Create crazy hype from a super exclusive guest list and then sustain it. Restaurants, it seemed, became the new nightclubs. But kids – look what happened to the music industry. I know you can't digitally download a meal.

Yet.

10

Never Complain, Never Explain

Warning: if you are not a fan of chain-smoking supermodels, you may want to look away now. Next up is the girl who is something of the hero of our story. For if there is any one person who proves time and again it can all be done, that you can defy convention and get away with it, change everything on a whim when it doesn't agree with you, have it all, have it every which way and have a complete blast every second you are doing it, then it is, of course, Kate Moss.

As a woman in her forties, I'm not sure it's possible to talk about lifestyle without ending up somewhere around Kate Moss. A coda here – I am, and always have been, obsessed by the girl from Croydon. Not as a person, but as an idea, a model for living, for cool, for chicness, for grubbiness, for naughtiness, for lols, for glamour. In short – for all the good and the bad. There's nothing that I haven't done that Kate hasn't done worse, nothing that I haven't done good that Kate hasn't done miles better. On a few occasions I have come face to face with her and it is not true what they say – about how you should never meet your icons. Kate surpasses expectations in the flesh. A very few women (and maybe the odd man, but I haven't met one myself) exude 'it'. You can tell they are there the moment you enter the room – there's an electricity, an excitement. Star power, they call it. Kate, most definitely, has it.

Like all our favourite icons, Kate has not surfed the celebrity wave of the last 25 years undamaged – indeed the opposite. When she had the foulest aspects of her life exposed, when she appeared to be the biggest cocaine-addled, man-obsessed, feckless no hope on the planet *on paper*, she somehow navigated her way out of it into an entirely bigger sphere of stardom. Never complain, never explain, as she famously once said. Skinny, yes, to the point of scrawniness, snaggle-toothed, short, even a little lop-sided, hair slightly lank, a bit dirty (the father of her daughter, Jefferson Hack, legendarily chatted her up with the line 'You smell of wee'), Kate was and remains the most beautiful woman on the planet for me. Maybe it's because she is the girl next door version of the supermodel, the accessible version – but that doesn't take into account the high-octane voltage of her image. She moves with precise and utter knowledge of what sexy is. She is not beautiful, in a way you could never achieve. Instead, she is fuckable, eminently fuckable.

I accidentally ended up on her hen night, the time she married Kills guitarist Jamie Hince and her bf Fran Cutler – a buxom Eastender with a canny eye for business and a ruthless ability to commoditise pleasure – organised Kate's hen at the Isle of Wight Festival. Kate borrowed a Tesco Florence and Fred poncho off one of us because she was cold in the backstage VIP bar. The next morning the poncho was on every national newspaper cover as the new tribal trend. Her mates – Sadie, Meg, Jess, Bella et al. – surrounded her like a flock of gaggling geese, cackling uproariously, throwing back the vodka, careering on and off the dancefloor, crashing into things, talking nonsense. They were a benchmark for every girl's big night out. Normal, and yet, so not.

Or the time I bumped into her – literally – at Glastonbury, hiding under a cap and Aviators, sucking on a fag like her life depended on it, grinning wildly (because it's rare she doesn't grin). Good times. Good times through the men, through the

scandal, through the public opprobriation, through the naked-
ness, literal and otherwise, through the shame, through the loss
of her closest friends, through her betrayal by others. Maybe
she's a horror underneath it all, but in my 20 years of working
in a business close to hers and in the 20,000 conversations I
have had with people who have known her and worked with
her, not one person has ever had a single bad word to say about
her. Instead they talk about how hard she works, and how loyal
she is to her friends and colleagues, and how much fun she is to
be around. How she loves a party – even now, her house in the
Cotswolds is a shrine to good times with disco balls, cabaret
bars, a music studio and rooms and rooms of dress-up and
walk-in wardrobes. Just like you would dream it, if you could.

'Kate gets knocked for being a party animal, for being this,
that and the other,' says her friend Serena Rees. 'But do you
know what? She has grafted so hard. She has done more shoots,
more films, more anything, that anyone. The reason you see her
everywhere and all those iconic images is because she puts the
hours in. Someone once turned around to her and said, "You
can't still be partying now?" She just replied, "Well, why not?
Why can't I have fun?"'

Kate does not compromise – she has not let children, marriage,
career, life, death, betrayal or humiliation compromise any of
her decisions about who she is and what she does. Not even age
– when she was asked in a recent interview about how she coped
with ageing, she flashed back, 'I don't do old.' Of course she is
rich, beautiful and successful and has the world's greatest hair-
dressers and beauticians at her fingertips, so of course she
doesn't do old. But, like everything she says and does, you have
to admire the chutzpah. There is a sense of timing about her, a
sense of humour that chimes perfectly with our sensibilities.

Jamie East tells a story about an encounter with her at
Jonathan Ross's Halloween party. 'It was a great party, in

Jonathan's back garden in his lovely house – it was just an enlarged family party for him. But playing the piano was Gok Wan, gossiping in the corner was Alan Carr, it was wall-to-wall celebrity, everyone in fancy dress. I went with my wife, which was great because Sarah hardly ever came to these celebrity parties with me. Kate walked past us and just grabbed me and went, "You're so fucking hot!" in front of my wife. Then she just walked off. To this day I don't know whether she was saying that because she meant it – or because actually I'd dressed myself up as a burns victim.'

As time has rolled on, Kate has become less important in our lexicon of glamour – Millennials have Cara, and Gigi and Karlie now; those big luxey brands have other faces to call on for their ad campaigns (although admirably Kate still manages to pick up one or two every season). But the nature of glamour has changed. Now that we have 24/7, real-time backstage access through social media and people's phones, the fantasy of those super-glossy photoshoots is less important. It is less believable.

We see the pictures of Justin Bieber arriving at the Calvin Klein shoot three months before the ad campaign hits the billboards. The paparazzi shots of Taylor Swift getting changed behind a towel on a New Zealand beach as she filmed her new music video hit ten minutes after the actual event: the video didn't drop for another month. Some even anticipate the moment: Christopher Bailey Snapchats his Burberry show models in the line-up before they file out on the catwalk. We have been backstage, seen the before and after pics, been talked through the process by every editor, creative and model long before we see the result. The finished product is nothing other than the final point in the journey. It is artificial, we know that now.

The secrecy and image conjured around Kate and her racy set would be impossible to replicate now – in fact it would just look ridiculous, haughty even. Glamour has changed. It is no longer P Diddy popping champagne in a nightclub, because we've seen Piers Morgan do that. It's not Gisele in a crystal-encrusted bikini because Myleene Klass has cottoned on to that game. Faye Dunaway poolside in her dressing gown after the Oscars is aped on every Instagram feed this side of Margate.

I think true glamour these days is something more wholesome – something you can invent for yourself, in your private time, away from the glare of a screen or a lens. Something that is not in the interests of showing off, but with the direct aim of pleasing your inner self. As the (fortysomething) writer Jessica Brinton wrote in an essay for *Vice*, 'You can find new glamour anywhere that reminders of the other glamour are not. Like along canals or in the countryside, and in the grounds of a stately home if it's at night and you don't own it, or sitting on a cliff naked with no one to see you but seagulls. The new glamour has a whole different relationship with the world because it isn't showing off.'

'In the Eighties Keith Richards doing a line of coke off someone's tits would have been glamorous because it was so out there, no one would have done it,' explains Jamie East. 'But in the Nineties, coke was everywhere. During the Britpop years London was snowing, so a story about someone doing a load of coke wasn't glamorous any more because they were doing it in pubs in Macclesfield. What the Nineties did was strip the glamour out of everything.'

The high life now is naff. Bloated businessmen like Philip Green cruise around the Med on gas-guzzling superyachts; whereas their cool new counterparts – the tech millionaires – wear sandals and go kitesurfing instead. Or climb a mountain, or run a desert. Fashion glamour is Stella Tennant in her woollies on a Scottish moor; it's thrift store chic and home-grown veg. It's doing five hours of fitness a week or reading a book for breakfast or taking in rescue dogs. It's wholesome, on your own terms and private.

Kate Moss can still shock and amuse (recently running off with the twentysomething son of her friend the Countess), but her beautiful and damned approach to living is nothing like as current. 'I used to worship Kate,' says Thomasina Miers. 'She was so drop-dead sexy, and her devil-may-care attitude was incredible. But she never spoke out about anything that mattered, and as I grew older I became really disillusioned about her lack of care. Cara Delevingne has already been on panels talking about feminism. She's taken a political stance. Our generation lost that political angle. We didn't care, we were nihilistic. The younger generation have got too much at stake to be nihilistic. They've got no job security, they're not going to own their own homes; some of them are thinking they might not be able to afford a kid.'

Millennials, as we know, are far too serious to think about partying or yacht hopping or who's in the band. They don't like to drink too much, they have much less sex than us, and they like to be in bed early so they can be up in time to work. They don't party, they worry. They don't celebrate, they care instead.

Kate's role has never been to make us care. It's been about knowing your own mind, knowing what you are good at and making the best of it through hard work, attitude and chutzpah. Kate doesn't do anxiety or stress. She does the high without the low. She parties through the comedown. Rehab? She goes to Chiva Som in Thailand. Detox? She 'over-refreshes' on the way back and calls the air hostess 'a basic bitch'. You never see the payback, never see the pain.

But Kate is an idea, not an actual person. Actual people do have payback from this sort of high-octane lifestyle. The photographer Amelia Troubridge was part of that scene, until it all got too much. 'There are consequences to that kind of living.

I woke up one morning and thought this is not right. Doing gear every weekend, rock 'n' roll lifestyle, everyone around me doing it. I thought, This can't go on forever. I'm not okay about the way my society is telling me to live and the way I'm living. So on 17 December 2002, I drove up to a rehab in north London, checked in, and stayed there on my own over Christmas and gave up everything. I had questions, and no one around me had any answers. So I went somewhere out of my comfort zone to ask questions about myself. Why do we do the things we do? Why is there this collective self-abuse?'

Pearl Lowe was on the inside of the infamous Primrose Hill set. Scandalous tabloid stories emerged about them, all famous A-listers involved in drug and sex parties, including plenty around Pearl and her husband Danny. 'There were a lot of girls and it was really fun. You felt part of a group and like you really belonged," says Pearl. "But I'm no good at taking drugs, I'm too sensitive. I was rock bottom, and ended up in rehab. I got sober for a year, then relapsed, then got sober for a year, then relapsed again. It was tough, really tough.

'So I made the decision to move the family out of London. A mum has to hold it together, and I wasn't holding it together, I was running out and coming back days later. Addiction is powerful, and because I am an addict there was no getting around it. It was brave moving to the country, and a lot of people hated me for it. There was a lot of stuff said about me [Pearl recounted her experiences in her memoir *Powder*], but I just thought it doesn't matter – I need to make sure my family are cared for. The people who stuck by me are with me today, and the people that didn't aren't, and that's just the way it is.

'It was painful, like grieving fifty people. When I lived in London my phone would ring off the hook – can you come here, go there, have lunch, I was right in the centre of it all. I got to

Hampshire and my phone stopped ringing, no one was texting me. It was strange – I had to live empty for a while.

'And Danny and I didn't fit in in Hampshire. People used to say to Danny, "Ha ha, you were in Supertramp!" Danny would say, "No, Supergrass." We were worlds apart. We enrolled the kids in the school down the road, which turned out to be the feed for Eton. I had pillar-box red hair. I remember Frankie going, "Mum, could you dye your hair please, and could you wear like those sort of chinos, a blue shirt. I stood out like a sore thumb and he was so embarrassed. He was only five and he just wanted me to be like the other mums.

'So we moved further west, to Somerset, and since then it's been fantastic.' Pearl lives in a beautiful Georgian rectory decorated in her trademark vintage style, and the house is full of children, musicians, sewing machines and dressing-up outfits. She has reinvented herself as an interior designer, has a line of children's clothes, and fosters around her family a broad circle of interesting, loving people. 'Now we've got too many friends again. There's lots of cooking, entertaining and walking. I often look at the kids and think, how would they cope in London if we had to move back? I think they are better off here. Alfie had the choice after school about where to go and chose Bristol – he's a bit scared of London. Ten years later, I'm still very pleased with my decision.'

'There's no way I can party anymore, it takes me *days* to recover!' screams a once notorious party girl. Now the mum of a two-year-old, the very idea seems toxic and hideous. As it does to many of the ravers, caners and good-time girls and boys. Fortieth birthday parties tend to be gruelling reminders of how age can be a barrier to such abandon. Fiftieths are even worse – and tend to be harder, as the kids are a little older and therefore a little more forgiving.

And it's not as fun as it used to be – of course it's not – to paraphrase Robbie Williams, who gave up partying because he had 'lost the keys to the magic kingdom'. Those first ecstatic nights were never quite the same again. People used to say the drugs changed, but actually what has gone is the innocence. Times and people change. Hangovers get worse. Work gets harder, children bookend your days – where is the time warp into which you can fit a bender?

But Kate Moss is still plugging away, and good luck to her. She is still throwing big birthday bashes at her Cotswold mansion, prancing about on boats, putting a premium on having fun. Launching a product line? Let's have a party! Get the old crowd down! Fan/stalker Instagram feeds like katemosslatest, wheresmossy and voguishcat track her every move so these days you can follow her life on a minute-by-minute basis. The fun clearly hasn't stopped, which is great, because these days I kind of feel she can party on so I don't have to.

Plus, despite what she says, I do like the way she is ageing. I like the way she cares less about fashion now – the girl who once launched a dozen trends a day has found a uniform of skinny jeans, boots and a blazer and sticks to it. Who's got time to try on all the trends now? Leave that to the bloggers. Her face has got fuller, flatter, more lifted and catlike. We know that look and there's a way to get it. She's launched an agency, as the number of campaigns she gets dwindles: so now she'll be in charge of finding the next Kate Mosses. She's got the same tight group of friends around her (love that) and she lives for holidays. She is always on holiday, and that's just what we live for too. (To the extent that I often find myself talking about my next holiday while I am actually on my current one.) And she is still smoking – like plenty of Generation X. The day Kate Moss picks up a vaper is the day vaping will become okay.

Never complain – take responsibility for your actions. Never explain – you are the creator of your own life, and you alone.

11

Namaste

In Britain we no longer live in a Christian society. When questioned, more of us say we have 'no religion' than identify some form of Christianity. Weekly church congregations have dwindled to fewer than 750,000. The collapse of the Anglican Church has been quick and profound, and it has happened most significantly in our lifetime.

This is hardly surprising to our generation, whose liberal values seem to be uncommonly alien to those of the Church of England. Abortion, homosexuality, gay marriage, corruption, paedophilia, contraception, divorce – none of 'modern' Christianity's views and practice around these issues chime with ours. The Church refuses to catch up, refuses to join in – incredibly it was only in 2002 that the Church of England decided divorcees could remarry. Gay marriage is still not allowed. It's difficult to believe these words as I type them.

But rejection of the Church as a pillar of our life has left a spiritual vacuum. Many who claim no religion will admit a belief in some higher power, and many of those allow themselves some kind of spiritual activity. So, in the absence of an organised religion that speaks to our own lifestyle and values, we have invented our own updates. Incense? Light me a Diptyque candle. Sacrament? Pass me a green juice, it makes me feel holy. Ritual? My weekly Vinyasa Flow class does that. The collection? Try justgiving.com. The book of Psalms? Deepak Chopra. Jonah and the Whale? Eat Pray Love. The Church has let it all run by. Like Kodak.

I went to church regularly in my childhood, at least up until my confirmation. I am familiar with its culture, because it is still part of the occasional weekend, Christmas and Easter. Even now, if I wander off a street into a church that's infused with incense, and listen to a preacher reading the Bible, offering wafers and fortified wine as the body and blood of Christ, I struggle to understand its relevance, although I absolutely feel its power. These hallowed, ancient buildings can bring serenity and peaceful contemplation – beauty even – but I wonder if I don't receive a similar experience now in a particularly good yoga class or in front of a magisterial Titian.

Vicars rarely have a voice in public life today; in fact they are mostly found on TV sitcoms. Or it is their robed, white, male elders making the news, espousing their antiquated and tortured attitudes to sexuality. Even when Christians began to be tortured and massacred by ISIS in the Middle East, the Church's response was unutterably feeble. In fact, I can't recall a response.

No one goes to church these days, other than to get their children into a decent school, do they?

Well, some do. It comes as something of a surprise when I ask June Sarpong to name her three favourite brands and, after the sunglasses Warby Parker and Apple, she names her third as 'God'. June we know is a switched-on, modern woman, conversant in fashion, music and political culture, bright, beautiful and sparky, and she is … a Christian?

'Yes! God is the ultimate brand – the brand of love! No bigger brand than that.' She explains: 'I was raised Church of England and went to church at an early age, Sunday school – we were all forced to go. We didn't enjoy it but then when I had my accident, the only thing that got me through it was prayer.'

A car crash when she was a teenager left June hospitalised for over a year. 'I got into the practice of prayer every day because I had so much time by myself and needed to stop myself thinking negative thoughts. I love the Bible. Whether or not you believe it's real is irrelevant. It has so many inspirational, uplifting stories, it's like the ultimate self-help book. And for my friends, whatever their faith, whether they are Muslim, Jewish or Hindu, their sacred text has the same impact. It gives me fulfilment and makes me grateful in life. When I've had my toughest times, the thing that's gotten me through has been faith in a higher power. Love God.'

Maybe Christianity just needs a reboot. 'I grew up Catholic and I despise the Catholic Church for what it did to my mother,' says the hairdresser John Vial. 'She was forced out because she was young, single and pregnant. And I could see the sexual frustration the churchmen had, who realised they were gay and the only way they could avoid having sex with women was by becoming priests. Then they couldn't control their urges because they were 20 years old and ended up with some altar boy. But then, when my mum died, I realised belief was nothing to do with Catholicism, I realised it was to do with a higher power. I definitely believe now.'

Recently an advertisement for the Church of England, featuring different types of people in different environments reciting the Lord's Prayer, was booked to run in cinemas before the new *Star Wars* movie. As a way of reaching our generation it was genius: the *Star Wars* audience was packed with nostalgic X-ers desperate to deliver their kids their own excellent childhood memories. And what is *Star Wars* if not an allegory for the fight between good and evil? It was exactly the sort of media buying the Church needs. But the UK's three leading cinema chains banned the advert, saying people had not come to cinemas to think about God, and that it could 'offend' people.

So organised religion is now seen as offensive, rather than integral. The Church has left it too late – our secularisation has gone too far.

Those that make the biggest noise now are academics like Richard Dawkins, whose rational, scientific arguments for atheism capture the headlines. Or popular scientists like Brian Cox, who communicates the latest theories in physics, including the suggestion that we live in a multiverse composed of an infinite number of universes. Is this where we find our wonder now? Do we no longer believe in the unknown, do we no longer sense the magic?

As the third wave of feminism takes root, it is tempting to look back in our culture, to the time before Christianity. In pre-Christian pagan societies women were venerated, particularly older women, as wise, spiritual leaders. It was Christianity that eroded women's equality in society, took away their elevated positions, their property rights, their earning power, their voice. It was Christianity that consigned women to a position little better than a domestic slave.

Furthermore, women were branded witches, and, as is written in Exodus: 'Thou shalt not suffer a witch to live.' From the thirteenth to the eighteenth century Christian men killed thousands of women as witches; they were tortured and then burned alive at the stake.

Only now are women beginning to find their place in the Church of England – there are currently nearly 2,000 ordained female priests to about 6,000 men. But it is far more common these days to find women in the care sector than it is in the Church. The refrain 'I'm retraining as a psychotherapist' has the same familiarity as 'I'm retraining as an interior designer/jewellery maker' once did. And let's not even start on the number training as yoga teachers.

For our need is greater than ever. Ten times more people now suffer from depression than in 1945, with up to 20 per cent of the population likely to suffer depression at some point in their lives. In 2013 there were 8.2 million cases of anxiety reported in the UK, with women twice as likely to suffer as men. There are two possible reasons for this – stress, anxiety and depression are increasingly diagnosed because they are now named and reported, or our life experiences and expectations have completely changed.

Happiness – our right to it, how to get it, and how to keep it – has become a national talking point. Its measure is sometimes used as an alternative to GDP for measuring the well-being of a society. Some successful corporations even have a 'chief happiness officer'. As a result, our emotions have become a resource to be bought and sold. The industry around the managing of our emotions – from books to drugs to apps to talking cures – has almost become a religion in itself.

It's particularly bad news for Generation X. A survey for the Office for National Statistics published in February 2016 found that middle-aged people are the least happy, with those aged between 35 and 59 reporting the lowest levels of life satisfaction and the highest levels of anxiety. So that's us, the ones who grew up expecting everything. It seems we now feel largely disappointed.

This could be down to our particular time of life – simultaneously caring for kids and parents, just as the pressures of work and mortgages reach their peak. Or it could be that the older generation are cut from a different cloth, a stiffer upper lip, who appreciate life a little more, expect a little less. They grew up in a postwar society that did not take prosperity and happiness for granted. Millennials, meanwhile, do not assume housing and education as a birthright; they see life changing rapidly before their eyes, and live with the notion that there is nothing certain about the future. They definitely expect less.

Generation X must also ask itself if the consequences of all those hedonistic years, and an unfettered celebrity culture of entitlement, not to mention easy money, has helped fuel this personal crisis. Is this the hangover from all that fun in the Nineties? Countless celebrities and 'civilians' (thanks for that term, Elizabeth Hurley) have ended up on the scrapheap, with the place that scooped them up itself becoming almost as famous. The Priory in Roehampton operated a revolving door as papped as The Ivy's, as stars came and went when it all got too much. Lily Allen, Kate Moss, Johnny Depp, Caroline Aherne, Robbie Williams, Paula Yates, Amy Winehouse, Pete Doherty and Paul Gascoigne have all done time in its treatment rooms. For a while a stint in rehab – whether it was The Meadows, The Priory or The Hoffman Process – was almost as de rigueur as P. Diddy's Mediterranean yacht party.

So how do we fix ourselves before we need to resort to expensive and dramatic treatment in rehabilitation centres? It's interesting how quickly the idea of 'healing' (when not at the hands of a medic, but something you can seek out for yourself) has gone from far out to right on. Remember 'New Age'? This was the term coined to describe every meditation expert, crystal healer, tarot card reader, astrologist and holistic medical practitioner in the early Nineties. In other words, everyone who didn't subscribe to orthodox medicine or an organised Church-based religion. It sounds old-fashioned now – perhaps because that Age is Now. California, way ahead of us for all this stuff, has led the way. They bought and repackaged yoga, meditation, macrobiotic eating and alternative 'healing' as acceptable tools for a Western audience.

Take yoga: it's a business now worth nearly £1 billion in the UK, and nearly £6 billion in the States. (Compare that with a Sunday collection plate.) It might ostensibly be a form of physical exercise, but it's the spiritual practice that often accompanies the classes – exhortations for you to be still, to listen to your body, to locate and acknowledge anxieties and stresses, to practise gratitude – that makes it so popular.

Its spiritual leaders have made fortunes. Bikram Choudhury, the man who claims to have invented 'hot box yoga', where you sweat through your poses in a sauna room, now drives around in a somewhat earthly white Rolls-Royce. Yoga does not exclude, it does not preach, it is open to all – age, size and culture neutral. Those who party hard at the weekend can pay their penance the next morning on a roll mat. In fact, so aligned are the two lifestyles that someone made a web series about it – 'Namaste, Bitches' – ridiculing the teachers who stay up all night doing coke to figure out their new class.

'You can't live your life just one way,' says the personal fitness guru Matt Roberts. 'There has to be balance. Our generation did get hedonistic and that still exists within us. But now we have this balance of doing ourselves good. Green juice, yoga and exercise do it for me, but I still like to see my mates and have fun. We definitely haven't given up on the good times. If anything now, with our kids growing up, partying is attractive again because we've got time to do it. But, being older, we need the payback more than ever.' You see – forgiveness.

And so yoga girl has become a fashion leader. The granddaughter of the Beatles' visit to India in the Sixties and the daughter of Madonna's yoga phase, she is the girl swinging her mat over her shoulder, clutching her green juice as she floats into her class, toned, honeyed limbs poured into lululemon leggings, ready to be absolved of all her sins.

But she has nothing on The Numinous. Set up by the British journalist Ruby Warrington, The Numinous – 'material girls, mystical world' – is a community of modern spiritualists who believe the universe is a divine force there to ameliorate your lifestyle with shiny fashion vibes and sassy incantations. Stories include: 'Hello Chakrubs, yes, it's a crystal dildo', 'Temple of Venus, a meditation for manifesting true love' and 'Adorn yourself, 10 high vibe talismans we love'.

Ruby recently brought her special brand of cool girl 'belief' to Selfridges for a pop-up Christmas display. 'It began as a platform to showcase a new generation of modern mystics bridging the gap between the mystical and the mainstream,' she says. 'It has now become part of a movement towards a global shift in consciousness that's about experiencing life – and each other – on a more meaningful level. The word "numinous" means "that which is unknown, or unknowable" – and in a world where our smartphones have become our talismans of choice, I want to explore ways to reconnect to this undefinable part of being human. With The Numinous, I guarantee you'll also look and feel more fabulous than ever.'

Big fashion tick there then. Ruby has a hashtag on Instagram called shitnuminousgirlssay, which includes such gems as 'I have a past life as a fashion designer so I let her pick my outfits'; 'I was thinking Wednesday too, why do we even text when we can just psychic schedule?'; and 'Our sex is so high vibe it must be like a sound bath for the neighbours'. Which I love, as it takes the high times and irony of our generation and translates what was once perceived as 'New Age' into, shall we call it, New Relevance? Or New Religion? Or, as Ruby calls it, the 'Now Age'.

The mindfulness industry is right behind, albeit with a little more official endorsement. NICE recommends it as a treatment for depression; it even has a platform at the World Economic Forum in Davos endorsed by Goldie Hawn. It is used to describe a conscious approach to anything from parenting to eating and encourages you to live in the moment, providing perfect respite to our fast-paced, anxiety-ridden world. In fact you could argue that the permission to celebrate the moment – whether that's the first spring blossom on the trees, your baby's first step or the taste of your single organic chocolate square – is what has overridden our prevailing cynicism. Suddenly, in the face of so much big crisis (war, corruption, disruption, uncertainty), the ability to enjoy the smallness of your own world has become the perfect antidote. (Although be careful not to take it too far, kids, it can very quickly pass for saccharine rubbish. You know – enough cute kittens already.)

Headspace (a self-proclaimed 'secular' tool) is one of the most successful meditation brands, promising 'if you treat your head right everything else will follow'. It was set up by Andy Puddicombe, a 43-year-old surfer from Bristol and ordained Buddhist monk, and Rich Pierson, a London advertising exec who says he was 'out all the time, drinking a lot, buying a lot of trainers, hanging out with d***heads, probably being the biggest d***head,' as he put it to the journalist Polly Vernon in an interview for *The Times*. At 26, Pierson collapsed and fell into depression. A friend suggested he see Puddicombe, who was treating depression with meditation courses at a clinic in the City. It didn't take them too long to work out there was mileage in their situation.

'We ended up doing a sort of a skills swap,' says Pierson. 'We'd do an hour of meditation, then go across the road to Starbucks, filled with City boys, and do Marketing 101.'

Once Gwyneth Paltrow, Emma Watson and Davina McCall had bought in (and posted about it), millions followed. Buddhist principles are a natural progression for those who grew up protesting over China's invasion of Tibet and the exile of the Dalai Lama and his monks. Endless gap year kids made the pilgrimage to the Himalayan town of Dharamsala to study the monks' teachings – which is why Headspace is the perfect form of lifestyle religion for now (and why we love it when the Dalai Lama comes to London, bugger the Beijing trade deal).

The pursuit of happiness, smartphone meditation apps, healing journeys: it all adds up to a greater emotional intelligence, a phrase once regarded by our parents with deep suspicion. Emotional intelligence, however, is now on the national curriculum, and regarded as the top ingredient in any leader. We can talk quite seriously now about nurturing ourselves, practising gratitude, understanding the heart space, demonstrating awareness and recognising moments when we are 'blessed'.

Just look at the explosion in self-help manuals in the last 20 years – there's no stopping the sales. From *The Power of Now* to *The Secret* to *Chicken Soup for the Soul* to *The Seven Spiritual Laws of Success*, these texts describe a modern religion, one you can design to fit your own life, 'whether you choose to recognise God as a spark of divinity that's external, to which you reconnect,' says the property developer and spiritual agitator Anton Bilton, 'or just awakening yourself to the humanist potential that's within you.'

Anton has spent much of his life in conscious spiritual quest. At the age of 50, he has concluded: 'Two things: first, that we are all structured by fears, and secondly, that the Buddhist mantra that all unhappiness stems from a denting of expectation is real. A simplistic analogy would be when you are unexpectedly invited to a party and end up having one of the best nights of your life – all because there was no expectation. If you can live your life with no expectation, you are living your life fearlessly, because the fear lies in whether the expectation will be met.'

The child of divorce, religious quester, society figure, father of five and now ayahuasca proponent, Bilton's journey is an interesting one. It began in the Church of England, progressed to the Alpha Course, has taken in some hypnotic regression and has ended in a very vogue-ish X-er activity: ayahuasca, a South American plant that contains the hallucinogen DMT. Native

American Indians have taken ayahuasca for centuries in spiritual ceremonies. Ingesting it leads to a hallucinogenic state of what its users proclaim as absolute truth. So how did a 50-year-old multi-millionaire come to dedicate himself to journeying on hallucinogenic plants in shamanic ceremonies?

'For much of my life, I was driven by fear. I'd seen my father leave my mother, and what had been a very luxurious lifestyle diminished dramatically in my teens when he moved to France and she stayed in England. As my mother was in a very sad place and using alcohol and Valium, I had to become the man of the house at 13 and it fell to me to look after my 11-year-old brother and my three-year-old sister, run the house and put my mother to bed. You've got two choices at 13: you either cry and give up, or you cut the emotion and solve the problem.

'There I was then, a little boy in a really dark place, bullied at school, terrible at sport, an academic failure with no self-worth. I went to church, thinking, what is this all about? And then one morning, carrying some toast back to my bedroom at school, I walked past a window – as I passed, this all-embracing fluorescent pink light suddenly appeared from the sky outside and held me in complete rapture. Everything seemed to go still, time stopped and a voice in my head said, "I'm going to give you something now, and there is no judgement as to how you use it." Then the bright light disappeared and I was left standing alone, absolutely shocked and thinking: What was that? Was it God? And what did it mean by saying, "I'm going to give you something now and there's no judgement as to how you use it?" It was all so real and yet equally so confusing, and it started my spiritual quest; I just had to reconnect to whoever that was.

'It was only when I left school for university that I started to recognise what the gift was. I began to make new friends and noticed how people would say, "What are we going to do tonight? Anton, what are you doing, can we come too?"

Suddenly, from being bottom of the class and not in any sports team, I had new friends and people wanted to do things with me. I realised it was a real gift – the gift of enthusiasm and leadership. The spirit of endeavour, if you like.

'I met my wife when she was 19 and I was 22, we got married and I became a workaholic. I didn't have any material wealth and I wanted to create it.

'I was driven by fear. I continued my spiritual search and enrolled on the Alpha Course. It was a fresh new way of teaching Christianity in contemporary, rather King James's 17th-century English. The priests wore jeans and T-shirts rather than dog-collars, and they spoke eloquently, sharing their personal doubts and sufferings; there was open, devout prayer where you really worshipped; you fully immersed yourself in deep reverence and gratitude for your life, and it felt very real and true. But in time I found the exclusivity a big issue. My questions about Buddhists, Hindus, pantheists, animists, spiritualists and all other religions were dismissed with, "Don't worry about them. God will deal with them in their own way." It just didn't feel right to me that there was some sort of exclusive "club" approach.

'Separately, my businesses had flourished and I still recognised the value of the gift I had been given. Then, out of the blue, my wife left me. It was a complete surprise. I had no choice but to go into my office and say to my team, "Look, I'm emotionally broken. I couldn't negotiate over five pence now, let alone a multi-million-pound deal, so please take control." They did, and without me sitting on top of everything as the control freak I had been our businesses continued to flourish. It took me about nine months to emotionally recover from my separation, but spiritually I was very disillusioned and sad. I felt betrayed, as I had tried really hard to be a decent man, work hard, build my businesses, be a good father and a good husband, and look after my family. Yet somehow I had lost the most important thing in my life: my wife and two little children. I was angry with my Maker. I'd felt that I'd played by the rules and tried my best, and even in my own acceptance that I'd failed and been neglectful, it just didn't seem fair.

'And at that moment it dawned on me that fairness wasn't the point. The purpose of existence had to be about a multitude of experiences and a multitude of self-judgements – the karmic wheel of reincarnation. My spiritual search continued but I was less interested in belief-orientated religions – books with parables and rules, filled with notions of original sin and salvation. I wanted something more direct, more experiential. I wanted to feel God's presence again like that time of my rapture at school.

'So I went looking for mystical experiences and did something that changed my life: hypnotic regression. I visited a renowned regression therapist and was hypnotised. After a long relaxation process I found myself in an underground chamber with stairs going down to a series of doors. I was asked to intuitively open one of the doors. Very suddenly I became furiously angry, overwhelmed with emotion, physically tense. A minute before I had been lying there listening to the jackhammer outside on a London street, thinking, "What are you doing here, it's 5.30 in the afternoon, you should be working!" Then suddenly, I was encapsulated by this immense fury, my body convulsing and straining on the therapist's couch. Visually, I felt myself rising up from and looking down onto a crumpled body somewhere in a desert tundra. I realised the body was mine, and I was the soul, lifting up from it. I had just died and I was furious. I then saw a review of my life; I had been part of a small group of nomadic hunter-gatherers, probably 1,500 years ago. We didn't know other people, we didn't stay anywhere for more than a few months at a time and we carried dome-like skinned tents on our backs that we slept under. It was a simple, mundane, survivalist existence, and the thing that was maddening to our life was that, once every few years, men on horses would arrive and take everything from us, rape our women, and anyone that resisted would get killed. I'd seen my father die in one of these fights, and I'd seen both my mother and wife raped and die this way. We didn't know who these people were or why they did it. It was an awful, fearful and unexplained way to live.

'At the time of my death, another military group had ridden into our village again, taking everything, and I was so sick of it I grabbed one of the men, pulled him off his horse and held him down on the ground, strangling him. Then he threw me off, rolled over and swung back on top of me and started strangling me. He was wearing a leather tunic and I could see the leather around his armpit was straggly, where the uric acid of his sweat had made it flimsy and damp. As I lay there hypnotised in the therapist's room, I could actually smell the strong, acrid stench of the leather mixed with his sweat. It was such a shock to smell it in real time. I continued to struggle and rolled him over, but his fellow soldier ran over and hit me in my back with a battle-axe and I fell forward onto my face. Strangely, rather than the axe, what hurt me most was grazing my forehead on the ground. I lay there, my spine shattered, knowing that I was dying, filled with a rage at the absolute futility of my wretched life and angry with my Creator. I came out of the regression shocked at the realness of the visual memories and especially at the emotional recall of anger and the vivid smells. My regressed life had not been glamorous or exciting. I was no hero, just a simple man from a small group, perpetually damaged by unexplained marauding troops. That simplicity made the experience even more real.

'After that experience I gave up on the belief-based religions, and focused on altered states of consciousness and experiential processes in my attempt to access the divine. I read a lot of books about near-death experiences, past lives, astral projection and altered states of consciousness created by shamanic drumming, sensory-deprivation tanks, psychedelics and indigenous use of plant medicines – all instances where people reported an alternative conscious state and felt a real connection to either the earth, nature or God.

'I think shamanic drumming helps to explain the current rave culture. Ancient shamanic tribal drumming practice is primarily about letting go to a repetitive beat in a meditative, collective trance state. You can see it in that moment when you've got people dancing for a length of time and there comes a moment where they sense a density in the air, it gets tangibly thicker and there's the presence of something other. Where the egos of all those involved have let go and their hearts are open as a collective. I've felt this during worship in church, I've felt it in a sensory-deprivation flotation tank, I've felt it during deep prayer and meditation in ceremonies in other temples and I've felt it on the dance floor. If you were the Creator, you'd look down at these people earnestly praying, meditating or dancing together and be pleased that your children are being focused on their sense of existence, being reverential, grateful, enjoying the gift of their life. As fickle as it may sound, I think it's important never to be guilty about celebrating one's existence with one's fellow humans; there is nothing that makes God smile more than seeing his children happy, mutually compassionate and at peace.

'A year or so after my regression experience I was staying with friends on the west coast of Mexico and we were sharing hypnotic regression stories. A fellow guest said, "You should drink ayahuasca." I'd read a lot about ayahuasca and was interested to try it. She knew a shaman who she had drunk with and who she recommended. So I jumped on a plane, flew to Ecuador – where it's legal – and had my first experience. I sat through the night, meditating for eight hours. You don't talk. Instead you're guided by the shaman's open prayers, songs called "icaros" and music. I cried tears of joy for a long time because everything I'd ever read about enlightenment, arriving in the void of existence with a sense of self-awareness yet without any material body, had happened. To feel the bliss of that place, the calmness, and to recognize that there is no such thing as death, gave me the overwhelming sensation that I had "come home"; I had returned from whence we came. The divine spark within had reconnected with its source. It was shockingly profound, life-changing, and it took away my fear of death and it took away my avarice.'

Since then Anton has moved his family to Ibiza and uses his UK base in Buckinghamshire – a vast and beautiful Palladian mansion, Tyringham Hall – as a centre to further research around the nature of consciousness. In the grounds is a temple, and inscribed on the wall is the following: 'Seek truth but remember that behind all the new knowledge the fundamental issues of life remain veiled.' He held a symposium there in 2015 to which he invited academics and scientists from all over the world, from Rupert Sheldrake to Dennis McKenna, to discuss alternative states of consciousness.

'Now I subscribe to a more gnostic view, that God exists as a cosmic mind, and we are sparks of that divinity. We are distanced from him when we are incarnated, and our intuitive subconscious recognition of him lies in our appreciation of beauty, music, love, compassion, kindness – all those things that we intuitively connect with and feel good about. When you do a good act, you know that he's glowing through you, his grace is shining through.'

Ayahuasca ceremonies have become quite the thing. Tens of thousands of tourists have travelled to South America to take part in ceremonies (the BBC even screened a documentary programme with Bruce Parry where he agreed to undergo a ceremony while being filmed). There are plenty of 'shamans' who will conduct ceremonies for you now in most major cities, but according to Louis de Rohan, a London PR executive, 'Doing ayahuasca with indigenous people in Latin America is a supremely spiritual and holy experience. In the end it doesn't matter if you think it's a genuine spiritual experience or a DMT trip, as what the chemical allows you to do is offload all your cultural conditioning and see who your true self really is.'

Of course, it seems only logical that a generation that has such a free and easy attitude towards drugs should solve their spiritual crisis with, um, drugs. The power of ayahuasca, claim its ambassadors, never diminishes. 'All the noise in your head is quiet, and the happy essential self is discovered very naturally,' says Louis. 'It happens every time you do it.' It's hardly a fun trip though – you spend several hours vomiting after ingestion, and then several more hours in a trippy trance. It is used in clinical conditions on patients suffering from PTSD or depression. Like a truth drug, patients claim it helps them face the root cause of the issues, rather than simply addressing the symptoms.

But its use by jaded thrill seekers to medicate the frustrations of Western living is having quite a profound effect. It is creating a band of revolutionaries willing to question the entire structure.

'Most people in the West organise their lives around financial gain, because they need to pay school fees or want a house,' says Louis. 'They don't think about the end goal, because our education system leads you to believe that what you need is to be professionally and commercially successful. So why are so many of us unhappy?'

Following a Catholic upbringing, Louis came out at 30, even though he had a girlfriend. 'It taught me everything I knew was wrong.' A few years later his business went through a crisis when he lost several big clients. He went on a paragliding course to try to clear his head (what was that about thrill seekers?) and, following a technical error, had a near-fatal accident.

'It focused the mind. I thought, there has got to be more to life than pitching for business and dealing with asshole clients. It's all about profit, and profit doesn't have a human side.' So Louis restructured his business and took a year off – in Latin America.

'What became apparent on my travels is that everybody in the West is completely fucked if they want to have any semblance of freedom. I realised that I was trapped through my sexual identity and my business and my Catholic guilt and I managed to blast all these things out of the water and make some brave calls. It takes guts to be happy, because being happy is following your instincts and understanding your essence – who am I, and what do I want out of my life? If it's having a farm in the Pyrenees then that's what you should go and do.

'The problem with Western culture is that there is so much literal, metaphorical and emotional noise. Fear of cancer, terrorism, manipulation by the media, marketing, limitations of education, conditioning, parenting – all of that. Most people can't even hear their instincts, because they don't have the space and time to do so. So they don't give their essential self the freedom of expression it craves,' says Louis.

Whereas 150 years ago many of us would have been in the fields all week, doing physical work in our natural environment and attending weekly church services, these days we are rushing round towns, clocking into workplaces and struggling to meet domestic and professional KPIs. We find instant gratification in short-term pleasure, whether that's a maxi tub of ice cream or a pint glass, and then we wonder why many of us are left with a spiritual void. Enter yoga, meditation, retreats, therapy, sabbaticals and, most extremely, ayahuasca.

Running off to South America and rejecting Western values doesn't need to be everybody's answer to a better life, though. More and more of us are using therapy to help find meaning – as many as 1 in 4 (compared with 1 in 5, five years ago), with women and those aged between 35 and 44 the biggest users (according to the British Association for Counselling & Psychotherapy).

'My mum and I came from a really poor family,' says John Vial. 'We lived on a council estate in Derby, and I remember in 1978 we moved house and got an indoor toilet. When my mum died a few years ago she left me £3,000, which was a lot of money to her. I didn't know what to do with it, and I ended up spending it on a watch, which my mum would have thought was scandalous. I was seeing a regressive therapist at the time who asked me to do a really simple thing.'

The therapist was operating on the theory that it is only you who can give yourself the answers. She asked Vial to pitch himself forward into the future, and imagine how he would like himself to be. 'A nice person, who isn't hysterical, who doesn't lose his temper and is happy,' was Vial's answer. The coach then told him to use the watch as the totem to remember that. 'Now I hold the watch every time I get nervous,' he says, and he reckons his mum would be very happy with that.

We are also becoming increasingly good at giving back. The charity sector continues to grow despite the recession – its income exceeded £70 billion for 2015/16. The generation that grew up with Bob Geldof, Greenpeace and Lonely Planet back-packing in developing countries is hyper-aware of its privileged position. As the inequality of society cuts deeper, those that are in a position to do something about it, do.

'I went to Eton, one of the most prestigious schools on the planet, but that feeling of being a good citizen was very much a part of our education,' says Ben Elliot. 'Very idealistically, straight after school, I went to go and work in orphanages in Romania. It stretched how I thought about life.'

A substantial part of Ben's business is now structured around the Quintessentially Foundation, a philanthropic arm that he dedicates 20 per cent of his time to. Charities in turn have become astute at getting people to exercise their giving reflex with regular monthly payments, and justifying Lycra-led pursuits with good causes (justgiving.com). Bono shepherds (RED), an organisation that encourages companies from Amex to Apple to launch products that donate a percentage of their profits to fighting AIDS in Africa. We tease him for being so tiresome as he swans around Davos in his sunglasses, but actually we secretly love the fact that a rock star can infiltrate such events. Comic Relief is another Generation X success story: led by entertainers, celebrities and glitzy media types, it has encouraged over £1 billion of donations in the 30 years since it launched.

But the charity sector is on the naughty step – unscrupulous fundraising activities has brought it into disrepute, likewise revelations that disproportionate amounts of funds are spent on fundraising itself.

'I support smaller charities, such as Women for Women International [which pairs westerners with women caught up in the aftermath of war] and The Circle, set up by Annie Lennox, just because you can see where your money's going,' says Alice Temperley. 'I like Women for Women, as you can have that direct link with one person on a particular project. You can see the difference. I do that now rather than Oxfam, because you see the results of your actions, rather than just putting your name to something and not knowing what the benefits are.'

Seeing our beloved celebrities and famous types throw them-selves into fundraising and charitable activities gives all of us ideas about how we can incorporate this sector into our lives. Following the financial crash in 2008, I wondered if the readers of *Style* magazine would be interested in supporting a charity alongside their weekly statement-handbag fix.

We found a charity that fitted the bill perfectly: Smart Works. Relying on donations from clothing companies, and an army of voluntary stylists and interview trainers, it gives women who are out of work an outfit for their job interview and some tips on how to conduct it. If they get the job – and over half the women who come through Smart Works do – they can come back for seven days' worth of workwear and accessories. For women who have been out of work caring for children or the elderly, or been in prison or are victims of abuse, the confidence boost a little good fashion can bring seems to do the trick. They come in, shoulders hunched, eyes on the ground, awkward and shuffling. They leave looking polished and confident, shoulders back, eyes sparkling. It's a simple but effective premise that delivers direct results.

When *Style* held its first fashion sale for Smart Works, the tickets sold out in days, and many hundreds of those who came brought bags of clothes to donate to the charity as well. Smart Works now has six branches across the UK and dresses hundreds of women. And supporting them feels good.

We are a generous and thoughtful bunch, and I would argue getting more so. We have given up on government and the Church being able to look after society's poor and disenfranchised, and instead have empowered the charity sector to do more. We roll our sleeves up and get involved, and encourage and sponsor others to, too. We are also at a time in our lives when our focus has shifted away from sorting ourselves out, and have more flexibility to give to others. The charity sector is benefiting. We like giving – we always have done and we will do more. Those collection plates just don't cover it.

12
Alexander Is Dead, Long Live McQueen

Alexander McQueen was 40 when he died. After a cocktail of tranquillisers and sleeping pills, he hanged himself in his flat in the dead of a February night, and was discovered, candle still burning, amongst his beloved dogs, the next day. A copy of the book *The Descent of Man* by Wolfe von Lenkiewicz was by his side, with his suicide note scribbled in the back: 'Please look after the dogs. Sorry, I love you, Lee. PS Bury me in the church.'

It was an appallingly tragic end for a man that had come so far. The sixth child of an East End cabbie, he had hauled himself to the very top of the fashion industry with hard work, blazing talent and a genius for attracting attention. He did this by doing exactly what he believed, which tended to be the opposite of what everybody else thought. Discovered and championed by his friend, the eccentric aristocrat Isabella Blow, they got on, he said, because she was like him: 'She doesn't care.'

It was such disregard for the establishment that made him so attractive. Uncompromising, controversial, romantic, innovative and creatively a genius, he was everything that true fashion celebrates. His collections were often accused of misogyny, but such accusations missed the subtleties. One, called Highland Rape, was actually a reference to the 'ethnic cleansing' carried out by British forces in the Scottish Highlands in the eighteenth and nineteenth centuries.

In his Fashion-able shoot for the magazine *Dazed*, he cast models with disabilities and commissioned specially designed pieces off designers like Philip Treacy and Hussein Chalayan. He invented 'bumsters', trousers with a waistband that sat halfway down the bottom, and often sent his models out with challenging and savage mouth and headpieces. For a completely uneducated, white, working-class boy, he transcended every stereotype. His training as a cutter on Savile Row gave him a pin-sharp approach to tailoring, but it was his inventiveness with fabric, historical references and ideas that made his collections so ravishing. Under the umbrella of the Gucci group, who bought a controlling stake in his brand, he learned to accept commercial imperatives, but never did this impact on the march of his ideas.

When he died, even the fashion world was surprised by how widely his story travelled. Something about his passing, about what he represented, resonated with audiences around the world, whether you cared about fashion or not. Savage Beauty, the retrospective of his work at the Metropolitan Museum in New York, became one of the most successful shows the institution had ever staged; when it came to London it was just as big a hit. I'm not sure the industry will ever produce someone of his standing again. The commerciality, its short attention span and the changing nature of its audience would probably not allow such a talent to be nurtured. He was a revolutionary, a true child of his time, but in the end he could not survive. That dark night in February 2010 marked the end of an era, and the beginning of something new.

Fashion is an exclusive language. Those who are conversant with its nuances and codes convey a superior knowledge that can leave those outside feeling slightly inadequate. This is intentional: boyfriends and husbands are often mystified by fashion. Most girls agree that true fashion is not about appearing sexy – let's face it, looking sexy is not that complicated. True fashion is about being in the know. In its highest form, like McQueen, it sits alongside music, art and film as the fourth pillar of the cultural estate. But it is also just clothes: look what I'm wearing, this is who I am. Geddit?

Over the period of our lifetime fashion has been fully democratised. Once an exclusive pursuit for the very rich, now anyone can own a flashy handbag or a pair of zhuzzy shoes. Magazines, blogs, newspapers – most media outlets cover it in some form, because as an industry it has become endlessly spawning. Spring and autumn collections are now punctuated with Cruise and pre-Collections, which also have their own show schedules. Then there are pop-up shows in new markets that the industry spies as ripe for some aspirational uniform. Rio, Havana, Tokyo, LA – hey guys, let's fly the world's press and our richest customers out there, put on a spectacular display, show off another 200-piece collection, our third this season, and pump out some product.

There's a famous story about the footballer George Best, who is lying on a hotel bed, sipping champagne, casino winnings spread all over the rumpled sheets and Miss World in his arms. The hotel porter comes in and asks, 'Mr Best, where did it all go wrong?' Well, I better hold my hand up and say, 'Guilty'. At *Sunday Times Style*, a magazine that has gone out to over a million middle England households every week, we became a significant cheerleader of the fashion industry's growth. As Derek Zoolander correctly identified, it's a Technicolor world of crazy characters and seductive glamour, whether that's Isabella Blow in her lobster hats, Naomi Campbell with her phone-slapping tantrums and blood diamonds or Tom Ford with his spanking paddles and python loafers.

It also has its share of clever types – mad pioneering personalities like Karl Lagerfeld, who behind his trademark goggles, has masterminded the rise of the biggest luxury powerhouse in the world, and deep into his eighties shows no sign of letting up. Or Christopher Bailey at Burberry, who saw the future and led the way for fashion in technology. Or Natalie Massenet and Anna Wintour (more goggles), who were masters of deciphering the industry for the woman on the street. Fashion enthrals young women and girls, provoking those who should know better to acts of rash expenditure. It dishes out great joy and confidence at the same time as incredulity and damning insecurity.

The first time I experienced the illicit thrill of expensive fashion was in Joseph, on Brompton Cross. I had just moved up to London and started working. Joseph at that time was the fashion destination for the Nineties working woman – a uniform of Helmut Lang trouser suits and black, black and more black. It was ruinously expensive (although not proportionately as expensive as it is now), but if you shopped the T-shirt racks and the sale you could usually find something.

It was the end of the day, the shop was emptying and I was ploughing through a rack of items when I found it. A black leather sheath dress, with an A-line skirt, split dangerously high up the back and a scoop neck swooping down into the cleavage. What a dress! I turned over the label. It was £600 – reduced to £300. I could hardly believe it. I raced it into the changing room – it fitted like a glove. I looked in the mirror and gasped at what I saw. It was possibly the first time I recognised the possibility that I had the power to look properly sexy.

But it was £300.

My salary at that time must have been about £1,100 a month, before tax. How could I justify it? And then he appeared behind me. A little man, with round gold glasses perched on his nose, a beautiful smart suit and a heavy French accent. He smiled at me and I knew instantly – it was Joseph Ettedgui himself.

'My dear,' he said, pausing to look me up and down, 'you should buy zat dress.'

He was right. I went on to wear zat dress on appropriate and inappropriate occasions for years and years. It made me sexy, made me vampy, made me powerful, made me killer on dates, work dos, nights out with girls. It became the ultimate, fail-safe LBD to pull out in all moments of crisis – classic, reliable, always one hundred per cent working. In recent years the amount of flesh it exposes has seemed less appropriate, but with a cream silk shirt underneath, a pair of black opaques and a slash of red lipstick it is as current as ever. It was, is and will always be a fashion triumph. I owe you many thanks, M. Ettedgui (RIP).

When I came to take my place in the front row, September 2002, I was an imposter with no background in fashion at all. I had been parachuted in by John Witherow, the editor of the *Sunday Times*, to transform his *Style* supplement into a glossy magazine for young women. Not many in the fashion fraternity liked this very much, and for my first season at the shows I had to squeeze my bottom onto the front-row benches as tutting fellow editors refused to move up: 'You can't sit with us.'

It used to take years to reach the top in fashion – long days steaming outfits in a windowless fashion cupboard, running around after grande dame editors exchanging their gifted handbags and picking up their dry cleaning. One famous fashion photographer keeps a Pantone card in his pocket and if his assistant fails to make his tea to the exact shade of brown he matches on the card they are fired on the spot.

Nowadays you can take a shortcut to the top via a blog, and if you have enough followers you're off. I remember when the bloggers first started appearing at the shows – upstarts, we sniffed – and laughed at them for their ridiculous outfits and craven desire to be photographed at every opportunity. They would hang around outside the show tents getting in the way of us – the real fashionistas! 'A circus!' the great Suzy Menkes called it. But over a few short seasons that circus outside became more influential than the one within, as the bloggers spoke directly to the customers. If they wore a piece of Dior, or Nina Ricci, or Celine, that could shift sales. That made them very important indeed. The front row moved up – albeit reluctantly.

But, oh, the glamour and riches of the fashion industry once you are on the inside. Coddled by every luxury fashion house in town, plied with free handbags and clothes, flown round the world to attend parties and shows, fashion's performance to the outside world is ostentatious and lavish. The meeting room at Dolce & Gabbana HQ is all black marble, gold thrones and red Baccharat glass. At Prada, Mrs P has a Carsten Höller slide fitted from her office to the ground floor. At Dior on the Avenue Montaigne, duck egg blue softpile carpets line the salons – Roberto Cavalli even has shaved mink lining the walls of his yacht. But make no mistake: it is thin gossamer between the treats and the business. Beneath every velvet glove is an iron fist. Feature us, flatter us – or forget it.

Milan always closes with the Armani show. Mr Armani has never quite recovered the currency of his Eighties heyday, but, as a smart businessman, he has continued to build an empire flogging the same clobber to celebrities and Chinese power wives alike. His reputation is fierce, his mouth pulled into a rictus grin as he takes his bow at the end of every show. No one who works at Armani has ever looked like they enjoy it much. What's more his shows can go on for up to 40 minutes (ten minutes is the norm), which, when you are watching the same short suit exit in 20 different hues of lilac, can be trying on the attention levels. Conscious his audience is not as appreciative as they should be, he plants fluffers through the crowd who spontaneously applaud and gasp with amazement at points in the show. How has he maintained this grip on an industry with such a famously short attention span? By spending copious amounts in advertising, of course.

When I inherited *Style*, our much-feared and dramatic fashion writer was the historian Colin McDowell, a portly old queen who liked to maintain his status on the front row by throwing dramatic strops if he didn't get what he wanted. If a PR refused to meet his demands he would stage a walk-out – a ploy he adored as it made him the centre of attention and appear very grand. It certainly kept the poor PRs on their toes. McDowell was banned from reviewing Armani shows as he had dared to suggest the collections were lacking in modernity.

Criticism was not something Armani liked to hear and my task was to woo Armani back, regaining the access and invitations. (The *Sunday Times*'s relationship with Armani has history: legend has it that after one particularly nuanced review, Mr Armani himself rang up the editor, then Andrew Neil, to vent his fury and unleash the ultimate weapon that he was 'dropping all the advertising'. As Armani ranted down the phone, Neil cut him off before he could finish: 'Mr Armani, I would like to inform you that from this point forward, you are banned from advertising in my paper.' Oh, the glory days.)

So there I was one Monday afternoon, at the last show of the Milan season, clapping politely through the sixtieth outfit of meh soft tailoring, thinking I had only 40 minutes to make my flight, tee up the issue for the following Sunday and prepare for newspaper conference on Tuesday morning. Conference was always an amusing affair. I would usually present my features list straight after 'foreign news'. Bush invades the Gulf, Pakistani secret service mole leaks support to United States military, Blair on his uppers with Chirac – and *Style*? Cropped trousers are the big news this season.

As I pushed my way out of the auditorium, the PR sidled up alongside me and whispered in my ear that Mr Armani would be throwing an intimate dinner for George Clooney tonight, would I care to join?

Of course this was not a question, and being currently single, it required no answer. I raced to the Via della Spiga to invest in a new pair of stilettos (obvs), before heading back to the hotel to brush up on George's films. Could this, I dared to fantasise, be the night that fashion changed my path forever? Could it?

Dinner was to be at Armani's new Japanese restaurant, and I arrived a few minutes late. The door was thronged – with fans, I presumed, but I could see the willowy English PR in the entrance. As I got closer it dawned on me that these were not fans – they were guests. The PR was ticking names off lists. Upstairs there were over 200 of us and I barely snatched a glimpse of George all night. But no matter – the PR had what she wanted, a room full of editors and press. A few hours later pictures of Armani and Clooney with their arms around each other flooded the news wires, and everyone admired how influential and cool Armani was.

My editor was furious I missed conference. I did not admit the reason.

Clooney was just the beginning of it. The race was on to coopt celebrities into the fashion brands' circle, for each label to seem more aspirational than the next. Donatella threw parties at her palazzo after her shows, littering every surface with ice buckets of Cristal. I danced with Beyoncé (literally – just me and her on the dancefloor in Donatella's front room), ate sushi on Cavalli's lurid purple yacht, shared a tête-à-tête with Tom Ford at Claridge's, watched Daniel Craig snog Kate Moss at a McQueen party, arrived at the Venice Film Festival by speedboat with Julianne Moore, binged on caviar at Pucci with Kylie and sat next to David Gandy more times than he would have liked.

I won't pretend it wasn't fun, particularly as those were the days before mobile phones. What was once a carefully staged photo opportunity for Armani and Clooney has become so much more powerful, with every blogger in the room able to publish each meticulously stage-managed moment, frame by frame. The result is, things are not quite so loose now. Be careful what you say and what you do – everyone is watching you.

Cool, then, has had to make way for popularity. Popular is not to Generation X's taste. 'If you think about the word "cool", it's a bit chilly,' says Claudia Croft, fashion editor of the *Sunday Times*. 'It isn't a friendly thing, it isn't supposed to be. It's "You can't be in our gang until we say you can." It's *Mean Girls*.'

Mean Girls does not earn you many 'likes'. Instead you have Cara Delevingne corralling alliances against the 'haters', and horsing around with her tongue out. Or Brooklyn Beckham falling off his skateboard, because it makes him appear – and here is a great Millennial word – 'authentic' to his six million followers. (Perhaps 'transparent' is more accurate.) Or Taylor Swift and her 'squad' hanging out on sofas with cats like the rest of us. Kendall Jenner has 50 million Instagram followers, thanks to her pictures goofing around with her family. When Estée Lauder signed her as their new face, sales rocketed – she brought an entirely new audience to what was then quite a 'mature' brand.

'Kendall is pretty, but she's actually quite dull,' confides Claudia. 'She's not interested in being wild or interesting. She's just focused on doing the job. She's conscientious.' No matter – she brings millions of young girls with her.

'Remember how that trying too hard thing used to be so uncool?' says Claudia. 'Chiara Ferragni is one of the world's biggest bloggers. She makes tons of money – something like US$7 million last year. The other day she was wearing a bomber jacket, and on the back it had embroidered "Follow me" and her Instagram handle.' Deeply uncool? Not to Ferragni and her followers. As the Balmain designer Olivier Rousteing, bfs with Kendall and co., asks: 'What's wrong with pop?'

Alexander Is Dead, Long Live McQueen   155

How different this seems from the days of Kate Moss, whose idea of cool is not to talk to anyone. She and her friends were an agonisingly closed group – hounded by intriguing tales of spats and fallouts. Pearl Lowe, Davinia Taylor, Lindsay Lohan – the gossip pages were for years laced with rumours of 'betrayals', those once held close now cast out for indiscretions. 'You had to be in. If you weren't in, you were dead,' says Claudia.

Cool is no longer about exclusive tribes – defined by the music you listen to, the clothes you wear, the places you go. With everything so transparent and accessible, you can go everywhere, with anyone and be all of those things just through the lens of your phone. You can do it in one outfit – and then change three times again that day. What makes you cool is not allegiance to a tribe, but the attitude of "I'm going to wear what I want." So Alexa Chung can switch from nerd to glamour puss via an M&S pie-crust collar, Laura Bailey can throw a duffel coat over her Chanel gown, Poppy Delivingne does double denim with a bikini.

It used to be much more straightforward. Fashion was a uniform, strictly prescribed. Once upon a time everyone wore Helmut Lang, and that was it. Now the offering is so vast and large, the only way to accommodate it all is to wear it all at once. And if you find that dizzying, you could do something completely different. Normcore. Normcore was a brief and rather wonderful moment to describe the utter rejection of fashion. It was – nothing. Not even trying. It was Zuckerberg in his hoodie and trainers before they got coopted back by fashion, it was Gap jeans and a crap jumper. As a fashion trend, however, it didn't last. How could it?

Where does this blogger-driven all-you-can-eat fashion buffet leave X-ers then? Are we post-fashion? What are the symptoms, what can you do? Giving up on fashion is a bit like giving up on youth and no way are we going to do that. I wonder, instead, if we are rising above it. Like George Best on his hotel bed, a parade of millions of pounds worth of Chanel clobber through the streets of Havana feels a bit wrong. What message are you transmitting here? 'Join the capitalist frenzy and look! One day you too can spend £5,000 on a cropped jacket!'

'The rise of luxury brands doesn't seem real,' says Serena Rees. 'It's just people going, "Look at me." I'm annoyed that every dress is £2,000. A dress for the day! It's wasteful and I'd rather do something better with that cash.' As Kanye West put it in one of his occasionally perceptive addresses, 'Beauty has been stolen from the people and sold back as luxury.'

Have luxury brands had their heads turned by the Asian markets and forgotten the home crowd? 'Definitely,' says Claudia. 'There are certain brands that never go out of flavour – like Hermès. Or if I said, "Would you like a Chanel bag?" You'd be like, "Get out of my way!" But what's the point of liking Dior? Who is even designing Dior now? You don't feel that invested in them because they're not invested in you. They've got into this system of creating lots of product, putting it into their shops and aiming it at new markets. So if you are a rich, Western woman who hasn't got the Hong Kong dollar, then what is all that product for?'

We still want fashion, but we want to stand out from the crowd. And the way we can do that is vintage. After all, we invented it. 'In the Nineties I had no money,' says Claudia. 'If I wanted a new coat I couldn't go to the high street because it was naff – it was for townie girls, not cool girls. If I wanted anything decent I found it in a vintage shop.'

This is where bands were dressing too. 'Fashion was important for us at the beginning of the Nineties,' says Alex James. 'There was lots of great stuff around, but it wasn't a luxury-brand thing. We all dressed from Deptford Market, which was on Mondays and Wednesdays. Clothes that you could buy for a quid, handmade boots and tailored suits. Graham Coxon's still got a lot of the clothes he bought. My best ever buy was this beautiful shirt, silk, absolutely lovely. I wore it until it fell to bits.'

Vintage is the real thing – it is authentic, with history and credentials and the fact that you will be unique in it, unlike all the other high street or luxury-brand clones. Now there are vintage dealers who can find you an original Courrèges ball-gown, and cool, one-of-a-kind shops, like The Vampire's Wife in Brighton, run by Nick Cave's wife, the model Susie Bick.

'I don't want to do the search through my screen, I'd rather go out and about,' says Serena Rees. 'I like antique markets, auctions, places where I have to go and find it. I enjoy the sense of discovery every time I find something.'

Generation X need clothes to feel emotionally right. To feel part of us, true to us. Our heads are no longer turned by the flashiest or most expensive things – we'd feel like idiots for having them. Neither do we want the same as everyone else. Millennials might be obsessed by 'individuality', but it ends up being in a very samey way. Boohoo is a successful shopping portal for young women, and it peddles a high street version of Cara Delevingne. Cara doesn't wear flashy clothes – she wears tracksuits and trainers, so what you've got to aspire to isn't that far from where you are already.

Meanwhile the great democratisation of fashion has spawned a toxic industry of fast fashion – cheap clothes manufactured in unhealthy, unsafe factories by workers who are paid a pittance for their servitude. Put your hands over your ears and don't think too much about it – if you ignore it then you can have a brand-new, on-trend outfit for Friday night and chuck it in the bin the next day. Disposable. Value for one night only. And then these clothes pile up and go to landfill (only a small percentage make the cut for recycling), and the earth groans on its axis again. Influential voices from within the industry are beginning to challenge the model. Women like Stella McCartney have made ethics the central plank of their value system. Journalists are beginning to express concern.

They don't need to tell Generation X girls. These women are well aware of what they are buying, the sourcing and the consequences. Millennials might make a big noise about conscious consumerism, but its X-ers that put their money where their mouth is. Generally, they have more money than Millennials, so don't need to shop at Primark quite so urgently.

As Annabel Rivkin, editor of the media brand The Midult, says: 'We were the first generation to consciously curate our own identities, and we wanted to make sure we did this in a whole-hearted way. We want our image to reflect our ideas, so that we are fully formed – so that we make sense as people. So we match our jeans to our ethical conversation to our choice of wine. We put ourselves together as packages.'

We signed the petition for better work conditions after the collapse of the Rana Plaza factory in Bangladesh. So how can we buy a skirt for £2 and throw it away two days later? In the same way we buy Fairtrade coffee, we might also buy organic cotton. We may not be able to resist the siren call of Zara, but an ethical jewellery brand that supports disadvantaged communities in Tanzania is very interesting to us. We make sure we take our unwanted clothes to the recycling centre or donate them to a charity shop. A secondhand market in designer clothing is beginning to mushroom, with marketplaces like Vestiaire Collective, High Fashion Society and Rebelle springing up to cater for recycling our expensive guilty pleasures.

What's more, Generation X girls are busy. We don't have time to fiddle about in front of a mirror getting our belt just right, or trying the latest print blocking. We need a uniform, or clothes that we can just pull on and go, but that still have that fashion tick. Just fashion enough. Clothes that speak to a lifestyle of work, kids and cocktails. Stella McCartney understands this better than everyone, and she should do – she's one of us. The Finery is a more accessible brand that has found success amongst this demographic.

McQueen now is a much tamer brand under Sarah Burton. In Lee's studio from the very beginning, she quietly took the helm after his passing. She designed Kate Middleton's wedding dress, and her shows are more romantic, less noisy. There is little controversy, though much still to admire. McQueen now is not a person or an idea, it is a store, a Royal frock coat, a heavy perfume, a statement bag. It is multiple ways to say I'm edgy, but as it is worn and carried by everyone from salesgirls to princesses, it has none of that rawness and danger that radiated around its founder. It is for everyone now – we can all sit with him.

And why not? It's just that, well … it feels slightly less exciting.

13

Flat White

Can you remember the precise moment when coffee became a thing? It was possibly TV. All those American sitcoms had young, groovy types rushing round New York with trainers in their handbags, clutching large paper cups. Much of *Friends* was set in a coffee house. Coffee was their centre of everything.

Those cups were the fashion accessory to a hip urban life; a US import at a time when we thought New York was cooler than London. The Seattle Coffee Company, Costa and Coffee Republic brought the trend over here; Anna Wintour started arriving at the shows with a Starbucks in hand. Gradually we all joined in, spending two or three quid a day to suck on great big milky cartons like babies' bottles, the warm, weakly flavoured confection washing down like mother's milk.

This is actually the UK's third attempt at a coffee boom: the first was the era of coffee houses in London between 1652 and 1750, which became the focus of intellectual debate around politics, law and the Enlightenment. Then, in the 1950s, there was a brief espresso-bar craze. Both came to an end, but it's hard to see this one going away any time soon.

Coffee is now an artisanal lifestyle choice. The nerd culture associated with beans, how they are sourced, roasted and blended, and then how those beans are ground and then steamed can be debated for hours. The flat white is a coffee that both Australia and New Zealand lay claim to inventing, its definition resting entirely on the proportion of coffee to milk. People are fanatical about its manufacture – when a Sydney coffee house took this to the extreme, serving a flat white in three glasses – one for the milk, one the coffee, one the water, there was global outrage. 'The end of days!' wrote thousands of Flat White apologists.

The Flat White is emblematic of many things we feel about food and drink. Coffee is a complex human right, ours to own and stylise, as integral to a good Western life as a cushion-plumped sofa. The rise of the independent coffee shop, and the shaming of Starbucks, has been a triumphant shift in consumer culture. No one wants the big brand any more, they want to support the little guy, the one with the authentic story about craft, passion and heritage. X-ers know all about this because we started it. With vodka.

Vodka was once our number one drink. Colourless, more or less flavourless, it fuelled our cocktail culture and was the most sophisticated way to get drunk (as discussed, we love to get drunk). Cosmopolitans, Sea Breezes, Moscow Mules, Skinny Bitches (vodka, lime and soda), Lychee Martinis, plain old vodka tonic, it was a bartender's dream. Somewhere along the way even bartending became a craft – bartenders became mixologists, just as people that work in coffee shops are now called baristas.

To begin with, Absolut dominated the market, but the distillers needed to find new ways to keep our interest. So began the boom in boutique vodka brands: Stolichnaya, Grey Goose, Ciroc, Snow Queen, Ketel One, 42 Below, all accompanied by stories of artisanal distillers in far-flung places like Kazakhstan and New Zealand. We didn't interrogate these stories too closely (too busy getting drunk), which was just as well, as the vodkas were ultimately coming from the same big beverage companies. But they looked great on the bar shelves. And our appetite for a craft story had been whetted.

What was happening in drink was also happening with food. The casual dining revolution started by Conran was catching on at home, extending to our ingredients and our home cooking. It was cool to cook at home, as Jamie, Nigella and everyone in between showed us. Cooking also turns out to be a healthy anti-dote to modern life, one that careers between office and online, commute and career.

'I don't think about any of that when I'm cooking dinner,' says Henry Dimbleby, founder of the healthy fast-food chain Leon. 'I like the flow of it. I've got terrible motor skills, can't draw, terrible handwriting, but with cooking I get that thing of flow. Cooking occupies just enough of your slow mind to switch the fast part off. It's very pleasurable in that way.'

It's also a very pleasurable way for us to express how in the know and up to speed we are. In the same way our music library and wardrobes are carefully crafted lifestyle indicators of our identity, so too are our kitchen bookshelves. Mine is a history of the last 20 years in food fashion, running from Alastair Little to Anna Jones and back again. All artfully arranged in a Pantone colour-coded format. (Overthought, I know.)

Tom Aikens's tale echoes how cooking made its way out of restaurants and into our homes. When Tom walked out of Pied à Terre, he went to work as a personal chef for a wealthy family, the Bamfords. They had made lots of money out of selling diggers and had bought a farm in Oxfordshire, which they were turning organic. Cooking for the family, he learned how to transfer his skills from Michelin kitchens to everyday suppers. Carole Bamford was also setting up a food brand named after her farm, Daylesford, a brand based on organic, home-grown ingredients treated simply.

'It was country-style, easy cooking: stews and casseroles, nice soups, stocks and pates,' Tom says. 'I worked on the farm and in the abattoir too, and saw how it all connected – which was a first for me because in that whole Nineties explosion of restaurants there wasn't a culture of locally sourced. No one gave a hoot. I got all my ingredients from Europe – there wasn't a link between what was being produced in the UK and the chef.'

When Tom moved back to London he knew what to do. He called his new restaurant Tom's Kitchen and bought everything direct from the farmer. 'We put the suppliers' names on the wall and started using them as the hero of the restaurant.' Farm to fork was born.

'It was the right time,' says Tom. 'People wanted understated, simple food.' The restaurant was packed – locals sat next to Hollywood types, passers-by dropped in with their dogs, even Wills and Harry tucked into shepherd's pie in the corner. It was a long way from the starched white tablecloths of the Nineties. 'I wanted it to feel like you were sitting in your own kitchen. It didn't matter if you wanted to have toast and a cup of tea or our seven-hour shoulder of lamb. You could just hang out.' Food was democratised – good food was for everybody, all the time, breakfast, lunch, dinner and everything in between.

Our new-found love of food was taking over everything. As clubbing culture came to an end (there are just under half the number of nightclubs in the UK as there were ten years ago), restaurants became the cool places to hang out. You could say Momo, a North African joint in the West End, started it – Madonna and Guy Ritchie used to eat there, and the bar underneath was always jumping. It was the beginning of the transformation of Soho from a breeding ground for bands, sex and sleaze (Alex James recalls Blur would hang out in pubs in Soho before dropping in on clubs and badgering them to play their tracks), to a gastronomic mecca.

Big money was also starting to wash through London as Gordon Brown's tax changes opened the doors to non-doms.

London became home to some of the world's wealthiest people courtesy of our new, lenient tax laws, and restaurants were the big winners. You could make far more money with tables and chairs and a class growth wine list than a bar with a sticky floor selling lagers to vertical drinkers. If you walk round Soho now you won't find many pubs and clubs; most have been replaced by tapas bars, hot dog joints and Asian soup kitchens.

'Soho is totally fuddy-duddy now,' sighs Alex. 'The kids have all gone east – eating dirty burgers probably.'

According to Thomasina Miers, it was the 2008 recession that helped fuel our current restaurant boom. 'It opened up property and landlords. It opened up creativity and shook the structure, which meant people could go out and do their own thing. Like our recession at the beginning of the Nineties, this one allowed young people to take the food culture and go and do it for themselves.'

Alex James has managed to surf the wave of both of the prevailing Generation X cultures. When Blur took a break in the early Noughties, he bought himself a farm in Oxfordshire and put down his guitar to make cheese. He began by launching a tikka masala cheddar with Asda, which horrified the foodies. Why wouldn't the man who brought us *Parklife* make food for a supermarket?

'Not everyone can afford 24-month Montgomery cheddar!' he says. 'It made me realise what a bastion of snobbery food is. People said you can't do this, but it tasted good, it was affordable and it was fun. Heinz copied it in the end.'

The cheeses he made on his farm – Blue Monday, Little Wallop, Goddess – began to win awards, and he became a food columnist for the *Sun*. 'I got loads of letters. It made me realise *everybody* loves food, whether it's KFC or grouse. Food is universal – everyone loves something delicious.' Not everyone is knocking up a three-tomato salad, though, and sometimes the food revolution, with all its attendant health and political issues, feels a very middle-class preserve.

'There's still bumper packs of Turkey Twizzlers going in the trolley. Wouldn't it be nice if we could all eat from the same menu like they do in France, bishops and postmen together? Here, food is still a class thing,' says Alex.

It is political too. Jamie Oliver has become our self-appointed minister for food, lobbying for sugar taxes and highlighting the strain obesity and dental health have put on our NHS. Henry Dimbleby was called on to advise the government on school dinners. Your stance on factory farming, organic, sourcing and sustainability is now all part of your food choice, just as Stella McCartney promotes meat-free Mondays, Gwyneth gave up factory-farm pork after a lecture from Leo DiCaprio or Ella Woodward credits her Lazarus-like cure to cutting out gluten. Having an intolerance these days is like having a Hill & Friends handbag. Just so hot.

Yes, food suits our lifestyle-obsessed culture very well. How different it was for our parents. 'My dad was brought up in the aftermath of the war,' says Alex. 'Bacon was rationed until he was in his twenties. We ran out of food and lost recipes and cooking skills. They weren't transferred from generation to generation like they were in France, Spain and Italy. It has taken us a generation to recover.

'Food was my first job. My grandad was a chef at a posh hotel in Bournemouth, The Royal Bath. He was mustard. My dad was a keen diver and he would go out in Poole Harbour and get lobsters for my grandad to cook in the hotel. He used to get huge ones, the ones that were too big to get into the lobster pots, gigantic, terrifying things. I never knew what I'd find when I opened the fridge – there could be a giant crab crawling around in the bottom.

'Then my grandad started a B&B, so I used to help him make

the breakfast. He'd lick his fingers, put them in the hot fat and turn the eggs over with his hands.'

But through a cycle of exclusivity, luxury, aspirational fine dining, coolification and lifestyle choices, it feels like we have finally come back round to where we started.

'Grow your own, that's what it's all about these days,' says Alex. 'There's something horrible about wanting to own a Ferrari. It's really flashy. But aspiring to own a pig – which probably costs as much as running a Ferrari, actually – nobody objects to that. It's funny how the pig has gone from being this totem of peasantry to something Elizabeth Hurley wants.'

Keeping pigs, chopping wood, smoking (food, not fags), craft beer, craft anything in fact, the return of vinyl, fixies, making a big fuss about your coffee. These are classically buttonholed as hipster activities, but although Generation X are probably too old to be classified as hipsters, they've definitely coopted plenty, not least the beards and the coffee. The Generation X hipster male is probably more likely to be 'Apple Dad', loping along the street in his Edwin jeans, Beats by Dr. Dre headphones, cross-body bag, with various pieces of Apple equipment tucked about his person. He will be on his way to some expensive coffee bar, for sure – the hipster might serve it to him, but the X-er is the one with the money in his pocket to buy it. If the lo-fi, craft-oriented hipster trends have taken off, its because us X-ers have bought into them too.

Much like the great coffee houses of the Enlightenment inspired new thinking in politics, arts and sciences, today's coffee culture has lent its name to the current boom in digital business: the flat white economy. And the flat white economy is a great place to look at how Generation X and Millennials have come together. We are going to have to learn to live and work cooperatively with each other for the next 40 or 50 years, as Millennials, you do not want to be forking out on pensions to keep us upright. You need to keep us engaged and working. You've got the innovation, the entitlement, the digital creds, we've got the business experience, the management skills, knowledge of the landscape. We are your customers, and as you have shown us with your coffee and your mismatched crockery and your jam-making and your homebrew, there is much to celebrate in a world that backs boutique, celebrates craftsmanship and a return to quality basics. You see no distinction between those values and our hyper-digitalised world – in fact you want them to coexist. Good by us.

And hipster culture has some interesting things to show us about masculinity – dudes covered in tats bending over hot grills flipping meat, chopping wood, dressing like a lumberjack, growing big, bushy beards. Apple Dad and the Mamil should take a look.

Henry Dimbleby, 46, now runs London Union with Jonathan Downey, 49. It is a proper crossover X-er/Millennial business that turns underused and derelict corners of the city into street-food markets, helping launch the careers of small, authentic food businesses. 'I'm quite excited about what we're doing,' says Dimbleby. 'Regenerating bits of the city that aren't being used helps rebuild communities.' Downey has a long track record in bars and festivals – if anyone knows how to create space where people can have a good time, it's him.

'At Hawker House down in east London, we've got 2,000 people a night coming down, socialising in a way that they can't find anywhere else,' says Dimbleby. In an increasingly automated age, you can't replace good old-fashioned hospitality and conviviality. 'What's more, it's properly cross-generational. You can go down to Model Market in Dalston and see 70-year-old couples there having a glass of wine – it's brilliant. I always say the best party is the one where at midnight, you've got your granny on the dancefloor with your six-year-old kid.'

14

Nothing Tastes as Good as Skinny Feels

Do you look good or bad for your age? Could you look better? Should you? How do you measure up against her further down the social media feed? Has he had work done? Are those extensions? Why is she always tanned?

If we were lucky, we may have been able to skate through our younger years without worrying too much about our looks – there certainly wasn't the scrutiny and there absolutely wasn't the pressure of every procedure going to fix every sort of problem. But age – it's a cruel thing. You catch sight of yourself accidentally in profile and spot the neck. That's you in your mate's picture and you look *old*. And fat. You scrutinise the changes in the mirror each morning and you suddenly realise that you can see your mother, and yep on a bad day, maybe your father too. Wrinkles and creases and bags and jowls and lines and bumps start to emerge all over the place, not just on your face but all over your body.

When I was in my mid twenties I decided to have some nude pictures of myself taken. (Actually, looking back on it, a rather pervy photographer 'friend' was doing a 'project' and asked me to pose. I said yes because I thought, this is me in my prime. I want a record. I drank a whole bottle of red wine and rolled around on the floor and he lit it very cleverly. Luckily it's all 'artfully' blurry.) What I do know is I would never submit to that now. I have gone from pride to shame in the intervening years.

And yet my body is so much richer now – it has born and nurtured three children, recorded bike crashes, bank holiday sunburns, sea scrapes and falls from rocks. Its contours etch out sleepless nights, delicious moments of self-indulgence, hungover eating binges, hours of effort in the gym. The backs of my hands are no longer smooth, but the rough skin marks the years spent working, typing, washing, lifting, handling, writing, doing. My hair is changing, my periods are changing, hormones are reorganising the distribution of my flesh. Why shouldn't I want to celebrate this more? Why don't I think this is beautiful?

Often it's because I'm looking at someone else and thinking, Wow, she looks good. Really, I could try a little harder. Look at that famous person who has just had a baby and is the same age as me, in her bikini looking hot. Must eat less, must exercise more, must get Botox. Right there is the fault line the beauty industry jumps on. Right there is your £75 worth of new moisturiser neurosis. While many of us grew up tossing up 'cleanse/tone/moisturise' with 'Can I leave my make-up on overnight?', nowadays we pay much closer attention.

And the beauty industry has a barrage of panaceas to help us. From serums to peptides, brighteners to BB creams, exfoliators to tone correctors, illuminators to hyaluronic skin tints, you can blow a fortune on trying to 'look a little better' – and we do, on average £40,000 on hair and over £100,000 on cosmetics over a single woman's lifespan (according to estimates from hairtrade.com).

But take it from someone who knows – the truth is few of these products have any kind of discernible effect. They might smell nice, they might feel nice, but creams make little difference, and they can promise all the nanotechnology and creepy science they like. Twelve years in an editor's chair meant I had the pick of every expensive unguent imaginable, and over that time I watched as a slow trickle of new product launches built up into a torrent, as the beauty industry learned to market more and more 'miracles' to an ever-hungry audience.

Every Estée Lauder Re-Nutriv chemical compound, every Clarins DHA-enhanced lotion, every niche Japanese beauty brand promise, passed across my basin top. I alighted on Crème de la Mer for many years (some cleverly spun myth about seaweed extract and Second World War burns), then switched to delicious-smelling oils from Vaishaly. Elemis's Pro-Collagen capsules had me convinced for a while, then I swore by Chanel's Sublimage.

But after such an expansive parade of products nurtured my skin for twelve years, one summer a friend gave me a pot of virgin coconut oil. You can use it for cooking, or spoon it in your coffee, she said, but then she leaned in and whispered that she used it on her skin too. Now this woman is a powerhouse – five children, three businesses, seventeen dogs, four houses and a lot of spare cash. But she uses coconut oil, £10 a jar. Admittedly, she liked it so much she bought the company, but still. I began to use it. It's not greasy, it smells delicious, it feels wonderfully pure and natural and – my skin looks exactly the same. Which leads me to believe that every skin product out there is built on utter bullshit.

There *is* one thing that works, though – Botox. I wouldn't have dreamed of Botox, until I discovered four out of five of my best girlfriends were doing it. Then I realised it was no longer a level playing field. Suddenly what seemed ludicrous a few years ago – injecting your face with a powerful poison to freeze it in its tracks – had become quite normal in certain circles. Reader, I tried it, and it works. It absolutely eliminates wrinkles. I can't say I have ventured any further into the invasive beauty world than this, but I'm quite willing to accept that an eyelift, a facial tuck, laser and lipo all work too. I'm just not sure how much I want to suffer for my looks. Ask me again in five years.

Of course there is a ridiculous contradiction in raw organic coconut oil on my face and botulin toxin in my brow, but that's the way we like it – both ways. That's why I have organic vegetables in my fridge and shelves of chemicals in my bathroom. We'll only wear 100 per cent cotton or silk underwear, but are fine with a spray tan. Most women I know like to preserve at least the illusion of a natural look because we think that looks earthy and in touch (however artificially it is constructed). Millennials, though – they love a full face. Millennial beauty vlogger heroines from Tanya Burr to Pixiwoo trowel on the make-up, with nothing regarded as more vulgar and shaming than a naked face.

Josh Wood tells the story of the time his friend Charlotte Tilbury popped in to the salon, and as a favour he asked her to make up his young assistant. He didn't understand why three days later his assistant resigned – apparently, her colleagues told him, the shame of having all her make-up stripped off in public had been too much to bear. 'Giving face today is what it's all about,' says Josh. 'Everything has to be perfect.' When your every move is documented on social media, you can't afford to get it wrong, and if you do, the judgement can be quick and damning.

I'm glad I am not a teenager now. How strong you would have to be to maintain your self-esteem amongst such digital company. As the editor of a woman's fashion mag I was often called upon to defend the use of airbrushed images, but what a fart in a thunderstorm that looks now next to social media – platforms that at once promote transparency, but at the same time kid us all.

'Everything through social media looks fabulous,' as hair-stylist John Vial says (clients range from Elle Macpherson to

Laura Bailey). 'All those filters means people are becoming more beautiful, the bar is getting higher, and resisting it is getting harder and harder.'

Supermodels used to be just that – superwomen who weren't really real, heroic creatures that were the product of hours in make-up and retouch. Cindy, Christy, Naomi, Linda, there's no way any of us ever entertained the idea we could approach them. But models now – well, they are just like you and me, except not. You can follow them on aeroplanes, backstage, at home with their cats, in a café having a coffee. Social media has normalised them, but of course they are still utterly unattainable in terms of beauty. Instagram gives you the illusion of sharing in a normal girl's every day but, as Annabel Rivkin puts it, 'they are not in any way inclusive. They are heavily curated, they are lies and they make everyone feel very anxious.'

What's more, the ideal of beauty has become increasingly difficult to achieve. From the comfy white flesh pillows of Renaissance women (because if you were plump, then you could afford to eat – thin was for paupers) to the time-rich, cash-rich, honey-toned limbs of models today, I know which one I've got more of a chance at.

'Gisele is a one in a trillion girl,' says Vial. 'Her look is utterly unachievable. Women of the Fifties and Sixties were curvy, much more realistic.' Worse, these modern icons are styled and photographed as if they just rolled out the front door and, Oh hi, there's a photographer. So snap me!

'We all want to appear effortless – but none of it is,' confides Vial. 'It's all thought through. Elle Macpherson looks incredible, amazing skin, glossy hair, how does anybody compete with that? But I can tell you that artfully "undone" look takes hours in the chair. First you have to have your hair blow-dried to make it glossy and sleek, then you use product and tools to make it look all mussed up. Takes work. Takes time. Takes money.'

Thanks, Elle. Thanks for shifting the goalposts as we get older. Fifty never used to look that fabulous, now it looks like thirty. There's going to be no letting go with Elle and friends running round. The rules are changing and there is no relief of an elastic waistband in sight.

'In her fifties, officially, Elle should have had her hair cut off,' says Vial. 'But our generation are not going to be told what to do, are not going to conform, on hair or otherwise.' Which is great in some ways, but corrosive in others.

'Women are competing really hard,' says Matt Roberts. 'Women in their forties in the media look fit, so that's the drive. They all talk about their working out and their wellness routines so the pressure's on everyone else to follow suit.' Great that it's possible for us to look 20 at 40 – but is it that great if it's only available to those with money and time to spend on themselves?

'It's not our attitude to ageing that's changed, it's our ability to do something about it,' says Vial. 'If you're in the know at certain levels, there's a surgeon for your eyes, a surgeon for jowls, for a semi lift.'

Age is fast disappearing as a marker of how you look – rather it's your commitment to polish, maintenance and glamour. Alpha women juggling work and home refuse to drop the health and fitness ball – there are endless tales of Michelle Obama types rising at 4 am to get an upper-arm workout in, or squeezing in a game of tennis before their 8 am board meetings. Karen Blackett, chairwoman of MediaCom, installed a gym in her garage so she could work out after she had put her son to bed. There's even a treadmill you can use as an office.

But what if we don't actually want to work so hard to look like that? How much of a prison have we made for ourselves?

There's pressure from both ends now – those bitches like Elle are not going to let us grow old, and we're damned if we're going to let the Millennials run off with the show. Just like fashion and music, beauty and ageing are not going to be an exception – we're going to keep up with Millennials all the way.

So Millennials, if we're still competing with you, where can you go? 'My experience of young people in the chair is they are truly insipid, with no point of view,' says Vial, and here I would excuse them by saying they are probably frankly terrified. 'They all want to look the same – long hair, a bit dolly dolly. Thirteen years ago I used to walk down the high street on a Sunday morning and see a broken heel, or a lipstick lying in the gutter. Now it's just clips of weave. They all want long hair.'

Where's their Human League side flick? Their Kate Moss elfin crop? Shirley Manson's pink do? Well, they dye their hair grey – the one thing they know would send X-ers screaming into the night (clever them). 'Actually, I think it's much harder for a younger woman to look modern than an older woman,' says Vial.

You poor young girls, I'm afraid we started this. It was under our watch that access to beauty became so democratic – the spray tan, the hair straighteners, the lip plumpers and the false nails all arrived together to make a bland benchmark you can now find on everyone from a Chelsea housewife to a Scouser teenager. She is the burka blonde – so called because underneath this glossy-lipped, bronzed, highlighted façade, very little personality is allowed to shine through.

You can picture her now, can't you, with her heel and her skinny jean, statement handbag and glossy hair. She crosses social divides, cities and towns – you'll find her from Salford to Salcombe, Birmingham to Belgravia. You'll even find her in the country, though her shoes will be a flat, knee-high boot and she'll be wearing a (fake) fur gilet. The burka blonde, while promoting greater access to the improving tools of beauty, has actually promoted conformity, narrowing our idea of what is interesting and acceptable. From Adele to Amanda Holden, everyone looks the same. Utterly ageless and cloned. For girls of colour there's Kim Kardashian and Amal Clooney – it's all too rare you'll find an afro.

So now it's up to us to get us all out of this mess. In our forties we've played with being radical – tattoos, dip dyes and upper-ear piercings have all been coopted by women having a youth crisis. (Guilty, I'm afraid – I endured two years of ear cartilage pain when I decided to celebrate my 40th birthday with a 'daring new piercing'. I couldn't sleep on my right-hand side for months – and for what? The excuse to buy a diamond hoop? That's what I told myself, but I'm afraid it was actually a lame attempt to appear more punk despite my advancing years. I eventually took it out for netball for one night and forgot to put it back in. It closed up two days later.)

Is there a way for us to be properly unconventional about ageing? After all, we have a lot more life ahead of us – the 100-year-old is soon going to be the norm, if not for us, then certainly for our kids. We simply can't afford to feel old yet. We've got decades ahead of us. Our relationships might end, and we might want to find new ones. Our jobs might end, and we might have to switch careers. Our quality of life cannot afford to take a dip yet, and for that we need to preserve our health and self-esteem.

'I still feel like I'm 22. I don't feel any different,' says Serena Rees, looking as grand and striking as ever. I wouldn't want to put on age on her – I absolutely couldn't. She still wears Westwood and looks a million dollars, but that's possibly because she is worth several million. 'I don't go clubbing any more, because I like feeling fresh and ready. I can't go out every night like I used to and work really hard, and I'm never going to not work either because I love it. But otherwise, I feel the same as I always have.'

Boomers never thought this way. For Donald Trump, 35 is 'check-out time'. 'My dad always said that no man looks at a woman past 30,' says Alice Temperley, 'even when my mum has aged so gracefully.' But it's not men's attention Generation X are competing for – it's women's. There are only a handful of graceful agers out there to inspire us as we hit the youth wall, from Charlotte Rampling to Patti Smith. Is it time to change the culture? Is ageing actually an opportunity for X-ers to become cool in a whole different kind of way?

'There is a backlash to all people looking the same,' continues Alice Temperley, 'like they've all been to the same surgeon. There is going to be a change. Our generation are becoming more alternative, holistic and relaxed. I was very freaked out about ageing, but now, as long as I can feel happy and secure and loved, it doesn't really bother me,' she says. 'Luckily my boyfriend loves my round bottom but at one point, it was just like, "Oh my God! I'm getting pictures taken – I've got wrinkles! What am I going to do about it?" Now I just let it go.'

Hmmm. What does 'Let it go' look like for Alice? 'More red lipstick. And boxing and yoga. And I try to walk everywhere I can and eat healthy. I don't do wheat and dairy and gluten. Or wine any more.'

No wine?

'No, just neat tequila or vodka.'

(This is also Liz Hurley's tip – you may want to add a bottle of Stolichnaya to your Ocado favourites.)

'I'm on this exclusion diet because I went to get all my bloods tested by one of Charlotte Tilbury's gurus. She said, "You need to cut out all of this, and then your body will feel better and your shape won't change as dramatically. You'll keep your body as it should. You have to do it for a month to feel the difference. I'm two or three weeks in."' At this point Alice helps herself to a biscuit I brought her. 'Nothing tastes as good as skinny feels' doesn't quite have the same ring in your forties as it did in your thirties.

But then, I think that whatever it is we are doing is working. Honestly I am much fitter now than I was in my twenties (when I did nothing – I certainly never rode a bike anywhere). I definitely eat better – you cannot avoid the nutritional advice these days. I know a lot more about what is good for me and I undertake a level of self-care I would not have dreamed of 20 years ago. I may be Tired All the Time and occasionally suffer appalling hangovers, but when I'm not teetering on the edge of sleep-deprived, anxiety-ridden collapse I feel strong and capable.

Fitness is what has done it. Size zero has made way for the athletic aesthetic – one that shows you run and punch and lift and work out. It's fashionable now to be toned. Gyms are cool places with hip music and trendy people. What you can wear to work out these days is also very incentivising. Which would you rather – a Prada car coat or a pair of Lucas Hugh running leggings? Or both? What says better things about you: a lululemon hoodie or an Armani sheath dress? Emily Maitlis jogging, Laura Bailey running, Victoria Beckham at Barry's Bootcamp, Reese Witherspoon at barrecorre, Gwyneth doing Pilates, everyone at yoga – any woman worth her tracksuit talks about her wellness routine these days. And the brilliant motivational campaigns like This Girl Can and Run Like a Girl taught the rest of us that the wobble and the sweat and the work and the skin flush was all beautiful and affirming, because sport makes you feel brilliant inside as well as out.

This is not a sensibility confined to women. 'Men don't want to get old any more,' says Matt Roberts. For them it's David Beckham, Brad Pitt, Johnny Depp or Tom Ford tearing up the rule book on what forty- and fiftysomething looks like. Or it's their psychotic boss who has given up booze, lost two stone and signed up to the Great North Run. 'Men know what shape they want. There's lots of guys who come into our gyms who want to look like Brad Pitt in *Fight Club*,' says Matt. 'But they want to stay healthy and lose weight.'

The X-er male hedonist has turned into the Mamil – the middle-aged man in lycra. The boom-and-bust, thrill-seeking raver has evolved into an exercise freak who flogs his two wheels to Paris and back, runs a triathlon, enters a Tough Mudder or an Ironman. The cycling explosion has offered men a double whammy – look good and feel fit, and you also get to geek out on all that extra kit and knowledge. Rapha is the brand that has nailed it with this community – marrying style, performance and experience in a recipe beautifully crafted for our generation of males.

'With guys, it's very much about going and doing,' says Roberts. 'The Etape stage of the Tour de France, or a 100-mile bike ride. It's about achieving huge performance targets. Then become very savvy in all the detail. They want to know about the tech, the fine details of training, the next event to take part in. They want measurements to be done on a regular basis to get more data back. Our gyms specialise in data, so for us that's real heaven. You want data? We can *throw* data at you.'

Fear – about illness and death and heart disease and cancer – is another great driver for the male fitness boom. 'I used to think going to the gym was for freaks,' says Ben Elliot. 'But lately I have become fixated by being healthy. I've seen two close friends in their forties and fifties drop down dead and I don't want that. We all want to live longer.'

Death is a spectre that is beginning to enter the Generation X universe. Plus there's the simple fact that as work, family and a social life converge, being fit and healthy makes it a lot easier to cope with all the demands. 'I'm boom or bust in the way I live my life,' says Elliot. 'I'm very zealous when I'm working and then I probably eat more ice cream, and drink more when I'm on holiday.'

All this adds up to a much more healthy male than our fathers ever were. Boomers drink more alcohol than us, have always exercised less, and certainly have not practised the healthy eating habits that have become the obsession of our times. Our men, or many of them, are model fit and slim, strong and healthy. Lucky us.

Now – do keep up.

15

Is It My Go on the iPad Now?

If you decided to start a family, this is a time when many things collide. Nappies, seas of rudely coloured plastic toys, insomnia, way more coffee than you would have believed possible, box sets (you're not going out any more), OFSTED registration forms, childcare.co.uk, Netflix bingeing, stroppy au pairs, fingerpaint, hummus, rice cakes, wet wipes, one-handed work calls conducted from the playground, vomit, diarrhoea, obsessive school angst and nits. Nightmare nits.

You also discover that you can't remember how to do long division too well, that the *Cutty Sark* is actually quite interesting, that Sunday afternoons are for homework projects, office FaceTime for bedtime, that supermarket home delivery proves there is a God, screens are the greatest cause of family discord, it costs a fortune to mend a cracked iPad, are we nearly there yet?, grandparents are great, grandparents are useless, there is no shame in bawling out sixteen verses of 'The Wheels on the Bus', Cornwall's actually a jolly good place for a holiday (as opposed to say, Istanbul), sex once a week is a treat. Then once a month. Then once in a while.

Your career, which you may or may not have spent years cultivating, is suddenly no longer the most important thing in your life. Your social life, once of huge importance, disappears, along with your huge network of friends, and your partner becomes your domestic co-worker as opposed to your heart-palpitating lover.

On the upside, there is an introduction to love like no other. Singularly the most important moment of my life was in the recovery room of UCH, after a 30-hour failed labour and a brutal emergency C-section, my hair standing on end, body filled with every drug known to mankind, clutching this squashed, battered piece of flesh as he latched on to me and took from me what he needed to survive. Nothing, nothing compares. As the days unfolded it felt like I had been living in quite a nice house all my life but I had never found this one door. Once I had opened it, I realised there was a whole other wing to the house that I had never known existed, filled with gardens and birdsong, sofas and sunshine.

Despite the medical and physical calamities, the unbelievably challenging sleep patterns (that thing X-ers say to each other about how you're really prepared for parenting because you're quite used to staying up all night? ha, ha, ha, not even close), the terror of making some kind of mistake (twelve hours bent over their cot to check their breathing the first time they get a cold), the bleeding nipples, the confusion, the learning curve – it was and is magical. We went on to have another one, and then another one (greedy mistake), because it was just too beautiful an experience to turn down. And the maternity leaves were undoubtedly a very nice break from working. (There was perhaps too much of this in consideration when we decided on the third.)

There are no words to describe the pressure the two-working-parent family has to deal with. For a group of people who did exactly what they wanted when they wanted and bugger the consequences, parenting is a physical, emotional and financial shock. Please, for our children's sake, let us look back on this moment in history and weep that we made it so hard for everyone.

No tax breaks on childcare; mums returning to work weeks after giving birth; ten-, eleven-hour days in the office so some lovely Slovenian girl teaches them their first word and witnesses their first step; the financial ruin as we struggle to maintain the punitive costs of living and working at the same time.

Through this, I have comforted myself that I will look back on the struggle and be glad that I kept my career going, as I will have something valuable and supportive to do during the years when my kids aren't at home any more. I hope I think it will have been worth it. What I do know is that at the end of my life I will look back and regret I didn't have more time with them when they were younger. And I certainly will not be wishing I had spent more time in the office.

First, a shout-out here to all those Boomer parents who pitch in. Grannies and Grandpas who do this – we love you. The breaks you give us are manna from heaven, and those who do nursery drop-offs and daycare when really you'd rather be in a nice chair with your feet up (or taking a houseboat trip across Kerala) will be sainted in heaven at the end of days. Thank you for picking up the slack, dealing with the chaos and the noise, bailing us out on countless occasions and reassuring us that we're doing a good job. You save us in more ways than you can imagine. I pledge to do all this and more for my children when the time comes.

But if, Millennials, we are frightening you with our tales of shock and awe around parenting, then be grateful that we have considerably broadened your options when it comes to having a family. Single parents, lesbian and gay co-parents, three-way parenting, adoption, step-parenting, inter-generational parenting – you name it, we've tried it, to the point where anything goes these days.

'We are on the crest of a wave,' says the mother and Midult founder Annabel Rivkin. 'Everyone has started to do it for themselves. This is solo motherhood as opposed to "single motherhood", a phrase that suggests there has been the slight tragedy of a divorce or trashiness of a one-night stand. But it's not a mistake – increasingly it's a solo voyage. I have five friends in my immediate circle who are pregnant or have just had a sperm-donor baby. And for them I'm a touch point as I've done it – they want to come and talk to me about it.'

So too have we relaxed the rules around relationships. Remaining trapped in an unhappy marriage is no longer so common, as divorce – and, crucially, civilised divorce – has become normalised. Many X-ers are victims of the havoc wrought by the family courts of the Seventies when husbands and wives were pitted against each other with the kids ripped apart in the middle. Or they grew up in households where the parents were in silent war with each other, grinding out each day in a conflict that poisoned the atmosphere around them.

Traumatised by their experiences, they would never inflict such pain on their own families, and have made wiser choices about their relationships and how they conduct them. You either wait till your kids are a bit older (the number of over-fifties who separated or divorced in the UK rose by 33 per cent in the ten years to 2013, according to Relate), or if you do it when they are young, it must be done in a civilised fashion. Like Chris and Gwyneth's conscious uncoupling – oh how we laughed, but actually, nice, no? And Helena Bonham Carter and Tim Burton with their adjoining houses that the kids can flit in between. Ulrika Jonsson is the poster girl for the 4x4 family (four kids, four different fathers), proving multiple partners for your kids is not only happily possible but also acceptable. Society will no longer judge your choices of how to do it – as long as you keep everything as happy and peaceful as is humanly possible. The conventional family no longer exists.

Likewise the extended family – that notion that it takes a

village to raise a child, that is a network of aunties and god-parents and elders – has had to morph now that grown-up children move away from their parental homes. Instead we spend years building collections of friends from school, university, workplaces and flatshares. Quite often these networks become family replacements. We are now more likely to holiday with our friends than our family in our middle age – or rent big houses and party barns to effect large gatherings of our disparate friend and family clans.

As parents we are much more open-minded about the future careers of our children. Fathers are no longer aghast that instead of a law career their son is becoming an actor or musician – because as teenagers we worshipped rock musicians. As babies we dress our kids in Pacha babygros and Run-D.M.C. T-shirts, conferring our own set of cool values on our offspring (not so very different from the Louis Vuitton Speedy on your shoulder, really). We venerate our kids and treat them as equals. We don't call them Sonny, a top-down authoritarian moniker, we call them Buddy or Bud because they are our friends. We take them on holiday with us, to festivals and to parties. They stay up with us at New Year, watch the same movies as us (Hello, Pixar!) and we discuss the news with them (honesty and openness at all times).

Childhood for everyone is a cause for nostalgia. It is a magical place and time, one that is unburdened by responsibility, surrounded by unconditional love. For many of us, though, childhood was complicated and painful. Those Seventies family law courts were devastating. In many ways Generation X venerates and protects its children more fiercely than ever. We adore and respect the sanctity of their moment (after all we have tried to hang on to our own childhoods for as long as possible), and as such we are the first generation to play with our kids on a flat hierarchy.

And we are also questioning the choices our education system offers. The education we had no longer seems right for our new, emotionally intelligent sensibilities, and certainly not for a world evolving as rapidly as ours is now. A wider choice of schools, championed by the Academies programme, has been welcomed by parents who want to encourage specialisation or the passions they see awakened and want to encourage in their kids. The factory-school system that grew out of the Industrial Revolution ignores the individual. Academy schools allow communities to design establishments and curriculums as they see fit. As workers we are at the coalface of industrial and digital change, but as parents we can only guess at the skills our children will need to address the challenges of the future. Suddenly qualities like perseverance, creativity, self-discipline, drive, entrepreneurialism, empathy and co-operation seem to be just as important as maths and science. In a world where robots will do all the heavy lifting – intellectual as well as physical – where will our children find their place? What do they need to learn to help them do that? Social and emotional learning, the desire – and ability – to explore and investigate, to speak publicly, to manage time, to see failure as a route to iterate, to be practical – all these need their place in our kids' education, whether that's through school or parenting. To learn to be, as well as to learn to know.

Importantly, they will need to locate their passion. As they get older we share with them our music, books and treasured cultural experiences, whether that's gigs or the ballet or an art exhibition (hands up: I took my firstborn to the Tate to see Gilbert & George when he was just four. I'm not sure it stayed with him). We take our daughters shopping in Topshop, we delight when we can start wearing each other's clothes. Some of our kids are beginning to become teenagers and many X-ers are now wrestling with what you say about sex, drinking and drugs.

Do you admit to your own behaviour? Or stick to the line that it's all going to screw you up?

The familiar fear and refrain for a newly first-time-pregnant woman is 'kids shouldn't change your life'. Not when as a generation we've put so much conscious care into curating our lives just how we wanted them. Surely you can just bundle a baby in a sling and carry on as you were. There's a beautiful picture of Alice Temperley in a hotel bed in Paris working on a laptop with a newborn Fox sleeping beside her. Victoria Beckham rarely appears without her family in tow – at fashion shows the entire clan plus little Harper are always sitting on the front row (NB: VB was never photographed pushing a pram. Harper was carried in her arms on top of Louboutins, chauffeur-driven limo waiting round the corner). My favourite moment was when baby Kimye refused to accept her front-row moment and had to be taken from the opening moments of a show mid-tantrum. Finally – and thankfully – some normal behaviour. Parents everywhere sighed with relief.

Meanwhile family-friendly festivals have sprung up out of an X-er desire to carry on partying with kids in tow – glamping becoming the more accessible version. Basically because you can drink wine beside the campfire and don't need to pay for a babysitter. Also, we love our kids, and we want them with us. Partly because we can't afford the staff (I remember one rich parent advising me quite seriously to take a weekend nanny, otherwise my marriage would be in mortal danger – as his was) and partly because when both of you have spent all week working you want to spend every spare second together.

The dread of a wedding invite dropping on the mat ('Sorry, while we love your children and want to spend as much time as possible with them in the coming years, we do hope you will understand we don't want them to be the focus of our wedding') could often mean a fourteen-day stretch of no quality time with your kids and a financially crippling outlay at the wedding as you struggle with gift, hotel, outfit and childcare. That's after you've spunked £500 plus on the stag in Estonia/hen in Ibiza/Champneys.

Partying with your children in tow can be hazardous, however. The desire and misguided idea of your ability to stay up all night still forms part of many an X-er parent's social agenda (albeit infrequently; let's face it, we can't physically hack it these days). There is an interesting trend in 40th birthday parties where parents who have been up all night are put in charge of the kids when they wake up at dawn. It's not pretty.

'We had such different lives from our parents, didn't we?' says Alex James. 'My dad was shipped off to Wales when he was a kid, evacuated. Can you imagine doing that now, knowing how much we care about our kids? They were literally put on a train with a card around their neck. I won't even let my kids have bicycles.'

Parenting inevitably came as something of a shock to Generation X. Used to having everything our own way, kids have a way of upsetting that matrix. Plus our easy liberal values are seriously put to the test.

'I floated through the Nineties, and then suddenly I became a sergeant major,' admits Alex. 'You know, "What are you doing? Put that down! Get over here!" That's the point where you grow up, I think. Parenting is a wonderful thing – it takes away all that self-absorption and it makes you selfless. Suddenly there's something you care about more than yourself.'

Alex, you could say, has fully embraced children, having had five of them, and then becoming something of a lifestyle icon by moving to Oxfordshire and moving in his parents and parents-in-law. 'A farm is a wonderful place to bring kids up.' He pauses. We're sitting in the hotel he escapes to in Soho (the only one that lets him smoke in the bedrooms). 'Well, they just want to play on their fucking iPads actually. I say, "Come on, we're going down the garden," and they say "No!" I have to hide a big jar of sweets right at the far end of the farm, so when I say, "Let's go for a walk" there's something to get them there. I love a walk. They're terrified of going for a walk.

'Still, I'm never happier now than when I'm cooking an enormous slab of meat on a bonfire in the garden with all the kids running around, all the grannies and grandads. That's the big extended-family dream, everyone just mucking about.'

There's also nothing like having kids for you to take your eye off the prize, whether that is career or cause or 'good art', all famous enemies of the pram in the hall. I've lost count of the number of highly motivated friends who, the moment kids have hit, have elected to make different decisions about how much time they give to work.

Or if they don't or can't make those decisions, despair about how much of our lives we have to give up for our jobs when we could be spending time with the kids. That's the refrain of the working parent – while the stay-at-home mum or dad mourns their lack of work and purpose and creativity in their lives. No one is completely happy because the truth is parenting has made us compromise, and compromise is not something we are used to. We fashioned our lives just how we wanted them, and now we rail against a structure which doesn't let us have it all (even though we thought we could).

'I've stopped worrying about me. You just want your kids to be alright, really,' says Alex. 'Having big dreams was something that happened in my youth. I remember staying up all night at Goldsmiths and talking about how shit money was and there should be something else instead of money. I remember my dad saying, "The status quo is the status quo and you've just got to get stuck in and get on with it." Of course it's important to look up and check where you're going. But I've got five kids and six cheeses and right now I'm just head down, arse up, pedalling hard.'

Instead, we obsess about the right way to raise our children. Whereas Boomers raised their kids in the 'all must have prizes' atmosphere of overpraise, X-ers have seen enough of Millennials and their famous 'entitlement' in the workplace to learn from those mistakes. Parenting culture has changed massively in the last ten years. Now we are told to praise effort not result, to encourage a growth mindset where our kids embrace and learn from failure ('Fail fast', as they say in Silicon Valley).

As the ex-education minister Nicky Morgan (X-er – 44, young son) said, 'People look at the X Factor winners or reality TV shows and they think you can have instant success, fame and money overnight. When I go in and talk to students about being a Member of Parliament, I tell them it took me 21 years from joining the Conservative Party as a 16-year-old to being elected as an MP. It's a long journey, but the reward is when you get there. The feeling of accomplishment is huge.' There is a growing realisation that it's not exam results that will lead to success, but teaching the virtues of 'resilience, persistence and grit' in young children.

Generation Z is also the first generation to be raised in the era of smartphones and iPads. My pre-school son is fluent in YouTube, and the diet of content it serves up to him is shaping his interests. For instance, he loves Spiderman, but he doesn't want to watch the original Spiderman cartoons on YouTube. He wants to watch all those – to my mind, spasmodic – home videos of adults dressed up as Spiderman leaping over cars on council estates. My nine-year-old is addicted to Vine – a video sharing platform where all content is limited to seven seconds. Research unsurprisingly reveals that our kids have a much shorter attention span to cope with the flow of content they consume over digital media. Why text a sentence when you can send an emoji or a gif?

Millennials, who are often painted as narcissistic brats who expect the boss to fetch them coffee, were largely raised by Baby

Boomers, who, according to many, are the most iconoclastic, self-absorbed and grandiose generation in history. Think Steve Jobs.

By contrast, Generation Z are the product of Generation X. We recognise the relationship of effort and reward. We know from our adherence to the hierarchy of cool that indeed there is a hierarchy – and it's up to us to raise individuals who can craft their own hierarchies and then choose where they want to place themselves on it. Our kids care about the environment intensely – they recycle, they raise money for school solar panels, they make posters to stick up round the neighbourhood entreating communities not to litter.

But are they also over-protected? There's a worrying trend amongst our generation of parents to obsess about safety – the legacy of the Madeleine McCann story means no children can now ever be left alone, for fear of a paedophile kidnapping. Kids under ten that walk to school on their own are frowned upon, and their parents sometimes even prosecuted. In the Seventies – our childhoods – kids were kicked out at the beginning of the day and told not to come home before dinnertime. Now any kid getting this kind of treatment would be equipped with a smartphone and told to text home every half hour so we know they haven't been abducted. Meanwhile, in cities, if they do have a smartphone, or even a smart bike, we worry about them being robbed at knife point (by other kids).

Then there's the air. It's polluting our kids' lungs with nitrogen dioxide if you live in cities – particularly London, where around schools and homes it's way over acceptable safety levels. Mummy bloggers obsess about BPA-free sippy cups, how to prep baby food safely, the threats of non-organic milk and the correct equipment for transporting your kids in cars (I don't ever recall wearing a seat belt as a kid). Food is a battleground for the values of your parenting, your choices identified as an indictment or badge of your parenting skills. Ice cube trays of mushed up organic vegetables have condemned legions of mothers to late-night sessions with a food mixer and punishing organic vegetable bills.

My ability to make my kids a novelty birthday cake (and I am no natural baker) became an absurd preoccupation that somehow helped assuage the guilt I feel for being so absent from my kids' daily life for time in the office. It's my youngest's birthday soon, and I notice Asda are doing a birthday cake where you peel off the icing to reveal a treasure trove of sweets inside. Honestly, my son would love this. He would love this a lot more than the carefully crafted six-hour baking session with a shark cake tin I'm thinking of embarking on. Why?

Generation Z have been dubbed the 'Homeland generation' because they have grown up in a post 9/11 world that doesn't understand itself, experiences horrific clashes of cultures and religion, and is terrified by the encroaching of tech on our lives and the speed at which the workplace is changing. The jobs many of us do now could not have been imagined when we first started out in the workforce – how can we prepare our kids for jobs in the future when we have no idea what that is even going to look like? An increasingly automated world will leave what for our kids? Will they even work at all?

'I feel anxious for my little boy,' says Alice Temperley of her six-year-old, Fox. 'I grew up in the countryside on a farm, with no nannies or anything like that, and had a very isolated, amazing childhood. Since then, I've kept myself locked up in my work and now it's a case of, "Okay, what's next? How are things looking for my little one? How are things going to change for him?" To keep people's innocence now is very hard. I had mine protected. My father's friend said to me the other night, "It's amazing, you're 40 but you're so innocent still." I've been lucky – I've always done what I liked and have this dreamy world of being and living my brand.

'But I'm also the first person in our family that's had a job where nanny help is essential. A life where the child gets picked up by a nanny, and the nanny looks after him after school. I feel terribly guilty, because he says to me, "It's all work, work, work, Mummy. It's all school and it's all work!" and that breaks my heart. Then I think of other people in my company who have longer hours and longer commutes so they drop their kids off earlier and get back later and don't have the constant childcare I have. It's extremely hard for working people and working mothers now. For my boy, he's fed up with work and he sees school as kind of work and just longs to not be at school and to hang out with me.'

Meantime children see their parents frantically trying to be with them and work at the same time – smartphone glued to their hands, eyes down. And so we pass on to our children the idea that these screens are the most important things in our lives – the things we are interested in that take our attention away from them. Put your phone down and count how many times your child looks up at you. Then imagine that every time he looked at you, you had been looking at your screen.

'It's worrying, the social world of web expectations for little ones and the ability to be able to read and learn and be interested in anything that's not a screen,' continues Alice. 'In the morning when Fox wakes up he's in the room. "Can I have your phone? Can I have your iPad?" "No, Fox. No, Fox." In the car, "Can I have your iPad?" "Yes, okay." It's like a drug. That is the younger generation's drug. Celebrity and now gadgets. What's next?'

Serena Rees, whose daughter is now a teenager, is also ridden with anxiety and exasperation at what she sees as the inability of this new generation to be prepared for the world.

'This generation are too mollycoddled. They're wrapped in a cocoon and aren't tough enough to go out there. Parents are paranoid and scared and won't let their kids go out in the street or take the bus. Kids need to have freedom. Instead they stay in and plug in to a screen. They haven't got confidence. Everything they see on the phone, laptops, TV, is not allowing them to get out there and be – so they don't have the confidence to get out there and be.'

When the latest Pokémon Go trend launched, everyone thought it was great because it got kids outside. But really? They were just wondering around with their heads in screens. On holiday in Cornwall the summer it launched, the sight of hundreds of children stumbling along clifftops and beaches with their heads buried in their iPhones is one of the saddest things I've seen. The sun was setting a beautiful crimson and none of them even noticed.

'My biggest predicament right now is what am I going to do with my boys,' says Anton Bilton. 'Do I bring them into this avaricious environment, where they're going to go through a schooling system that's going to teach them if you work really hard at school you're going to go to a great university, and if you go to that university and work really hard you might be lucky enough to become a great lawyer or a great banker. Then, if you work really hard there you might be lucky enough to save some money, and if you're really lucky you might be able to get yourself a small flat. Is that really what I'm raising them for?'

No one is more aware of our kids' predicament than the Generation X parent. Whereas our parents thought that all we needed to do was work hard, get good grades, go to a good university and everything else would fall in to place and progress would carry us further down the river, X-ers can see that Millennials are going to be the first generation who will not have better standards of living than their parents. Things are going to get worse for them, not better.

'I think, what I've got to imbue in them is the notion of happiness without the quest for more,' says Anton.

We are beginning to do something about it. Some of us, where we can. Women in leadership positions are able to make their own rules. Take Alison Loehnis, CEO of Net-a-Porter, who leaves the office at 5 pm every day. She clocks back on later from home, but this gives her time with her kids every evening. There are many who would say the dawn of the 24/7, always-on work culture took away our freedom. But I think for parents it has helped deliver it. Consider Karen Blackett, the chairwoman of MediaCom, one of the world's biggest media agencies, who at 45 is the single mum of five-year-old Isaac.

'I had my son when I was chief operations officer for EMEA, so I was doing lots of flying around Europe. Halfway into the pregnancy I realised I didn't want to be with Isaac's dad. Five months after Isaac was born we split, which was when I came back to work. Then about year later I was promoted to CEO. My initial thought was this is brilliant, then – how am I going to manage this? I'm doing it on my own, it's a big gig, there's five offices, 1,200 people, 200 clients, how can I possibly do this?'

Senior enough to set out her stall, Blackett went back to the business and accepted the job on the terms that worked for her.

'I'm just as productive and committed as I've always been, but my hours are going to be different. I was able to do that because I had equity in the agency with my reputation, I was senior enough and I had some brilliant working mums who had gone before me, showing how to be a committed working mum – at home and at work.'

The few women of our generation who are in leadership positions are now beginning to change the playing field in terms of what's expected. And hooray for that. But there is still a long way to go, especially for women further down the ranks.

'Not all women have a person near them to role model and

talk to,' says Blackett. 'And you can see the lights go out in some, especially when it comes to kid number two. They ask themselves, how the hell am I going to do this? Because it's hard, bloody hard, and anybody who says they've got it down is lying. And it changes all the time.'

As CEO, Blackett began to address the problem. 'I banned the phrase 'work–life balance' because it's negative. It means there is a constant struggle, a winner and loser. Instead, it should be about how you blend what's important into your work – because work is life and life is work. I launched a programme called Project Blend, developed by a maternity coach. There is an app that tracks the six most important elements of your life. You define what those elements are – because my blend is different to your blend. This allows you to have a conversation with your manager about your blend, and how you need to be flexible to manage it.

'My six things were a happy child, effective child support, fulfilment at work, progression at work, exercise and fitness, and my time. Then you have to put a KPI next to each of the six things. For my fitness, I just don't have time during the day, so I turned my garage into a gym so I could hop on the treadmill when I had a moment. Also I prioritised 'my time' – getting time to be Karen the woman, not Karen the chief exec, or the chairwoman, or the mum – just Karen. I love sport – so getting time to do or enjoy sport is my time. If I can go off to a yoga retreat for a weekend, that's like going to a spa for a month, because I get that much more back. You have to know what your criteria are and then track their progression.'

Frighteningly organised, but then Blackett didn't get to be CEO by muddling through. And she's not stopping there: 'I think we can do more: part of the issue is the cost of childcare. So once you've had your child you get a baby bonus of one week's salary. That will help you purchase some of the stuff you need. Then when you come back for the first year you get a 10 per cent pay rise to help cover the immediate costs. You need that elevated cost because you are now working to pay nursery fees or a nanny. We've introduced this for men as well as women.

'Mental preparation is also really important – so we have maternity and paternity consulting. When men become first-time fathers, this hunter thing takes over – I need to get promoted and earn more! So coaching now happens during pregnancy, and when they come back we have absolutely seen less damage to the pipeline as a result. It's also been good for managers who don't have children managing people who have just had their child. And from people who are caring for elderly relatives too. It is allowing people to talk, to be more flexible. To have the conversation.'

Also, we have to remember that what success and happiness look like is different for different people. Not everyone wants to be CEO. 'I'm all for Sheryl and leaning in, but sometimes you are exhausted because you are doing too much leaning,' says Blackett. 'For me, feminism is being allowed to have the choice. What hasn't quite worked is everybody else's attitude around it. That's what has not changed yet.'

We're on it, Millennials. We want to hand you a better experience than ours.

16

Amy Winehouse, RIP

In the way Diana's death should have changed things but didn't, there were two events at the end of the Noughties that finally gave us collective pause for thought. By now 'celebrities' had become little more than social totems we had manufactured and pursued, bred and hunted.

The first of these events was Britney Spears's meltdown, the second the death of Amy Winehouse. 'These two things changed celebrity reporting forever,' says Jamie East. 'They made everyone take a long, hard look.'

Britney had gone from being a pre-pubescent schoolgirl Lolita whom everyone conspired in sexualising, to a shaven-headed, unhinged nutter. Two unseemly quick marriages, a stint in rehab, a psychiatric charge and a custody battle culminated in her losing it with a paparazzo and attacking his car with an umbrella. The pictures of her meltdown went viral, the storyline of her, her young children, husbands and family was laid bare. I remember watching the pictures unfolding as they came through the news wires – it was a horror show.

'After Britney's meltdown,' says East, 'I said Holy Moly would never again use, publish or pay for any pictures that showed anyone in any kind of distress. We were the first site to go, "I'm not being part of this."'

Eventually Britney's father intervened and Britney today is 'back on track'. But it was to be no such happy ending for Amy.

'We were being offered pictures of Amy being woken up,' East continues. 'The paparazzi were ringing her doorbell at four in the morning, smashing glass all over the front door so that she would come and answer the door dishevelled, then run outside and cut her feet on the glass. Then the headlines would be: "Drug-addled Amy Winehouse seen wandering the streets at 4 am with cut feet".'

As these two events turned public taste, Twitter was born, providing every person in the land with a forum to be as opinionated, funny, rude and insulting as they liked, directly to whoever they liked – celebrities and civilians alike. Twitter, says East, 'killed off celebrity websites overnight. Perez Hilton, Holy Moly, Popbitch, Dlisted, the lot. Because no sooner could you run a story about some celebrity somewhere, than the same celebrity could pop up on their own Twitter feed, post a picture of themselves on a beach and say, "Yeah, thanks mate, I'm fine actually."'

Celebrities now had their own direct line to the public, and the mystique around their lifestyle was chipped away at again. Gossip could now happen person to person over the digital garden fence, removing much of the power from the celebrity news feeds. Now everyone could run their own news feed, form their own opinions, share their own props and insults.

Facebook, and later YouTube, Twitter, Vine, Instagram, WhatsApp, Weibo and Snapchat have conjured a world that empowers each and every user to have their own channel, their own shot at fame. These days, with only an internet connection and a smartphone, you can put your life, your thoughts and yourself up to scrutiny, build your own audience and fan base, become your own publisher, and have your own advertising and branding stream. It doesn't even have to be any good: sometimes it seems all you have to do is empty the contents of your shopping bag, share your self-harm scars or demonstrate your way with a mineral foundation.

This alone can net you millions of followers, because all we now crave is a connection – a portal to a world where there is someone like you who you can identify with in some small way. We all now have that portal in the palm of our hands, 24 hours a day, seven days a week, wherever we are in the world. For the Millennials who have grown up with this lifeline, it has become indispensable, a breathing tube to a world they exist in with greater meaning and significance than perhaps the real world. Take away their internet connection or their battery life and they genuinely begin to panic. Unlike us, they do not know a world without it. This is their community, watching in bedrooms and at bus stops, watching each other broadcasting from bedrooms and bus stops. This is their 'cool', their 'rave in a field'; down a series of interconnected wires and via millions of handheld screens. A confessional world of broadcasting boys and girls next door.

The YouTube generation is crowned and presided over by imperial global celebrities like the Kardashians, a family whose willingness to share their live births, divorces, weight gain, periods, miscarriages, catfights and sex changes has won them mass globalisation and the ultimate commoditisation of the human condition. It started as a reality TV series, but has masterfully utilised social streams to maximise its power.

The success of *Keeping Up with the Kardashians* (and there are a myriad of successes in this family now, from fashion to pop to TV), and the shortcuts offered by talent shows like *The X Factor*, promise instant riches and fame in this new digitally fuelled landscape. Justin Bieber was discovered on YouTube in 2008, when his video was spotted by the American talent manager Scooter Braun. South Korean star Psy, with his viral 'Gangnam Style' video, was an overnight success thanks to

YouTube, subsequently receiving thousands of endorsement deals, from noodles to alcohol to fridges.

Such democracy of fame has now spawned some quite bizarre trends, leading to unlikely celebrities. For example, in South Korea a craze for 'gastronomic voyeurism' has emerged, with some 3,500 people running live-eating blogs. It is reported that South Korean Park Seo-yeon (known as The Diva) earns £5,600 a month from advertising and donations for live-streaming herself eating huge and elaborate meals in her Seoul flat, with thousands of fans logging in daily.

Platforms may come and go (Friends Reunited, MySpace – names that feel like ghosts from a recent past – have been notable casualties), and some are going to be better at financing their free model than others. But even if Twitter or WhatsApp fail to monetise themselves, the concept will never go away. The model is there now – it has proved there is an appetite for 100 million people to stick random thoughts up in real time. Facebook is currently cleaning up the advertising dollar, but the signs are usage is slowing as younger users migrate to new platforms like Snapchat, where live video holds greater currency.

'People our age think Snapchat's a fad – it's not,' says East. 'Kids are platform agnostic, they'll WhatsApp, Facebook, group text message, they see no distinction.'

Andy Warhol was right – everybody now does get their fifteen minutes. No longer do you need to play gigs in spit-and-sawdust pubs around the country to gain an audience, do stand-up after closing time to a room full of beery punters, put on variety shows from Hull to Hove out of the back of a van on a diet of Ginsters and crisps. The flip side to all of this, to my jaded X-er eye, is a decline in quality. Art schools cost £9,000 a year these days, so why would you bother with that when you can clock up your 10,000 hours in your bedroom? You don't have to go anywhere to win approval, fame or notoriety any more, but I'm not sure it actually produces a better performer.

Some talents have twisted the new platforms expertly to suit their acts; a comedian like Marlon Webb uses the seven-second Vine platform almost like haiku to perform his 'watermelon' gags, while Vine also works perfectly for the 'fails' genre (arguably better than TV's *You've Been Framed*).

So who can Gen X admire in this quagmire of bedroom celebrities? And does it even matter? I know very few who feel like the YouTube stars talk to them. I know some who have tried to become one, but somehow the low production values and seemingly unedited flow that the medium promotes don't chime with a generation brought up on MTV videos, glossy magazines and the carefully constructed notion of cool. We still crave our celebrity fixes, though – hand us the *Daily Mail*'s sidebar of shame, and it's like crack cocaine to Whitney Houston (and we know how that ended).

Here we learn about Victoria Beckham's latest airport exit, Little Mix's Jade's (Who? Care!) dramatic new hairdo and Nancy dell'Olio's unfortunate stumble from a taxi. It's gripping stuff. Drip fed a diet of celebrity incidents second by second, these are the new Holy Moly and Dlisted replacements: columns and columns of pictures and non-stories ranked on an algorithm that measures square inch of flesh versus number of global clicks. The more you click, the longer the story sustains. Few are immune. Douglas Coupland claims he starts his news consumption with the *Mail* every day, because 'if the front-page story is a wardrobe malfunction, everything's fine with the world.' Even staunch third-wave feminists admit their addiction – although they claim they confine their searches to 'right on' celebrities like Lena Dunham and Amy Poehler.

How can the lavishly expensive, 20-page Annie Leibovitz photoshoots compete with this highly distracting, low-quality, mass-audience content? I remember when Tom Cruise married Katie Holmes and they had their daughter Siri, they chose to control their image to the world with a high-production photo-shoot in *Vanity Fair*. It was luscious stuff – Katie in taffeta ball-gowns posing on a forested mountain side with a grinning Cruise at her side, the cuteness that was Siri smiling beatifically on her lap. Carefully controlled pictures, carefully controlled words. The cost of the shoot, which doubtless took days, then weeks in post-production and design, just could not be justified now, as all the pictures would be scanned and posted online within seconds of hitting the news stands. And no one would have believed them anyway.

Vanity Fair, *GQ*, *Elle* and all their glossy brothers and sisters who adhere to a line of celebrity glamour from the good old days have had to look elsewhere for revenue and audience – namely online, where digital advertising budgets cannot fund expensive photoshoots, or stories where writers spend months following their subjects around to gain a detailed biographical portrait. No – online it's a quick snap and a clickable headline; three seconds of audience attention is all you need to win an audience to sell to the brand that's advertising next to you.

There are notable exceptions – the *New Yorker*'s year-long investigation into Scientology was one of the magazine's most successful digitally, the interest in it eventually spawning a film. (Ironically, Scientology has been made most famous by its asso-ciation with Tom Cruise.) Journalists like to use this example from the *New Yorker* when they pin their hopes on a future of quality digital content and an audience able to consume some-thing that is long in its form.

Likewise Tom Hodgkinson of *The Idler* says their most widely shared stories are often their 1,500-word essays. 'I'd actually interviewed Jeremy Paxman for an event and we had filmed it. It was a funny interview and we had cut it down to 15 seconds or whatever "snackable" size Facebook told us we should, and it didn't do anything. But then we had a seriously long essay by someone no one had heard of called "Philosophy is the cure for workaholism" and it went bonkers.'

Perhaps these examples are the start of a backlash – after all, we will all sit through ten hours of long-form drama on Netflix now. But so far they seem to be notable exceptions, rather than the rule.

Do you grow out of celebrity culture? As the mailonline's sidebar of shame demonstrates, we are as addicted as ever. I am still fascinated by those women I grew up with – Moss, Beckham, Aniston, Angelina. Like me, they are at the same point in their lives, juggling career, family, children, age, fashion, mid-life. I do want to know what they're wearing (though slightly less than I used to), and I'm always morbidly delighted to hear when the ones I'm jealous of trip up. Mostly, though, I still want them to inspire me. It feels like I know such detail about their lives now, it would be impossible for me not to still harbour some interest.

When *Grazia* magazine launched in the UK in 2005 as a weekly off-stand fashion title, it was something of a publishing sensation – but the reality was it was selling itself on a very small number of celebrity storylines, and it was those celebrities driving the sales. Victoria Beckham, Angelina Jolie, Jennifer Aniston and Kate Moss were catnip to us, (with a side-serving of the fifty best skinny-jean styles), it didn't even matter if the stories were true. Almost every week it was Aniston – was she or wasn't she getting married?, was she struggling to have children?, was she still bitter at Brad for dumping her for Angelina?

Over in the States she was having a similar effect on sales for magazines like *People* and *US Weekly*, which doggedly pursued her every move for some new plot twist, imagined or otherwise. You can blame the magazines, but the weekly sales figures told the truth – we were all complicit. Editorial sources at *Grazia* claim the best weekly sales were always with Aniston on the cover. Aniston finally hit back last year, posting a response to the stories of her phantom pregnancies on the digital news website *The Huffington Post*.

'For the record, I am *not* pregnant. What I am is *fed up*. I'm fed up with the sport-like scrutiny and body shaming that occurs daily under the guise of "journalism", the "First Amendment" and "celebrity news".'

Good for her, but I think she understands that Jennifer Aniston the person is a long way from the narrative we have constructed for her, and almost doesn't matter any more. And, you might say, with her mineral water and shampoo deals she has done quite well out of it.

Beckham, who never seemed quite one of us, never entirely comfortable in her own skin (bit embarrassed by her Spice Girl days, tried fashion on for size and bought her way in, seems rather desperate and clingy with her husband), conversely embraces the fame. She has relentlessly traded up her stock with media coverage, whether it was selling her wedding pictures to a gossip rag or promoting her fashion line on the cover of *Vogue*. When scrutiny in the UK was not going the way the Beckhams wanted it they moved to America – where they introduced themselves with a raunchy shoot in the high-fashion *W* magazine. They have never complained about the coverage or the intrusion; for them it is their life and career, and they have been shameless in allowing their children to become part of it too – whether it's Harper on David's knee front row at Victoria's shows, or casting Romeo in the Burberry advertising campaigns.

But Victoria (the Victoria I know from her public profile and the rumours that swirl around her, as opposed to Victoria the actual person) also achieves much that I now admire – happy kids and a roaring work ethic, remarkably well-maintained looks, grown-up fashion, plus she has achieved the ultimate lifestyle fantasy of hiring my favourite interior designer to do up her London home. (Jealous! Fascinated!) I did meet her once or twice on the fashion circuit where she would earnestly explain every detail of thought and production that went into her collections, desperate for approval and credibility. And I once sat through a three-course lunch with her at which she only managed to eat a tomato (gripping item of gossip, now as it was then).

Angelina is a super siren that you simply would not believe if someone made her up. Wearing her lover's blood in a vial round her neck, strutting the red carpet in designer gowns, adopting a rainbow collection of children from around the world, reinventing herself as a human rights campaigner and improbably turning up at the United Nations to petition for the end of violence against women in war. Who couldn't help but feel *schadenfreude* when her global nomadic lifestyle with Brad finally hit the buffers? When tales of their kids' lawless lifestyle began to leak, their endless roster of nannies, their up-all-nights, their insurrection that resulted in accusations of violence, the lurid detail of Brad's supposed 'drug and alcohol' abuse, and Angelina's flights to sanity in five-star hotels. Thank you, we all breathed. It seemed an utterly unrealistic approach to love, work, parenting and marriage – and turns out it was. We all returned to the 9–5 and frozen pizza for tea with a great sense of relief. And that, there, is a genius depiction of the role of celebrity – how it serves to inspire and comfort, intentionally and unintentionally.

As for the others, well, third-wave feminism has given the celebrity world something to think about, and delivered back some substance. How we love kooky Lorde and her Facebook page, Ri Ri is never going to fail to amuse with her quite refined and brilliant fashion styling (care less about the music, I'm afraid), Taylor Swift has her supportive squad of 'besties'. We even like the fact Rupert Murdoch, at 84, embarked on his fourth marriage – to a supermodel. The conflation of digital voices means there are always a myriad of views now on the significance of all of these events – haters and fans, fans and haters.

The ones I admire still need to be cool, I'm afraid, or have some admirable qualities about them. Cool is still in the hands of a few arbiters, ones that can court high and low culture together and sprinkle a new look over the top (see the work of Generation X-ers Katie Grand in *Love* magazine, or Charlotte Stockdale and Katie Lyall in *Garage*). Or it's celebrities taking on something current and demonstrating it fluently in thought and action (Lorde on feminism) but not tragically and out of context (Benedict Cumberbatch on refugees, when he embarrassingly chose to close his performance on stage as Hamlet with a mistimed political rant).

It's not caring what people think and going your own way (never complain, never explain). It's plugging away at something and making sacrifices and in the end contributing with something valid and admirable (Beckham). It's entertaining me with incontestable talent (we forgive Kate Winslet and her marital adventures – her latest husband is a man who changed his name to Rocknroll – because her acting is just so damn good). It's being literate with the visual language of modern culture (Kimye, you know it – exposing her bottom in *Paper* magazine, a magazine no one had heard of). Let's face it, there isn't anything a celebrity can do these days that isn't going to provoke a whole load of intelligent, derogatory, infantile, insulting and witty commentary, so perpetuating an image of cool is almost impossible. Anything you build will be instantly deconstructed. Perhaps you only win it when you die – see Bowie, Prince, Rickman, Winehouse.

But these are celebrities with canons of meaningful work behind them, even, in her few short years, Amy Winehouse. Will

YouTubers Zoella, Alfie Deyes and Ella Woodward leave the same legacy? The pernicious influence of this explosion in celebrity culture, this great groundswell of access-all-areas fame, is a vacuum of greatness. Where is the greatness now? Swamped as we are by mediocrity, it is hard to find examples of the inspirational quality we had in the past – Nelson Mandela, Princess Diana, Martin Luther King, Mohammad Ali.

'We don't have greatness in our generation in the way that previous generations did,' agrees June Sarpong. 'Whether you liked Margaret Thatcher or not, she was a great woman. Everything about her life was set from a place of excellence. There were no half measures, she gave it her all. But there aren't many great characters in our generation. We idolise a lot of people who are brilliant, but they're not great.'

Greatness is conferred by changing the course of history, of society, of culture for the better. 'I love Usain Bolt, but he's not Mohammad Ali,' says Sarpong. 'You have to have done something to win greatness. You have to have purpose, something a "bit more", and I don't think our lot do yet. But we're not finished yet, we're coming.'

Perhaps the zeal of Jamie Oliver may turn out to produce something great. Perhaps he will resolve our obesity issues and our twisted approach to food. David Beckham's footballing academy might morph into a great vehicle for social mobility. Angelina Jolie might change something in conflict zones. The Google founders Sergey Brin and Larry Page may yet do something with their billions, whether that's flying their signal to the Serengeti via hot air balloons or solving the problem of petrol and diesel consumption.

Perhaps the greatness is yet to come.

17

Going Green, Finally

If there is one thing Greenpeace, Friends of the Earth and later the Soil Association and agitators like George Monbiot have demonstrated it is that we have not been treating our fragile planet properly. We have not been paying it forward. Political progress has been slow, but as a generation we have done way more than any other in terms of individual responsibility to alter our habits and respect the environment around us. From litter to plastic bags, recycling to organic, deodorants to Fairtrade, buying seasonal to being conscious of air miles, we have adopted and championed every one of these initiatives. And while our Millennial colleagues might be right behind us in terms of agreement, ultimately the influence rests with us as we are more powerful economically and socially.

'Millennials will tend to make a lot of noise about ethical shopping and collaborative consumption without actually putting their money where their mouth is,' says Annabel Rivkin of The Midult. 'Boomers aren't interested, they are in it for themselves. But the Midults are the ones that actually buy Fairtrade. These are people thinking truly cross-generationally because they have old parents, friends starting to get ill, school-age kids and they want karma on their side. That means that morality comes into their consumer decision-making: we buy the Fairtrade bananas, we don't buy T-shirts made by children the same age as ours.'

It might be self-interest induced by mid-life anxiety, but it also might be part of the fact that as a generation we have always wanted to be passionate, admirable and influential with our voices. And of course, we wanted to be cool – and because we were young and we cared, adopting green credentials became the cool thing to do, not least because as schoolchildren we all wanted to give money to the *Rainbow Warrior* and save the whale.

From a consumer point of view, the Green Movement suits us perfectly, and we have turned it into something of a lifestyle. I feel good when I buy Ecover over Persil, when the Abel & Cole box lands outside my front door, when my recycling bin over-flows faster than my actual bin (I know, simple pleasures). It marks me out as responsible, modern and knowing. Parsimonious Boomers used to shout at us for leaving the lights on (the expense!) – now we turn them off because we know it's cooler to be energy-saver than energy-waster. I can dress up the economic need for a staycation as a lifestyle choice – so much more hip to be taking the train to Northumberland than a plane to Ibiza! Right on supper-party conversations centre around underground heat pumps and going off grid, while the ultimate badge of honour is to serve up your own home-grown veg. A window box of herbs is amongst today's most aspirational urban home accessories.

'Sustainable' literally became the new black when the accessories designer Anya Hindmarch launched a new tote in 2007 emblazoned with the slogan 'I am not a plastic bag'. Made out of unbleached cotton and retailing for only £5, she turned environmentalism into a fashion statement. The bag was produced in partnership with We Are What We Do, a non-profit campaign group that has set out to change the world in small steps. It was a consumer sensation: with only 20,000 produced it became the must-have accessory of the moment, with imitator versions springing up on Ebay and the genuine article changing hands for hundreds of pounds. It even went on to be chosen as the *Vanity Fair* Oscar-night goodie bag. Does it matter that we lusted after this bag because it had achieved fashion holy grail rather than the fact that it was not quite what it seemed (the bags were actually manufactured and imported from China, which somewhat dented their credentials)? Of course not. Making green cool has worked; behavioural change has been far more effective than political diktats.

Lifestyle movements have been far more successful for us as a generation than any kind of civic change. Where is the fun in that? The actual implementation and administration of our ideals has held much less fascination for us. Under the influence of Steve Hilton and led by David Cameron and George Osbourne (all Generation X), the Tories made one of the main planks of their 2010 election campaign their green credentials – even changing their party logo to an oak tree and sending Cameron sledging in the Arctic. It helped rebrand them and got them into a coalition government.

But once in power, many of their pledges were dropped. Onshore wind and solar subsidies, watering down incentives to buy a greener car, the zero carbon home target: these were the environmental policies that helped them look attractive to Generation X voters, but all fell by the wayside. Did we complain? Barely. Either because we thought they were boring, or we sided with the Boomers and thought them an unwelcome distraction from the spending cuts the Tories insisted we needed following the 2008 economic crash.

Boomers have a different view of the environment. It can probably be summed up in the views of the iconic 60-year-old American chef Thomas Keller, who said he did not see it as his place to set any kind of example: 'With the relatively small number of people I feed, is it really my responsibility to worry about carbon footprint?' he asked the *New York Times* back in 2012. 'The world's governments should be worrying about carbon footprint.' As one of our most influential chefs, he demonstrated his views to be totally out of step with the legions of cohorts coming up underneath him, with their microbreweries, local cheeses and regional sourcing.

'Wahaca is about to achieve carbon-neutral status – we are the first fast-food chain to do that,' says Tomasina Miers, the fortysomething owner of the Mexican chain of restaurants, Wahaca. 'We have installed special designs so the heat from the fridges and freezers goes to heat the hot water in the taps. That way we don't have to have water boilers. Everything we use – from the detergents that clean the tables, to the recycling we do with our food waste to compost, even the paint our graffiti artists use decorating the walls – has to be non-polluting. All our materials are reclaimed or recycled. For me it was a massive driver: if we were going to open this really fun restaurant, we had to be environmentally responsible.

'But how do you run a Mexican food chain without importing chillis from across the world? In my darkest hours I sat there thinking, where is the planet going to be in 20 years? When's oil going to reach its peak? It was not a good environmental place to start from, setting up a restaurant where all the ingredients come from the other side of the planet. So we make sure all our meat is British, all our fish MSC certified, that we use local producers wherever we can.

'I'm a social activist,' she says, 'but as someone who cares deeply about life, environment and the planet, am I going to be an MP? Of course not. Your life would be completely intruded on. Whereas if you just get on and make a noise yourself, you can get stuff done. A few years ago I got a band of chefs together and we reared eight pigs on Stepney City Farm on permissible food waste and held a feast for 5,000 people in Trafalgar Square.

Loads of restaurants took part, because it was a necessary response to the ludicrous European law that got passed after the foot and mouth outbreak. The law bans feeding livestock on food waste, resulting in an increased need for crops, which means we are cutting down forests at a horrendous rate, affecting all our weather cycles.

'We're doing it at my kids' primary school too. The mums have all got together to build a garden on some common land nearby, because all the research shows British kids lag behind in general welfare; many inner-city kids never see parks or green spaces, never value the environment because they have never been shown it. All free time is screen time. Research shows the positive impact gardens and being outside can have – on learning, on social cohesion, on communicating and breaking down barriers on cultures and backgrounds.

'It is normal now for people to get off their arses and do stuff like that because you have no faith now that the government will do it for you. You've got to do it yourself.'

Children have only helped drive Generation X's green zeal further. I am very proud of the way our schoolchildren are so passionate about their environmental responsibilities. Our local home zone in north London is plastered with posters from the local school asking people to pick up their litter, drive slowly and respect their surroundings. My kids can spot a solar panel at a hundred paces, they recently raised money to have them installed in their school, and my nine-year-old's recent project was debating the relative merits of wind and nuclear. When your kids tell you to compost your food waste – well, you get it.

18

Will House Prices
Ever Stop Going Up?

Ooh, let's hope not, because that wouldn't suit any of us at all
well, would it? It may have taken some of us longer than others,
but chances are, if you are Generation X, you own some element
of the home you live in. You might have a whopping mortgage,
but yes, you've done it – you've clambered on the ladder and
you can look down pityingly on those grasping around beneath
you.

Maybe you are one of the really lucky – or simply older –
ones who got in early, played the market and are now sitting in
something substantial, or even own more than one property.
Maybe you've got a weekend pad, or a holiday home, or you are
part of the buy-to-let industry making a tidy sum from some
Millennial tenants on the side.

You may have been able to upgrade your home several times,
and maybe now your house is detached, with a garden, a
paddock, a pool, or a tennis court. Maybe you live in a smart
part of town, and obsessively check in on Zoopla several times
a day to see how far local prices have gone up. What fun, playing that fantasy property game – if I flog off my home now, we
could swap it for something twice the size in the countryside
(and become subsistence farmers!), or move abroad (and learn
Italian!), or downsize (and have no mortgage!). Perhaps your
chic little Clapham maisonette could buy you a Georgian rectory

in Leicestershire – the commute wouldn't be so bad, would it? Or your Acton two-bedder could get you a starter house in Colchester (then we can have a garden!). Or a chateau in France, or a finca in Spain. Or maybe you could move to Surbiton, pay off your mortgage, and never work again. Just think what your life could be like ...

It has been a feverish pursuit, a golden ambition, for much of the last 40 years, owning your own home, ever since it was enshrined as a social right by Thatcher with her Right to Buy policy. Only now is the dream receding, slipping from our grasp. Boomers have had the best of this asset inflation in the property market, and are properly dug in. Many of Generation X have also managed to reap the rewards. Many of us got in at the last minute, through a shared ownership scheme or a dodgy mortgage provider, and are clinging on by the skin of their teeth. And as so many of us have all our equity in our houses, all our savings, our pensions even, a crash would be disastrous.

'We have no plan beyond our houses,' says Annabel Rivkin of The Midult. 'Millennials on the other hand are much more agile, they are much more like New Yorkers or Parisians, less obsessed with owning a piece of the world, happy to up sticks and move wherever life or work takes them.' But for Generation X, approaching or deep into families, our house holds a lot more jeopardy.

As a result, we love our homes. In fact we fetishise them, pouring as much love and attention into them as we once did our wardrobes or our record collections. Farrow & Ball paint charts are now as keenly observed as new season cruise collections. Graham & Green furniture helps us look a little artisanal, and we pepper in some industrial chic or upcycled factory clobber for 'originality'. On the walls you'll find digital art, framed family photos of everyone looking relaxed and picture-perfect on a Scottish loch, Cornish rock, park picnic rug or Maldive beach (delete as appropriate). Neon signs, wall hangings, graffiti art, Abigail Ahern's artisanal cacti collection, Sophie Conran's earthenware kitchen pots and Henry Holland for Habitat cushions – you can dress your home now almost as quickly, cheaply and fashionably as you can yourself. And for a generation obsessed by cool and lifestyle, it is only right we should extend the same indicators to our living space.

Thank God, then, for Ikea, the H&M of the interiors world. This other high-volume, low-cost Swedish megabrand has, like fashion, democratised home-styling, at the same time as encouraging rampant consumerism and the disposability of goods. Everyone can afford a new kitchen now you can get them from Ikea on interest-free credit for less than a grand – and we can splurge on scatter cushions and shelving called 'Bobby' whenever we fancy now, as it's so goddamn cheap. For Generation Rent this is a boon – every time you move into a new letting, you can afford to do it over just how you want it.

Meanwhile our homes have changed to accommodate our new flat-structure households, ones where friends live together well into their thirties, and kids are afforded the same importance as their parents. Obsessively we knock through to create the sort of one-space living areas that reflect our family and household values – hey, we're really fluid about our eating/ living/relaxing, everyone just hangs out together. The kids are just like us, they shouldn't be locked away (although I'm increasingly jealous of friends who have hived off a space that is kids only – a playroom where they can stash all the plastic coloured crap kids trail around; or better, somewhere that is adults only – Daddy's porn room as one friend likes to call it, 'My mum cave,' says another).

Everyone hangs out round the kitchen island, where we are busy fetishising our food and our cooking, now the focus of the home. It's here we have our discos after dinner – here's a mirror ball to prove it, we still love a dance, you know. Opulence in a townhouse, mid-century modern in a cottage, contemporary Italian in the loftspace, vintage in the studio: we knowingly reference our nostalgia as we refashion it for the way we want to live.

And now that we are in our forties, we go out less and so our living space has become even more important. Going out costs too much money, we have kids, we're tired, we work from home, there's Netflix. We're still social, but not in clubs or raves any more, we do it at home instead. We want big, long dining tables on which we can throw inclusive kitchen suppers – sure, bring who you like, come when you like, we're so relaxed around here. Just turn up if you feel like it. Bring a bottle and we can recreate those Nineties rave communities right here in our kitchens. Why bother with a nightclub (when you don't even know the doorman any more), when you can DJ for yourself at home? There's room for our record decks (vinyl's back in, which is great, because we've all still got it from the first time round) and our bars are well stocked (wheel in the vintage drinks trolley, Steph – so *Abigail's Party*, we just love it!). Bookshelves line our walls, carefully curated to show how well read we used to be (before kids and Kindles), with backdated issues of *Vogue*, *The Face* and *Q* to show off our historic style credentials.

The objects that equip our homes define us – our NutriBullets and KitchenAid mixers (ah, but what colour?), our Daunt cloth book bags, our animal skin hides, Tom Dixon lampshades, Neptune kitchens, fluffy Berber rugs and Le Corbusier armchairs. Our copper-bottom saucepans, our Ercol sofas and G Plan sideboards – the antiques Boomers treasure so much are not modern enough for our tastes. Twentieth-century furniture is what we collect now.

Yes, we love our homes. They are the safe harbours from the madness outside, dressed to express who we are and how we want to live in these confusing times. And aren't we lucky if we own them. And – yes – smug.

But what if you didn't make it? What if you are still renting in your middle age – is it so bad? Some of us did not manage to make that deposit, didn't have that conversation with the mortgage lender.

'I worked abroad between the ages of 25 and 29, like loads of people did, and came back just at that critical moment when house prices were starting to accelerate,' says my friend Flo, 44. 'Within a year or two of being away, all my friends in their late twenties had suddenly become totally obsessed with house prices – I came back and it was all they could talk about. I found it bizarre. I had been in Australia with a whole group of itinerants, and then in New York where it was quite normal to rent, so this new obsession just seemed weird.

'I didn't have any money at the time – I was working, but living hand to mouth, and my boyfriend was really pressurising me to buy. Eventually we borrowed some money for a tiny deposit and bought a one-bed flat in Walthamstow – this was way before Walthamstow was in any way a good place to live. It was in the wrong part of town and I found the flat stifling for my spirit. A year later we split up and sold it. We made a bit of money, but not much.

'Everyone kept going on about how I had to get on the housing ladder, but prices were going up so quickly. I didn't buy the one-bed flat in an odd part of town again, because I just wasn't thinking like that. Instead I was shocked – really shocked by how commercial everything had got. I still am shocked.

'Now I find myself in this big bucks world, and I have to keep a check on myself when I visit friends. Ones who bought a tiny terrace in Bristol and now live in a seven-bedroom house in Frome. I have one friend who married someone rich and moved to the South Downs. I crashed at her house after a party once and when I woke up in the morning and walked into her kitchen I almost fell over – it was an atrium. Absolutely mind-blowing. All my closest friends live in vast houses because they have spent the last 20 years working their way up the ladder, whereas I was earning without any sort of view to building up equity.

'But my values are still the same. I don't need much money to be happy. When I visit my friends I have to remind myself that we are all the same people, they are no more happy than me, they have mortgages to worry about. I have to remember to keep these things in proportion.

'As a renter you are an itinerant – I don't mind as I never get bored. But the pay-off is I'm not settled. Not settled in my personal or professional life, I'm always flitting from one thing to the next. I actually spent last summer staying at my parents' house, because I had to move out of my rental as my landlord was selling it. Maybe I'll be able to buy something in Margate eventually, but it will be tiny and I'll still be coming to London to work as that's where all my work and connections are.

'I have to remember not to get caught up in the idea that you have to have a lot to feel like you have succeeded, as it's really pernicious.'

Flo is a wonderful exception. She doesn't talk about property or schools when she comes round, she consciously doesn't measure herself or how well she is doing or where she lives or what she owns: instead it is her friendships, her work, her social life, her passions and her cultural inquisitiveness that define her. Remember that next time you wake in the middle of the night sweating about catchment areas, Ofsted ratings and loan to value ratios. Think of Flo next time you sit next to some bore at dinner who bangs on about their property success and how clever they have been: 'Well, when I was in my twenties I bought a flat in Notting Hill, and sold it for this, made two hundred thousand. Then, I borrowed another couple of hundred, bought a house, now it's worth a million, and that's tax free. Took some capital out, bought a buy to let or two, done very well, haven't I?'

Living in a time of cheap money, we and the Boomers have been able to over-leverage, and so far there has been little punishment for it. It's not only in property prices – inflation has happened in virtually all assets from gold to oil, art to fine wine, watches to classic cars. For a certain class and age group, every time they spent money, they made it. Wealth just came.

'The ease of wealth creation by simply buying a property with a large mortgage and waiting for its value to rise has no skill to it, it's pure luck,' says Anton Bilton. 'Those who have benefited from this asset inflation have created their wealth not from entrepreneurialism or saving, which previous generations would have done, but have instead lucked-out on continually rising property values. It's given them a false sense of entitlement.'

Bilton has created millions out of property investment in the last 25 years. And it worries him. 'I bought my first flat 30 years ago for £100,000 and I borrowed £80,000. But now, that flat is probably worth £800,000. So, how would a young person today get the deposit he needs to buy the same flat and the earnings requirement to borrow the rest? For those who don't have family financial help it's impossible, which means if they want to live and work in London they have to buy at the far edge of the city or outside and commute. It's wrong and it's a politically motivated social mistake.

'By allowing wealthy, non-resident foreign investors to buy into London, residential prices have spiralled out of the next generation's reach. As a nation of house lovers we have blindly sold our children's birthright to live in their capital city to speculators.'

It's not just in town centres, either – it's happening in the countryside, too, where second-home owners have forced out locals by pushing up prices. X-ers might just about be okay if we managed to hang on to their coat tails, but the size of our mortgages may be more than we can handle if prices start to go the other way. Boomers, as we know, are sitting on fortunes. And hanging on to them too – they have little intention of downsizing their big houses and freeing up the market. Why should they move out of the homes they have lived in all of their lives? But for the generations below us, the property game has changed forever.

And now our capital city is littered with half-empty towers built by Chinese investors for super-rich foreigners. Foreigners who may not either want or be able to afford them any longer. Much of London's prime central property is a safe haven for cash moved out of unstable foreign economies, repositories for mystery fortunes of dubious sources. 'The American authorities have recently initiated a law for New York and Miami that any buyer purchasing an apartment over £3 million must name the true beneficiary,' says Bilton. 'So its ownership can't be hidden behind Cayman Island companies, or anything else. They suspect, and quite rightly in my view, that city residential property is the great money-laundering instrument of the world. The way to unfathom the money flows is to start seeing who the real owners are.'

But there is a more pernicious effect from this economic golden age. Those who grew wealthy off the back of asset inflation have not had to struggle for their wealth; they have not known a war or loss or atrocity. And so, there's less gratitude. As a result, 'There's a lack of pioneering spirit and entrepreneurialism,' says Bilton. 'Instead wealth creation has been modelled on the back of other people's wealth – the hedge-fund model. It's shocking that such huge fortunes have been made by people who simply manage other people's money with no shared downside risks to themselves.

'You also see it in executive pay. FTSE 100 company chief executive salaries with associated bonuses today can reach £10 million a year,' he says. 'If somebody made £10 million 25 years ago it was because they had come up with a clever idea, worked hard all their life and sold their business. Now, you get that for managing a business someone else built.'

One CEO I know was let go after just three years, having taken the company down a disastrous route. I used to walk past him at the lifts at 6 pm sharp every day, coat on, briefcase in hand, rushing to his chauffeur-driven limo to get home. Most of the rest of the building were still working. When he left, not only did he collect an enormous severance payout; he also took his negotiation to the wire over a lifetime allocation of the company's Twickenham and Wimbledon tickets. This attitude and renumeration policy doesn't create novel thinkers or pioneering leaders. It creates politically minded, difficult people, whose vested interest is not in the quality of the company's product or the well-being of its workforce, but the short-term share price by which their bonus is measured.

'The managers who earn these salaries have an overwhelming tendency to cronyism,' continues Bilton. 'Twenty-five years ago, a senior partner in an accountancy firm or a legal firm probably earned £250,000 a year, a huge amount of money. But then that person had dedicated their life to becoming intellectually advanced, focused, dedicated to their profession, providing good advice to their clients.

'Now, that would be the salary of a mid-level accountant or lawyer, and instead senior partners are earning millions a year. They can charge this much because of an unspoken cabal that exists around the provision of advice to big corporates.

'Chief executives of large listed companies surround themselves with crony advisors – merchant bankers, lawyers, accountants – and it's in everyone's interest to maintain a high level of fees, because when it comes to remuneration committee reports, everyone wants to maintain the evidence that "this is what it costs to run a big company; this is the cost of the advice I need – I get paid this much because he does over there." It feels that in the higher echelons of management everyone looks after each other and leaches the system. Legal, accountancy and investment banking fees have far exceeded average wage inflation over the last 20 years and simply shouldn't be where they currently are.'

This is the system Generation X are inheriting from self-interested Boomers who have not been paying it forward, who have taken as read the idea that society just keeps on getting richer – so pocket what you can in the process. The Digital Revolution has begun to disrupt these big businesses and many of them do not have the wit or the talent to cope. Big business deserves to fail if it can't get its house in order, but it's causing enormous damage in the process, whether that's in a BHS pension scandal or a BP oil spill.

And digital disruption is not going to level the playing field – in fact, quite the opposite. Just as the Digital Revolution looked set to recalibrate the system, the new X-er-led hegemony of big tech has started to flex its muscles. Apple, Facebook, Amazon and Google, the four horsemen of the digital apocalypse, are buying up anything that looks remotely like a threat and behaving with the arrogance and imperialism of the very structures they looked to replace. They have huge monopolies now, and as they get bigger they are swallowing more in their path. Business as a force for good, don't be evil – did someone forget something here?

The Mark Zuckerbergs, Sergey Brins and Elon Musks – the Rockefellers of our generation – are megalomaniacs. Zuckerberg may have set aside 99 per cent of his $50 billion fortune for charity – but only in a structure that he controls. The vast wealth they are amassing is confined to limited workforces. What's more, they are not paying taxes but funnelling their profits through tax havens.

The Nineties may have been the decade where class barriers came crashing down, but somehow in the Noughties we allowed money to build them all back up again. The enormous glut of stock-option wealth generated by the explosion of financial markets, new technologies and the management of the investment of these absurd windfalls has created a new strata of the privileged classes.

In front of us, they have created a parallel universe of big boats, five-star holidays and crystal-encrusted bikinis. They have second, third, fourth, fifth homes in London, Hong Kong, New York, Gstaad, St Barths. Their children are taxi-ed around the world in private jets, and they have pushed up house prices and private-school fees, the cost of luxury goods, travel and hotels. Costs that leave everyone else barricaded on the other side.

They have run away from the rest of us, and the gap is only getting wider. The top 1 per cent of the world's wealthiest now own more than the rest of the world put together. One in nine meanwhile do not have enough to eat. Oxfam reckons the world's richest 80 people have seen their wealth double between 2009 and 2014.

What should we do about it? We, the X-ers, who are in charge now, and the Millennials, who will be soon. These are Oxfam's suggestions:

- Clamp down on tax dodging by corporations and rich individuals.
- Invest in universal, free public services such as health and education.

- Share the tax burden fairly, shifting taxation from labour and consumption towards capital and wealth.
- Introduce minimum wages and move towards a living wage for all workers.
- Introduce equal-pay legislation and promote economic policies to give women a fair deal.
- Ensure adequate safety-nets for the poorest, including a minimum income guarantee.
- Agree a global goal to tackle inequality.

Meanwhile, and irritatingly, the rich have stolen some of our pursuits and made them distinctly uncool. 'Going to nightclubs in the late Eighties it was about what you wore, who you knew,' says Kris Thykier. 'Yes, it was hierarchical, but there was some sort of democracy in terms of how you got in with that crowd. Now, nightclubbing is simply about how much can you pay for a table, that's the charge of entry. Money as social currency has become central.' Nightclubs are suddenly about sparklers and champagne buckets. Being on the guest list is simply a purchase, not a signifier of being in the know.

Maybe this is the inevitable conclusion of commodifying cool. Nightclubs have become vulgar playpens for the uninteresting. Likewise the acquisition of stuff – watches, handbags, designer gear – no longer seems that desirable. Once your Hermès handbag or your dad's Patek Philippe said something classy about you. Now they are edging on 'nouveau'. Buying things for the sake of buying them is something of a social disease – and given space in our homes is at such a premium, where do you store it all anyway?

'We have reached peak stuff,' declared the chief sustainability officer for Ikea, which is a marvellous example of having your cake and eating it. But then there is such a glut of 'stuff' these days, it seems to be losing its value. It's like when you chuck out the mountain of kids' toys that have lain unplayed with for months: when only a plastic lorry and a spinning top remain, they suddenly find they can play with both again.

'I'm streamlining everything at the moment,' says Alice Temperley. 'Selling the house in the country. Flogging off my vintage cars. All these things – you just don't need them. You need your health and your family and there's no point in all this clutter.'

Experiences are where we are choosing to spend our money instead – holidays and travel, food and good wine. 'There was a period where the acquisition of stuff was a route to fulfilment,' says Kris Thykier. 'But actually if you had a better watch, a better car, a better suit or pair of shoes, would that be as fulfilling? Nowadays I spend my money on food and drink. I like being generous and hosting, I like going out and seeing people, and I travel. These are the things that I enjoy. I probably spend much more money on experience than I do on stuff.'

'People are definitely becoming less materialistic,' says Tom Hodgkinson. 'They want to do things instead – just look at the way festivals are booming. We were asked to set up an Idler tent at the Secret Garden Party. It was challenging what we were asking of people – I was amazed they wanted to come and listen to talks about Socrates at 11 am on a Sunday, but they did. People seemed to like learning stuff, so out of that we grew the Idler Academy of Philosophy, Husbandry and Merriment. The idea is with philosophy you're studying the arts of good living; husbandry is the practical things like how to bake bread and keep bees, and merriment is the third element of a fulfilled life – singing in choirs, dancing lessons and playing the ukulele. At Festival no. 6 last summer we had 400 people doing swing dancing to hip hop outdoors in the rain – it was so joyful!' And a long way from a magnum of Cristal in Chinawhite.

It may well be that the experiences we sought so relentlessly from our rave days have now passed through a period of over-consumption in the Noughties, left us feeling slightly sick and moved us on. After buying and spending, acquiring and amassing, we have come out the other side looking for skills and education. Kitesurfing and Tough Mudders, growing your own and learning Latin.

'Hedonism still defines us as a generation,' says Tom, 'so we are always going to bring a sense of fun and community to whatever it is we do. Education is the new drugs! It's such good fun, you do it in groups, you laugh. There's something empty about hedonism eventually and it's not very good for your health. Education is about discovery and mind-expansion, new perspectives, showing an interest in other realms out there.'

Meanwhile we need to rethink property for a generation that may not know home ownership. We need accommodation that is accessible to those who work on public-sector salaries – doctors, nurses, firemen and policemen who are integral to the smooth running of our towns and cities. We need to create spaces that cater to a new, flexible live/work model, for a society that is always on, 24/7, that will no longer be housed in offices. We need flexible work/live spaces that encourage communal collectives and can accommodate short-term, project-based teams.

The prototypes of these new co-living spaces are just opening. One, based in London's Old Oak Common, charges from £225 rent per week and includes bills, concierge, linen and cleaning. Also included is a co-working space, a spa, rooftop terrace, themed dining rooms and 'disco' launderette.

This all sounds good for freewheeling Millennials, but what about those of Generation X who are still stuck in flats and maisonettes with multiple children because we can't afford a terrace house with a patio garden? What's going to happen as we get older? Do you really think Generation X are going to accept the care-home model?

'I'm hoping we make brilliant old people's homes,' says Miranda Sawyer. 'The way we treat old people is a disgrace, so I hope we reinvent that. It should be similar to the way clubs work – you could have like a rave old people's home and a Britpop old people's home, but mix up old and young. It should be: your name's not down, you're not coming in – because you know which old people you'll want to live with, in your club, you can see them a mile off. Why not take over those awful caravan parks in seaside resorts? Everyone living separately but together.'

Annabel Rivkin has the same vision. 'I think we might end up in communes. There's a place in Paris called Babayagas' House, which is a women-only old people's community care home that I rather admire. Me and a few of my friends want to sell our houses and pool the proceeds – a bit like free schools, we might do free care homes. And probably single sex.'

Babayagas' was set up by a group of Parisian women who wanted to keep their independence but live communally. A bit like the Golden Girls, if you like. Publicly funded, the building contains 25 self-contained flats with 21 of those adapted for the elderly, while the ground floor houses a university for senior citizens. Maybe chuck in a disco ball and a wine bar and that would suit us very nicely.

As one of the first Babayagas' residents declared as she settled into her new home: 'To live long is a good thing, but to age well is better.'

19

The Speed of Things

We are breeding a short-attention-span culture. One of tweets and texts, second-screening (when you watch TV and play on a phone/tablet/laptop at the same time), an always-on, 24/7 culture that necessitates endless multitasking. We are developing toxic digital habits like keeping your phone next to your bed (guilty), checking your social media feed in the lift (guilty), quelling your restless child with an iPad (yep), trying to take a photo or video of everything (from a scenic view, to a band at a gig, to a milkshake – not everything is an Instagram moment ... Oh wait – yes it is).

With the deluge of stuff coming down our channels, content providers are fighting for our attention. Facebook's advice for video creation is to create something that grabs you in the first two seconds. We are promiscuous, restless readers and viewers. We've got a fear of being present, with a perpetual quest for distraction. It takes discipline these days to stop and focus, to collect our thoughts and think, to put down our phones and look up. The speed of things and the pace of change are dizzying. Look away for a moment and something has happened – you missed it.

There is less permanence in the workforce (zero-hour contracts), in the longevity of products (Google Glass), technology (another software update?) and in consumer trends (sous-vide cooker, anyone?). From banks to newspapers, institutions that have lasted for hundreds of years are now hanging in the balance. Tomorrow's world is not visible any more, not in the way it used to be, not even as a TV series.

Many of us don't take the time we need to stop, pause and reflect (try leaving your phone at home for the day. It's a release, once you've let it go), which is why stress, anxiety and depression diagnoses are going through the roof.

But maybe that is something to do with our sleep patterns. Lying awake in the middle of the night, or insomnia, is often described as an affliction, but it could actually be the best time to digest the day. In fact, there is evidence from science and history that the standard eight-hour sleep pattern may be unnatural.

In the early Nineties, psychiatrist Thomas Wehr conducted an experiment in which a group of people were plunged into darkness for fourteen hours every day for a month. It took some time for their sleep to regulate, but by the fourth week the subjects had settled into a distinct sleeping pattern. They slept first for four hours, then woke for one or two hours before falling into a second four-hour sleep.

In 2005 historian Roger Ekirch of Virginia Tech published his book *At Day's Close: Night in Times Past*, detailing more than 500 references to a segmented sleeping pattern – in diaries, court records, medical books and literature. These references also describe a first sleep that began about two hours after dusk, followed by a waking period of one or two hours and then a second sleep.

During this waking period most people stayed in bed, read, wrote and prayed. Many prayer manuals from the late fifteenth century offered special prayers for the hours in between sleeps.

Ekirch found that references to the first and second sleep started to disappear during the late seventeenth century, and had disappeared entirely by the 1920s. He attributes the initial shift to improvements in street lighting, domestic lighting and a surge in all-night coffee houses. As the night became a place for legitimate activity, and as that activity increased, the length of time people could dedicate to rest dwindled.

The theory is that these middle-of-the-night waking hours were actually a time for contemplation, a time that we have lost. If we wake in the night now we are fearful of the next day, haunted by unresolved issues and anxieties. But maybe they are that magic 25th hour – the extra bit in the day we all wished we had.

I found that pregnancy-induced insomnia was not half so scary as any other type of insomnia. If we can't sleep, we tend to think there is something wrong with us; we lie there in the dark, magnifying all our worries until it seems like the world is going to end. But if we can learn to relax, the time can actually be productive.

My first baby was a terrible sleeper, and some days I would go into work having had just an hour or two of sleep. Although it was awful, it didn't break me, and now that I know I can get by on so much less sleep than I thought I don't panic when I am lying there awake in the dark. I am able to let my thoughts wash over me and examine each of them calmly as they arrive. Which is a comforting form of meditation.

Generation X have a very different view of work from Millennials – we still talk about work–life balance, distinguishing between them as separate parts of our lives. 'I'm working really, really hard,' despairs fashion designer Alice Temperley. 'You get to this stage and you know you're not young. My parents say, "Alice, why are you still working so hard?" I tell them they don't understand, it's not easy running a business. But at the same time I'm thinking, "Actually, you're right. What are the most important things?"'

If we are building a future where there is no separation between work and play, what is that going to do for everyone's minds? At The Pool, a digital publisher of women's lifestyle content set up by the editor Sam Baker and DJ Lauren Laverne, twentysomething journalists populate the site all day long. They don't break for lunch, they don't stop and chat, it's heads down. How different this was from the newsrooms of my day, where fag breaks, going for a 'quick coffee', breaking for lunch and gossipy phone calls to mates broke up the shift. Not to mention hiding in the fashion cupboard goofing around with the fashion editor. And when these Millennial journalists leave the office, they have to make sure the site is pre-programmed to slow-release content through the night. It keeps going even when you don't. How far that seems from the old night shift and night editor model newspapers used to have.

'Maybe they won't get caught in the rat race like us, maybe the younger generation will be cleverer than that,' says Thomasina. 'Paid-for education won't be an option, everyone will be renting, they will have fewer children for environmental and economic reasons. Maybe they won't want it all in the way we do.'

Perhaps we expect too much; perhaps as a generation we are just plain greedy. We want the nice life of the boomers, with the careers, travel and consumer benefits we crafted for ourselves. Yet we also want fun and fulfilment on top of that. At this pinch point of our life, the scale of that desire is coming home to roost: we look up at the boomers in their nice, relaxed retirements, voting in more economic and political advantages for themselves, and our pension and mortgage statements arrive, and we want to weep.

But there's no use despairing – we need to design things better for ourselves and for those coming up behind. If we must pay off accumulated government debt, and we must work harder for longer, we might as well enjoy it, or design it in a way that works for us. If you're a mother trying to get back into the workplace, or a displaced digital refugee, or a business owner struggling to adapt and survive, you already know this: we need to evolve.

The media industry is a case in point. As upmarket, intelligent brands have seen their audience leach out to digital platforms like Facebook and Twitter, they have to learn to adapt to survive. Those that cosied up to these new digital giants, giving away their content for free, are realising it's an endgame: the digital giants are making even more money, they are making even less.

In the face of a blizzard of unedited content, where does the confused reader go these days? When you think about the events of the last few years, having economics, global politics and ideas explained properly is more important than ever. The rise of extremism that we see in the success of Trump, Corbyn, UKIP and their equivalents throughout Europe is hardly surprising when you think most readers live in the echo chamber of the supposedly 'publisher agnostic' feeds of the digital giants. With such small teams managing the digital news feeds of so many millions of people, it is not surprising that the unconscious bias of platforms like Facebook has been exposed as inherently biased.

After all the liberalism that we ushered in during the Nineties, the young, feeling angry and hard done by, are becoming more extreme in their attitudes. The rise of the Corbynistas is threatening to engulf the Labour Party, UKIP displays worrying tendencies towards absolutism, and extremist political groups on both the left (Greece, Spain) and right (France, Austria) are becoming more powerful all across Europe.

But is your Twitter feed any worse than a tabloid newspaper? It's certainly more immediate, but is rarely held to account or bears any scrutiny around truth. Digital is slowly killing off responsible journalism, which requires investment and time.

Working at the coalface in 'legacy media' organisations has not been much fun for the last few years. Tighter budgets, greater productivity demands, dwindling ad revenue and dwindling audiences have meant we are all working harder, for less.

'In the Nineties, I was so much richer than I am now,' says Tom Hodgkinson. 'When I was 28, I did comment pieces for the *Guardian* for several hundred pounds. I did one for them recently and they told me, "You'll get £210 if it goes in the paper, otherwise £150 if it just goes up online." When I got paid they only gave me £100 – ridiculously, I found myself ringing them back haggling over £50. Likewise I did an op-ed piece for the *New York Times* recently and only got $100. These are top papers. Your name pops up in these and it looks like you are doing quite well, but you might actually only be earning £100 a week.'

Amelia Troubridge, a photographer whose award-winning work has been published in some of the world's most prestigious magazines and newspapers, says work she used to spend days producing is now being done for a fraction of the cost. Lower production values by less experienced photographers are an expedient route for squeezed budgets.

'I feel like the younger generation is being pitted against our generation. They are much more accepting of how they are going to have a humbler life and their skills around digital are something we cannot keep up with. I need younger people working for me to produce the job that I'm now expected to produce as a photographer. I don't have those skills and I don't have the mental ability to learn those skills. It's not just about being a photographer now – it's a multimedia thing. You've got to actually be a celebrity and sell yourself. I chose to be behind the camera because I didn't want to be paraded in front of everyone else. There's a nice anonymity to photography that as an English person I always rated. I think there's something quite good about being low key. But suddenly you've got to shout it to the world every day about how awesome you are, and that penetrates every moral I hold on to. To see myself on that level is very uncomfortable.'

Technical innovation and audience reach have replaced creativity. So we have Brooklyn Beckham, aged 17, shooting the new Burberry campaign and sharing the images with his several million Instagram followers. The Millennial world sees no irony, has no creative bars – it measures itself in followers, likes and fans.

'The Nineties were so easy,' continues Amelia. 'I could do a job, earn one or two thousand pounds and have a great life for a month. I could buy a flight to Brazil for £300 and stay there and make that budget stretch. We had options – we could live in London, our great city, for much less money.

'But it's much easier for people to make their own content now – brands have their own newsrooms. You can hire a photographer now to go and do a shoot for you for hundreds whereas before you would have spent 20 grand. You see the people who were really flying in photography six or seven years ago have been flattened. The kind of pictures that do well these days are not gritty or challenging or edgy – it's just lifestyle. It's not over-thought. It's people looking happy, celebrating, enjoying luxury goods, enjoying a luxury lifestyle.' A long way from the sort of haunting black and white photography you used to find in the *Independent*'s Saturday Review.

But the game is not up, it is just changing – changing faster than most of us can keep up with. Trying to find new revenue models for great brands like *The Times*, the *Guardian* and the *Telegraph* is challenging, but not impossible. For a start these companies are not agile or innovative by their very nature: they are historic, large, populated by many who do not want change, who do not see the scale of the disruption. Trying to get print journalists to file copy three or four times a day for hungry digital news feeds is just the start of it.

Where a journalist used to work on instinct and an editor used to commission stories he or she felt were relevant, interesting or important, they now have a digital dashboard of trending content starkly displaying their readers' proclivities. What succeeds online is a stark reflection of the reality of human tastes: the moment a woman nearly drowned; a toddler being beaten up by her parent; ten new drugs you've never heard of; the cutest cat you've ever seen. To the horror of some newsrooms it can even be commercial content that tops the most-popular list – stories commissioned and created by brands as a form of advertising.

New media can launch products quickly and shut them down quickly if they fail. They blend advertising with their editorial teams in a way that makes newspapers shudder, and run paid-for live events to help monetise their content. Newspapers spend years agonising over the morality of these things, then when they finally come round to it, realise the ship has already left the harbour.

But there's no doubt – the ride is a thrill. Many of the most successful new media brands still don't turn a profit, but suck up rounds and rounds of investment based on their audience growth. Whereas those that opted for paid subscription models, like *The Times* and *Sunday Times* newspapers, are turning a profit. Increasingly, slowly, people are beginning to understand that you have to pay for quality content where you will be uninterrupted by the blinding deluge of hysterical digital advertising you find everywhere else: the success of *The Times*, Netflix, Spotify and the *Economist* all prove this.

'The danger with resting on your laurels is someone fifteen years younger can then do something you can't,' says Matt

Roberts. 'Unless you're really on it, with tech in particular, you're a dinosaur. You've got to stay connected.'

Roberts is currently reinventing his fitness business. 'I am trying to use digital to globalise my brand. I want as a consumer to be in a fitness class in LA at ten o'clock on a Tuesday morning. I want to do that from my living room. And I want to be in the class in Tokyo at two in the afternoon. We're using the strength of my brand to cherry-pick the best fitness offerings around the world, working on some great tech that will place cameras in all those studios and will broadcast live out to you. You can be a member on this site and we can monetise it.

'If you're anyone who's been inspired by doing things in our generation, right now you need to make a step,' he continues. 'I think we have three, four or five careers in us. And it's exciting: finding what the workplace is doing, which areas are growing, identifying the expertise you've built up, where your knowledge has got you, how you can take that on.'

'Work is both a gift and a duty,' says Pope Francis. But the trouble is, duty never really featured high on the X-ers to-do lists. Work for us has never been about that postwar, knuckling-down mentality, nor has it been about the Eighties need to make money. It's been about creativity, passion, invention and entertainment. Work should be fun.

But in this time of wage stagnation, zero-hour contracts and almost full employment, job satisfaction is increasingly rare. *Marketing Week* in January 2016 ran the cover story: 'Overworked and Undervalued: a marketing profession working long hours with little promise of new opportunities'.

Words like 'Shatterday' and 'Shunday' are being deployed to describe what we used to think of as the weekend. Ever-increasing consumption and demand are making increasingly less sense. Interesting product growth is now around artisanal, lo-fi trends. In the fashion industry, brands are finding that it's the highly wrought, timeless pieces that are selling, rather than the transient, seasonal items. Not everyone wants to consume cheaply and quickly. Not every business wants to strive and grow. Not everyone's definition of success is the same.

Richard O'Connor and his wife Birgitte Hovmand set up the brand Chocolate and Love to produce a 'fairly traded, organic' chocolate product. He is a social entrepreneur, she is a lawyer. It was following the birth of their daughter that they decided they wanted to live a different sort of life. They sat down and asked, 'What's the dream? If we run a business together, what do we want to do? We came up with one rule and it's our number one rule today,' says Richard. 'We're going to start a business that we can run from a beach. One, in brackets, that we're proud of, that does good. And every decision we make has to go through that rule first.'

For several years the family lived between Denmark and Scotland, while taking month-long breaks round the world. 'I wasn't allowed to call them "vacations",' says Richard. 'Birgitte insisted I call them "workations". We would hire a nanny wherever we went, and she would take our daughter off on trips and to the beach. Then at two o' clock every day we would stop working and it's family time.'

They tried California, Cape Town, anywhere with good skiing – and eventually settled on Majorca, where their daughter is now in school. 'About 90 per cent of the parents at Sophie's school are entrepreneurs,' says Richard. 'Majorca is something of a lifestyle destination – it has 23 international schools.' Now they live five minutes from a beach, and every summer plan to travel for three months. Chocolate and Love they describe not as a business but 'a passion project'.

Lifestyle business also allows you to take the thing you love and turn it into a living. The hipster movement, although much derided, is actually a lovely example of bringing the slowness of

artisanal craft into the modern world. Coffee shops, micro brew-
eries, baking outfits, craft emporia all celebrate the care and
attention that go into making a product excellent, celebrating a
skill and consciously consuming. Running your own business in
many ways gives you the freedom we craved in the Nineties –
and digital has kickstarted and facilitated a start-up boom.

'I think we're the beginning of an alternative movement,
questioning the way we live,' says Temperley. 'We're the beginning of a massive change. The world below us has transformed
into something we don't really know yet, and we are like the
modern-day hippies. The techno generation underneath are
going faster and faster, while we are trying to simplify our lives.

'I'm tired of the cycle of it all, the cycle of deliveries, the
seasons, the shows,' she continues. 'When I started there were
hardly any designers on the fashion schedule, and now it's
flooded. I don't want to be floating in this sea of people. I want
to do what I want to do.

'Forty is a good age to put it into perspective. I'm running a
creative business, and, ironically, I want to be more creative.
I have people in the company that are creative for me, and
production facilities that make the dresses. But I'm not stitching
and making and painting and doing things myself. So, I need to
slow it down. Make a product that's not got such a massive
churn-around. Do the stuff that's real and more tangible. Why
do you have to deliver four seasons a year and deliver different
times within that season? It's very fast.

'So, my new schedule is one day of just leave me alone, no
gadgets, no nothing, where I sit in my studio and paint and
create. Then three days in the office, and another day to do
whatever I feel like. A project or something unrelated to
fashion.'

Which sounds nice, but the economy still needs to grow. For
all our extra hours, our productivity is flatlining. Generations X

and Y have still got a massive job on to pay back the Boomers' debt. But maybe Alice actually has the answer.

'After putting in that structure, we're 30 per cent up on last summer. We've got our groove on now. I'm not shooting from the hip any more, I'm more focused. Because I don't want to work crazy hours, I want to be with my little boy. Everybody is so good at taking on more – now, I say no a lot.'

The hairstylist Josh Wood, whose name is now a brand on the shelf at Boots, says he is driven by work, to the point where he feels like he has become its prisoner. 'Every morning, when I get to work, I see this guy in Costa sitting there with a book. I watch him, and for half an hour he never looks up. Who, at 8.30 in the morning, has the kind of life where they can do this – where they allow themselves to do this? It makes me think "Sod the Prada shoes and the business class, I just want a life." I'm first in and last out my office every day. I've never read a book in the morning all my life.'

There is a collective sense of exhaustion amongst even the most successful members of our generation, but they are not allowing themselves to let up. 'I am haunted by this slight feeling I have failed,' continues Josh. 'I feel like I constantly need to do more, feel like I have never quite got it right. If anything I have a greed for constant change and evolution – I love setting a goal and moving it.'

'When people say, "Why are you doing so much, why don't you just calm down?" I say, "What's the benefit in calming down?"' says Martha Lane Fox. 'Life is short, you should try to work hard. That's pretty much the only things I believe in: be nice to people and work hard. I don't think it's that complicated.'

Then she pauses, and adds: 'I think it's also really important to drink too much champagne.'

20

Where We Are Headed

Last summer I attended an advertising conference in the south of France. I was taking clients and there was a mistake with the booking, and I ended up staying in a swanky five-star joint up in the hills above Cannes. Sitting out by the pool one evening admiring the view, I was joined by a silver-haired American man. His wife had just bought a house in the area, he said, and they were staying here while she finished off the interior décor. They had come from the Hôtel du Cap-Eden-Roc in Antibes. 'You know? That place where all those famous people stay,' he drawled, sounding a little resigned. A few days before they had been in Monte Carlo, but 'So many hills! I had a gall bladder operation a year ago and it's no good for that.'

He was curious as to what had brought me to the south of France. I explained I was at a conference that used to celebrate creativity in storytelling, but these days was mostly concerned with technology. It seemed, I said, to be populated by young men running round championing distribution platforms that had names that frequently skipped all the vowels. Sprinklr; xAd; DataXu; InMobi; OpenX; AppNexus; Mblox; YuMe. He looked baffled (as well he might), so I politely enquired, 'Do you like this hotel?'

'Well, yes,' he said, and then sighed. 'But there's only so much wine and cheese a guy can eat and drink.' He looked around at the rolling hills and terracotta-topped houses dotting the wooded landscape, and shrugged his shoulders as if he were faintly bored. 'I didn't want my wife to buy the house here, but she insisted. After all, what else is there to do?'

Oh. He told me he was in the cheese industry. He must have sold a lot of cheese.

That night I flew back to London. It was the day of the referendum on the European Union. I was late and when I arrived home the first results were beginning to trickle through. The consensus had been it was going to be close, but 'Remain' were going to pip it. People voted for the status quo. Remain was the culmination of so many of the achievements the world had worked towards for the last 20 years – globalisation, multiculturalism, economic growth through free markets, social libertarianism, the European Court of Human Rights, the validating of workers, parents, migrants, prisoners, gays, the disabled, students, any ethnic minority you care to name. Funding for the arts and the sciences, a health service and a tech industry built on the best of talent from all over Europe, all over the world.

It was a world, dare I say it, envisioned and fashioned by Generation X: a generation who have grown up feeling European, living the European dream. We learned European languages in school, mostly French, German or Spanish, we Interrailed around the continent before university, we week-ended, holidayed, worked and partied there. Our friends live there, in Paris, Milan, Rome and Lisbon. Back in the UK we are friends with Poles, French, German and Dutch people. We are European, in lifestyle, business and society. Mostly, it suited us.

But our parents, they are not so sure. Many never left the country, or only did so when they retired. Holidays for them were Margate or Prestatyn, Penzance or Whitby. Their honey-moons were in Devon or the Cotswolds – never mind the stag parties in Tallinn. Our music comes from Mali and Cuba, theirs was home-grown, with the odd bit of Beatles-inspired sitar. Our food is from Vietnam and Peru; when Claudia Roden introduced Middle Eastern cooking to Britain in the late Sixties it was considered fiercely exotic. Our fashion is Uniqlo, Zara, Helmut Lang, Dolce & Gabbana, theirs was Laura Ashley, Mary Quant, Ossie Clark, Biba.

My friend Natalie, who turned 40 last year, has just had a baby. Her daughter has a half-Welsh, half-Mauritian mother, and a father who is Saudi Arabian but was born and lives in London. My friend Louise is Danish, but she was brought up in the UK and now lives in Paris. My next-door neighbours are French, my son's best friend is Muslim, my yoga teacher is Croatian. None of these people feels any different from me. But somehow, somewhere, fear has crept into the national psyche, especially outside the magnetic melting pot and powerhouse that London has become.

Now this was not *our* vote. Generation X do not do fear. We are not anxious in the way Millennials are, and we do not fear 'immigrants' and an 'erosion of sovereignty' as our parents do. We are old enough and experienced enough to have witnessed change and young enough to have relished its advantages.

In the aftermath of the vote, this letter appeared in the *Financial Times*:

We are the 48 – years old as well as per cent.

We have small houses and large mortgages. We went to raves and we stopped fighting at football matches. We got very drunk one night in 1997 then felt betrayed because of Iraq. We like being European and we understand the world is interconnected and complicated ... We have friends in other countries and we're embarrassed. We feel ... the need to apologise in person to our Polish friends at

the school gate. We've explained to our kids ... we'll still
be allowed to go camping in France.

We are lecturers, nurses, systems analysts and
engineers. We are the civil service. We run small
businesses. We work for large, foreign-owned companies.
We aren't in charge but we are the backbone of the
country. We can't leave because our kids are at school
and our parents are getting old ... We didn't prepare
ourselves for this because we didn't believe it could
possibly happen.

We want a plan B, but we haven't worked out what to
do yet. We will. We want our country back.

Robert Gross

Twickenham, UK

As one of the comments underneath the letter read: 'I wonder if
the 48-year-old from Scunthorpe shares your view?' But as well
as a regional bias, when the vote was broken down it was clear
there had been a demographic bias too. Sadly, the turnout of
18–24-year-olds was only 36 per cent, and 25–34 was 58 per
cent. Generation X turned out between 72 and 75 per cent,
while the over-55s had an over 80 per cent turnout. And the
over 55s voted mostly to leave.

A week after the Brexit vote was the 100th anniversary of the
start of the Battle of the Somme, in which over a million soldiers
lost their lives. For our generation this is just a story. For the
postwar generation it is nearly a memory. They feel the fragility
of the world more keenly than we do.

Growing up in the Forties and Fifties my dad still remembers
rationing, the first time he saw a banana. The postwar generation worked hard for the prosperity they now enjoy – they have
consistently voted on an economic play that has given them
wealth that outweighs their children and grandchildren's.

Pensions for them were a life's goal; growing up we were constantly being urged to save into one. My parents wanted me to join the professional classes, study law or medicine or get on the graduate training scheme at a nice company like Marks & Spencer. There they saw safety, a 'proper' life. They were, and remain, baffled by the media, technology, the creative industries. They do not talk about 'happiness' or 'emotional intelligence' but instead they 'keep buggering on'. They fear burglars and pickpockets, they trust policemen and judges.

This generation may have invented the Pill and rock 'n' roll, it may have burned its bras and urged each other to 'turn on, tune in and drop out', but very few of them were actually able to live it – that was the gift they gave to us. Most Boomer women married young, had children and gave up work for a domestic life. Sure the Seventies feminists fought for equal pay, but this is a fight we are still having. LSD and pot might have been around on the Kings Road in the Sixties, but they took a lot longer to reach Milton Keynes and Warrington. Instead it was our generation that benefited from a more independent life for women, an alternative view of the job for life system. It was our generation that picked up the anti-apartheid baton and installed a black president in the White House, it was under our watch that class barriers were broken down, homosexuality celebrated and normalised, gay marriage allowed and the great legacy of Thatcher – social mobility and entrepreneurialism – delivered.

Pay It Forward?
One of the most shared memes at the end of 2015 was the words attributed to Steve Jobs on his death bed. They weren't actually Jobs's words, but, like most things on the internet, that didn't seem to matter:

*'At this moment, lying on the sick bed and recalling my
whole life, I realize that all the recognition and wealth
that I took so much pride in, have paled and become
meaningless in the face of impending death. Now I know,
when we have accumulated sufficient wealth to last our
lifetime, we should pursue other matters that are
unrelated to wealth ... Perhaps relationships, perhaps art,
perhaps a dream from younger days. The wealth I have
won in my life I cannot bring with me. What I can bring
is only the memories precipitated by love. That's the true
riches which will follow you.'*

What do you want to change about the world now? This is the
question I asked everyone while researching this book, and
almost to a person the reply was 'inequality'. It is what we feel
most keenly now. Generation X reorganised the value system.
We worked for love, not money, we prioritised our friends, families and relationships, we worked to make things better, more
socially equal, to create more opportunity and more wealth –
but here we are: it hasn't turned out quite right.

'If you look in the Seventies probably 75 per cent of the men
and women who would have made up the *Sunday Times Rich
List* inherited their wealth,' says Ben Elliot, whose company
Quintessentially – a lifestyle concierge company for the super-
rich – services the new money. 'Today 75 per cent of them have
made their wealth. The question you're asking is what is left
behind. If you're in a place where you could see no hope and
you don't feel opportunities are going to knock for you, there
should be ways and means. We need more organisations like the
Prince's Trust, which is an excellent model of giving people
opportunity, developing their skills and sponsoring them.'

Those who have been left behind have now had their say. Last
year, 2016, delivered two shock results: in Brexit democracy

triumphed and the majority (just) voice was heard, while Trump gained sufficient electoral college votes to become the new US president. Globalisation, liberalisation and wealth creation have not delivered enough to enough of us. This is the backlash to the changes we have wrought.

Generation X have also had to engage with the increasing demands of work–life balance. They have been the cannon fodder in a world that has exponentially increased, if not productivity, then the actual number of work hours worked. As digital culture has consumed us 24/7 we have had to work out where our families, our friends, our relationships and our own time fits in.

Millennials look on absolutely aghast – many of them cannot imagine adapting their lives now to include children and a family of their own. As the Millennial Emma Gannon, author of the girllostinthecity blog and the book *Ctrl Alt Delete*, a memoir of a girl growing up online, observes, 'At work I see these really hardworking, ball-busting business women, but then I also see them as mums. I see them panicking, "Oh shit, I'm late to go and pick them up!" or just drained after a mental weekend looking after children. I see them pulled in very different directions and their situation terrifies me. It makes me think perhaps I do actually have to choose between work and motherhood, which is really sad. And could I really have children, because the sacrifices scare me. Maybe it would just be better if I don't.'

Sometimes our struggle feels like a war of attrition. The two-working-parent family is now the norm and has spawned a culture of frantic childcare arrangements, a loss of freedom (that quality we all fought so hard for) and a life of ridiculous micro-moments where you are simultaneously worrying about a spelling test, a presentation at work, the last time you saw your husband and whether you have run out of laundry powder.

The fallout has been an obsession with happiness, what it constitutes and what it means. Simple, meditative practices like baking a cake, planting a flower bed, embroidering a cushion, even writing a letter, have taken on a totemic meaning of self-determination and are celebrated as antidotes to modern life – the sort of things that not so long ago would have just been a regular part of each day. The ability to balance life and fun, home and the office, care and duty, analogue and digital, children and friends, parents and lovers has become a dizzying juggle that claims many sacrifices along the way. As such, the 'lifestyle business' has become a sort of X-er mirage: a way of life that pays your way and allows you to live in the way of your choosing. Whether that is managing a surf school, opening a bakery, making jewellery, running a B&B in Costa Rica, teaching yoga or subsistence farming in Wales, we endlessly obsess about these mythical careers that allow you to work on a hangover, see your children, be in touch with nature, exercise your creative spirit, fuel your passion, answer your vocation, pay into society and the world, and live your life in the way we fantasise about.

The criticism often thrown at British small enterprise is that it never scales into a world-dominating brand. The UK has not spawned a Google or a Facebook or an Apple in recent years. Where is the twenty-first-century East India Company? Is this because the ambition of our generation lies elsewhere or is it because we are scared to commit to one thing? Famously, we have creativity in spades, but lack commitment to take that creativity from one cultural movement to another. Our values are based on cool, and cool is transient. We would rather cash in for comfortable millions, than scale to what is known in Silicon Valley as 'unicorn' levels – when your company is valued at over a billion. Isn't 'billions' a bit vulgar? A bit undemocratic?

We have not wanted to grow up, we are childlike in our approach, we nurtured nerd culture, comics, nostalgia, school disco – what is rave if it's not a grown-up version of a children's birthday party with everyone dressed up in bright colours running round high on sugar, going a bit mad? We held on to our youth for as long as we could, till the Millennials took it back. Whereas Boomers wanted to grow up quickly – the world of their parents was not a nice one, they wanted to get on and set things right, and they knew just how to do it.

Meanwhile the proliferation of the media is busy disposing of a pluralistic spectrum of voices (university campuses have voted to ban tabloids like the *Sun* and the *Mail* as they 'fund hate'). Instead, social media and its algorithmic culture allow users to live in an echo chamber of their own opinions and beliefs (Facebook was roundly attacked for handing Trump the presidency – many were simply not aware of what everybody else was thinking). Technology is promoting Millennial exclusion zones where you can 'safely' inhabit a world constructed around your own desires, rather than reality.

Now we have children we have had to wave goodbye to youth, and mortality is beginning to stretch its cold fingers into our lives. Friends and family have begun to be touched by death and disease: we are not going to live forever, as Liam Gallagher sang it. As parents we have been forced, finally, to articulate to ourselves what kind of life and world we want to have and we want our children to have. Generation X venerates and protects its children more fiercely than ever: we adore and respect the sanctity of their moment (after all we have tried to hang on to our own childhoods for as long as possible), and we play with our kids on a flat hierarchy. They are our friends, our equals.

As we crest the middle of our lives, we now have the conscience, the insight – it is our turn to fix the world. But, like children, childlike, we didn't have plans – how could we when the world has changed so much? Most of us would never have imagined the jobs we do now when we left school, and the chances are those same jobs won't exist in ten years' time – we will be doing ones that are currently unimaginable, ones that haven't even been invented yet.

The rising spectre of artificial intelligence is also emerging as a challenge. Doom-mongers threaten a world where there are no jobs, where machines will perform the functions of workers and our children will be left floating or 'useless', as the historian Yuval Noah Harari has it. Translators, designers, doctors: in as little as 40 years' time the need for humans in these professions may be almost gone. How do we prepare our kids for this? They will need to be resilient, super-adaptable. They will have to know how to find their passion, how to be happy, how to flourish in an economy where they may have no function.

'Actually I think it might be a rather utopian future,' says Tom Hodgkinson. 'Everyone will need a citizen's income, and will be required to work less. Paying people not to work was the political idea *The Idler* had 25 years ago and one we still adhere to today.' Rather than strapping a virtual reality headset to our face to pass the time, perhaps we can all study Aristotle and the ukulele instead.

Still, while our generation may not have had much of a plan, that has opened us up to spontaneity – we are ready for newness and change. A few years ago my parents joined my husband and our young family on our summer holiday. I had heard about a little train that went up a nearby mountain – it was locally quite celebrated. I suggested one morning that we should take this train, and so we drove to the station and boarded. It was indeed a glorious ascent, the Pyrenees soaked in August sunshine, and the dramatic peaks and crags appeared suddenly as we rounded each vertiginous corner.

We arrived at the top exhilarated. 'What are we going to do now?' asked my dad. I had no idea, but clearly we were in some hilltop village, so my husband loaded the baby into its pram and we wandered off to find a restaurant. Eventually we found one with some tables spilling out on to the street and we ordered the local rosé. It turned out to be a lovely afternoon. Several months later my dad pointed out that that was pretty much my approach in life. Take a trip and see what happens when you get there. Not his style at all, but one he could see had its benefits – as it had that day. What he didn't say was: what if the restaurants had been full, or there had been no restaurants, or the wine had been awful? Then where would we have been?

But how can you make a plan until you know where you are going? With no predetermined outcomes you keep yourself open to opportunities, you are able to be nimble, spontaneous, reactive. This keeps you looking outward, looking up. I wonder now, though, if the lack of a plan might be problematic. I wonder if this next phase of our life might need more vision, more structure.

Perhaps our love of irony is a clue here. Cool, which we have been obsessed with all our lives, can only come with a healthy dose of irony, the ability to stand back and observe, dispassionately. Postmodernism, which we have so enthusiastically embraced, maintains that there is no high and low culture, only culture. You can play lawn bowls ironically and enjoy it just the same. Art is graffiti and it is classicism, great music is the Pet Shop Boys as much as it is Elgar. Irony has stopped us facing up to reality, because we are not really doing it, we are doing it ironically.

Well, now we are. The world feels a much more serious place and no one we trust is in charge. It's time we made a plan.

So let's:

1. *Invest in Millennials and our kids – they are the future*. The love and devotion we pin on the next generation means that in everything we do we are paying it forward. Unlike Boomers, who expected life chances to improve, we can see that this is

not going to be the case. The houses are gone, universities cost money, maybe too much money. The world is splintering, peace is precarious. Our environment is in peril, our climate is changing. We may not have spearheaded any huge causes, but actually we practise low-key activism every day in every choice we make. We need to acknowledge now that whatever we do, however small, will lay the ground for those after us. Our kids might not own their own houses – but what can we do for our grandkids?

2. *Age enthusiastically.* Age should not wither us, but encourage us: we've got to live it large as the clock is ticking. As the finishing line hoves into sight (hopefully still a long way off), that should give us more incentive to embrace every part of life as much as we can.

3. *We are experience junkies – let's use that.* Let's live life in the moment, be exploratory and open-minded. Anxiety, like guilt, is a useless emotion. A waste of time. Next!

4. *Recover liberalism.* We own it, it's a good thing, let's champion it – louder. A world where extreme views are violently pitted against each other cannot be a happy place. Inclusivity, multiculturalism, tolerance and peace are the only way forward for an increasingly global society. We must listen to everyone and ensure that the fruits of success are shared equally. Executive salaries need to bear a relation to the workforce that enables them. Opposing voices need to listen to and understand each other.

5. *Be authentic.* I'm sorry, but that is not a hipster word, it is a Generation X value. Social media profiles are not authentic, living through social media is not healthy and nor is it real. We crafted our identities by going places, physically, to experience them. We chose tribes and dressed, talked and behaved like we belonged. We actually did it – we do it – in real time, face to face. Now we are older we don't need to pretend to be

part of something we are not – we don't have to pretend to be posh, or working class, or fashionable if we are not or we don't want to be. We recognise who we are now – and we know we are cool because it is the real thing, we have spent our lifetime crafting it. That conviction should drive us. As progress accelerates beyond our control, it is important that we can view change for what it is, distinguish the good from the bad, sort through the different shades of grey. Not everything in the name of progress is good and we should call that out as and when we see it. We know what's cool and what is not cool.

6. *Step on it*. We are driven, perhaps by the power Thatcher instilled in us. We have already experienced the ultimate power of dismantling a country and putting it back together again. Millennials might be inheriting it, but we did the legwork. Leaning in is an exhausting idea, but we have to refine our lives in a way that gives us the most personal pleasure at the same time as contributing to the world in the way each of us sees fit. This requires strategy, a plan.

7. *Look up*. There is nothing more profoundly depressing than the sight of kids wondering around the streets like zombies, their noses in their Pokémon Go apps. Raise your eyes and check out the views. It's pretty magnificent.

And finally … a word on joy. It appears to have been forgotten. If there was one thing rave culture taught us, it is that you can throw your hands in the air like you just don't care, and it is ecstasy. For a moment, for a night, you can turn to the person next to you, whoever they are, you can smile and you can feel the purity of happiness. That right there, my friends, is the reason to be alive. You can spread it to your neighbour on the dancefloor, you can show it to your child, you can smile at your boss, you can share it with your friends, you can comfort your parents with it too. Life is long and holds many terrors, but actually what are we here for, in this incredibly short space of time, if not to enjoy ourselves, marvel at the world and each other, see as much of it as we can and hand it on to our children.

In the words of Alex James, 'Are we just going to carry on wearing skinny jeans and going mental at festivals until we're 80? I fucking hope so.'

Appendix

June Sarpong

June was born in Walthamstow in 1977 to Ghanaian parents. After a car crash as a teenager that left her hospitalised for a year, she built a career as a presenter for Kiss, MTV, Channel 4 and latterly for Sky with the current-affairs chat show *The Pledge*, and ITV, where she is a panellist on *Loose Women*. She is a lifelong Labour supporter, and campaigns to get more kids involved in politics.

Three favourite brands?
1. Apple, because they make amazing products and are a brilliantly run business. But then you think – what could they be doing in the world with all that money they've got? So my next nomination is:
2. Warby Parker, who make cool, beautiful glasses. But when you buy a pair they train somebody in the developing world to become a mobile optician and then give them a kit to sell the glasses. It provides training, jobs and sexy glasses. It's a great model.
3. God, the brand of love. No bigger brand than that.

Three objects you can't live without?
Lipgloss, a push-up bra and green juice.

What were you wearing in 1991?
Fluorescent leggings. Still love to wear them now (though perhaps not the fluoro).

Who did you admire in 1991?
Oprah Winfrey. A smart businesswoman who has heart and humanity. And Margaret Thatcher. I like strong women, even if I don't agree with them.

What was fun for you in 1991?
Partying, my life revolved around it.

What is fun for you now?
Surprisingly for a city girl who grew up in a concrete jungle, I like hiking and spending time with nature.

What do you want to change about the world?
I want a more equal society.

Are you still cool?
I still am in the know about young people. I know it because I'm genuinely engaged with them.

Tom Aikens
Tom was born in 1970, and grew up in Norfolk. He is a 'crazy, passionate chef', who careers between his restaurants, which are now on several continents. He has two young daughters, Violette and Josephine, with his partner Justine. There's always a sour-dough in his fridge.

Three favourite brands?
1. Oxo, because my mum used to use it on a Sunday with roast chicken.

2. Rolos. I grew up next to the Rowntree Mackintosh factory; there's something about their soft caramel centre.
3. Converse: I've worn them from the age of 20. You can wear them with a suit or jeans, put them in the washing machine when they get dirty and they only cost £30. And they're cool.

Three objects you can't live without?
1. A kitchen steel I bought at a fleamarket in Paris when I was 24. It can sharpen anything and everything.
2. My mobile gym.
3. My Apple laptop. I have everything on it, all my recipes, all my photos. I burst into tears when I thought I'd wiped it.

What did you look like in 1991?
I had a terrible hairstyle, bleached and permed. I wore horrific pale jeans, which I would team with some insane tie.

Who did you admire in 1991?
Pierre Koffman, because he was a brute, but fun with it.

Who do you admire now?
People that go beyond what you think is humanly possible. Marathon Man is a guy who has run a marathon every day for a year. He's a postman, but he's done it to get recognised. Which he did: he got sponsorship from Lucozade and now holds the record for running the longest distance ever – 380 miles non-stop without going to sleep for four days.

What was fun for you in 1991?
Going on holiday to Praia da Luz in Portugal. Parties, windsurfing and lots of nice girls.

What is fun for you now?
Making gingerbread with my daughters. And Ibiza.

Richard Reed

Richard's first business was Two Men Went to Mow: a lawn-mowing service in his hometown Wakefield that charged £2.50 an hour. After a spell in advertising he launched Innocent Smoothies with his two best friends, which they eventually sold to Coca-Cola. He now runs JamJar Investments, which he runs as a not-for-profit, investing his fortune in everything from an insomnia app to a subscription shaving service. He also writes books and has impeccable taste in music.

Three favourite brands?
Innocent (obviously), Greenpeace and Pacha.

Three objects you can't live without?
My iPhone, despite years of persevering and resisting with a BlackBerry. A wok, because it's bloke cooking – you can do it quickly, easily and in one wash-up. And my belt. At my age you need a bit of flexibility around the girth.

What was fun for you in 1991?
Music, clubbing and dancing.

What is fun for you now?
Group holidays.

What were you wearing in 1991?
A grey marl T-shirt and anything from Diesel.

What do you like wearing now?
A grey marl T-shirt and skinny black jeans.

Who did you admire in 1991?
Anita Roddick, because she showed business could have a purpose. And Prince.

Who do you admire now?
Alexander McQueen. I went to see his exhibition and discovered the line, 'He hoped his clothes would make people a little bit scared of the women who wore them.' All fashion tries to make you look attractive to the opposite sex – how disempowering that actually is. What McQueen did was empower women.

What do you want to change about the world?
Inequality. Everyone is born with same amount of talent and work ethic, but not with the same opportunity to succeed. Access to opportunity is what makes people successful.

Are you still cool?
Do skinny black jeans count?

Pearl Lowe

Pearl was born in 1970 in Bethnal Green and has been a singer, songwriter, fashion and textile designer, model, author, stylist, interiors expert, TV presenter and spiritual lobbyist. She fled the Primrose Hill set in 2005 and now lives a bohemian life where she combines all her skills with a rail season ticket from Somerset to London. She once took her husband to Champneys after a particularly long party and almost killed him by leaving him wrapped in seaweed in a sauna.

Three favourite brands?
Chanel, Dolce & Gabbana, Zara.

What were you wearing in 1991?
White Levi's, vest tops, Gucci loafers.

What do you like wearing now?
Pencil skirts and shirts. I'm going for the power suit over vintage dresses these days.

What three things could you not live without?
Nurofen, reading glasses and my diary.

What music were you listening to in 1991?
Nirvana and the Pixies.

What music are you listening to now?
Elliott Smith, Neil Young and Hope Sandoval.

What did you want to change about the world in 1991?
I used to get really upset about the treatment of animals. All the big cosmetic companies were testing on animals. It made me so angry.

What do you want to change about the world now?
The school system. It's unfair people have to pay to have a good education and not everyone has access to that. All schools should be free.

Danny Goffey

Danny was born in Oxford in 1974 and got his first set of drums from his parents when he was ten years old. He formed the band Supergrass after being expelled from school. He had his first son, Alfie, with Pearl at 21, then went on to have another, Frankie, and a daughter Betty. He now fronts the band Vangoffey. He is a committed cook (once reaching the semi-finals of

Celebrity Masterchef) and has perfected the art of sticking a beer can up a roasting chicken's bum.

Three favourite brands?
YouTube, Waitrose, old Volvos.

What were you wearing in 1991?
Velvet suits, glitter, women's clothes.

What do you like wearing now?
Breton tops, cheesecloth and cardigans.

What music were you listening to in 1991?
I was 17 and really into the Manchester scene. Stone Roses, Happy Mondays, Inspiral Carpets. Active 8 by Altern 8 was out the summer I hit the rave scene really hard – one glorious early Nineties summer, I forget which. Songs like this spun around our tiny brains as we danced about with strangers.

What music are you listening to now?
Nick Cave, Ian Dury, Talking Heads. Radio 6 & 4. I also spend a lot of time listening to my children's needs.

What did you do for fun in 1991?
Illegal raves around the south of England. Five boys in an old red Ford Fiesta looking for convoys to join and arriving in strange fields full of eclectic young people. Marvellous fun. I was also playing in a band with my brother called the Jennifers. Early experience of the toilet tour pubs.

What do you do for fun now?
Writing words and music for Vangoffey. Cooking for friends and then eating and drinking with them. Watching the football. Helping my kids realise their dreams.

Karen Blackett

Karen grew up in Reading, in 'mini Barbados', the daughter of West Indian immigrants who taught her 'You're black and you're female, so you have to try twice as hard.' She had a pension at 20 ('I'm so sad') and a flat at 22. Fascinated by psychology and human behaviour, she went into advertising and is now chairwoman of MediaCom, the country's largest and most successful media agency. She has a son Isaac, who is five.

Three favourite brands?
Net-a-Porter (before children), The Outnet (after children). Also love Not on The High Street and Michael Kors.

Three objects you treasure most?
A framed photo of myself and my son; two paintings by Heidi Berger (a German artist who lives in Barbados); a Monies bracelet.

What music were you listening to in 1991?
The Roots, De La Soul, Jackson 5 and N.W.A.

What music are you listening to now?
The Roots, Ed Sheeran, Lauryn Hill, Beyoncé.

What were you wearing in 1991?
A tracksuit, as I was always doing sport.

What do you like wearing now?
Now? If at work, heels and a colourful dress. If at home, leggings and a Sweaty Betty top.

What did you do for fun in 1991?
The student union and clubbing.

What is fun now?
Time with my son: horseriding, surfing, watching *Star Wars*.

Who did you admire in 1991?
Nelson Mandela, Oprah, Sir Trevor McDonald, Daley Thompson, Sir Garfield Sobers.

Who do you admire now?
Hasn't changed. But also includes Mo Farah, Jessica Ennis, Malala Yousafzai.

What do you want to change about the world now?
I want to champion this country's creative industries on a wider platform, and champion diversity for the fruit salad of thinking it delivers.

Sum up Generation X?
Thoughtful, empowered, dynamic, hungry for more.

Alex James
Alex grew up in Bournemouth, then moved to London when he won a place at Goldsmiths College. There he met Graham Coxon and later Damon Albarn; the three formed the band Blur, which went on to dominate the Nineties Britpop scene. After writing his memoir about their rollercoaster ride through fame and excess, Alex moved to Oxfordshire, where he took up farm-

ing and cheesemaking. He is still just as skinny, tall and cool, and smokes just as many cigarettes. Specialist subjects: his award-winning Goddess cheese, astronomy and space travel. He is also the only rock star who has managed to successfully land a call sign on Mars.

What are your three favourite brands?
Oxford University; KPM (vintage library music label); sunny Bournemouth.

What three objects can you not live without?
Guitar; 2 Group cappuccino machine; sharp knife.

What were you wearing in 1991?
Deptford Market chic; charity-shop razzle dazzle.

What are you wearing now?
Skinny jeans, ancient baggy T-shirt, high tops.

What music were you listening to in 1991?
Pixies, Prince, Kirsty MacColl.

What music are you listening to now?
Rossini, Prince, Major Lazer.

What did you do for fun in 1991?
Hot knives, magic mushrooms, Long Island Iced Tea with orange juice. Went out for breakfast, looked at the moon through a telescope.

What now?
Bonfires, naps, go out for dinner, try to get a handle on the Riemann hypothesis, play murder in the dark with the kids.

Who did you admire in 1991?
Jeffrey Bernard, Albert Camus, André Gide, Kim Deal, Des
Lynam.

Who do you admire now?
Prince Philip, Lee Child, Arthur Conan Doyle, Florence Welch,
Fearne Cotton.

What did you want to change about the world in 1991?
I just wanted to mess around.

What do you want to change about the world now?
I probably spend more time trying to preserve things that I care
about than trying to make things different.

Define Generation X:
Anyone smoking in the back of a 747 on the way to NYC with
no luggage.

Matt Roberts

The chiselled, Action Man figure of personal trainer Matt
Roberts can often be seen jogging in St James's Park alongside
one of his celebrity clients, from David Cameron to Elle
Macpherson. A contender for Olympic sprinting, he dropped
out of training when he realised his partner Darren Campbell
was probably going to be better than him and set up his fitness
brand instead.

Three favourite brands?
Apple, Porsche (because I'm a sad car person) and Tom Ford
(for his unashamedly ambitious belief in his own image).

What were you wearing in 1991?
Levi 501s; Grolsch bottletops on my Dockers; Paisley shirts.

What do you like wearing now?
Zadig, Boss, Prada.

What was fun for you in 1991?
The Hacienda in Manchester. I was training back then, so I was always the driver.

What is fun for you now?
Travel, my kids and cooking curry: I'm a glory cooker.

Who do you admire?
Bill Gates. I spent a small amount of time with him; he was super-humble, interesting.

Objects you can't live without?
My phone – my whole life is on there. And my tennis racket.

Serena Rees

Serena graduated from club kid to entrepreneur via Agent Provocateur, the erotic fashion brand she founded with her then husband, Joe Corré, son of Vivienne Westwood. Joe and Serena met in 1992, and grew AP into a brand that spanned 13 countries with over 30 stores. They sold it in 2007. Serena now advises and invests in new business. She has a teenage daughter, Cora, and is the partner of former Clash bassist Paul Simonon.

Who did you admire in 1991?
Vivienne Westwood, John Galliano, Alaïa. But I didn't want to be anyone else, I just wanted to be myself.

And now?
As above.

What brands do you admire?
Apple, Absolutely Fabulous.

What did you want to change about the world then?
To be heard, to change people's attitude, to make the world a better place.

And now?
To be heard, to change people's attitude, to make the world a better place.

What objects do you treasure?
Photographs, my art and book collection, all the strange objects I've collected on the way.

What music did you love in 1991?
Rock 'n' roll, punk, Sixties girl bands, Bowie, the Stones.

Now?
I still love them all!

What did you want to change about the world in 1991, and what now?
I admire everyone who has managed to do what I wanted to do then: to be heard, to change people's attitude, to make the world a better place.

Jamie East

Jamie grew up in Derby and had his first taste of celebrity with the band the Beekeepers, making the top five of the Indie charts and the front page of the *Derby Evening Telegraph*. Then he got a job doing overnight shifts as a graphics operator at Sky News, 'my first experience of miserable graft'. There he learned to code and pick up celebrity gossip, which led him to launch holymoly. com, a blindingly irreverent celebrity gossip site he eventually sold to Endemol. He is now a radio presenter for Virgin and the *Sun*'s film critic.

Favourite brands?

I wallow in the smugness of my brand loyalty. The removal of choice is a wonderful thing, it's a luxury not to have to worry about what you put on every day. A guy finds the perfect white T-shirt and now he can spend more time thinking about the things that matter. For me it's Nudie Jeans, Oliver Sweeney shoes, American Apparel T-shirts, the motorbike brand Deus Ex Machina – and Brylcreem, because it's served me right, man and boy.

Who did you admire in 1991?

Michael Hutchence. He was sleeping with Kylie on ecstasy: when you are 17 you think, 'That would be quite a phone call home.'

Who do you admire now?

My eldest son. He is 22 and getting on with it. Like me, he was slightly above average at school, never going to make uni, knew it was up to him just to get on with it. All his mates are just leaving uni now and he's already earning £30k in a job at an e-gaming company he really loves. That's as good as it gets.

What did you want to change about the world in 1991?
The welfare state so I could be in a band and sign on.

What do you want to change about the world now?
Invent a bullshit filter. I'd like to get rid of all the people slowing progress down. There should be compulsory retirement at 55.

John Vial

John was plucked from obscurity in Derby to join the Vidal Sassoon apprenticeship programme in Manchester in 1991. 'I had arrived. At that point, you couldn't speak to me because I was just too fucking fabulous.' And he was. Within five years he had become creative director, working on fashion shows and shoots around the world. From city power women to the A-list, editors to top models, his scissors have become the one-stop confessional shop for those seeking identity, security, glamour and style.

Three favourite brands?
Apple, obviously. Coca-Cola, because it has never lost its way. Disney, because it is as important to kids now as it was when it was founded. I'm 47 and I still love Disney.

Three favourite objects?
My Hermès watch, bought with the money my mum left me when she passed away. My scooter, because without it I would have left London by now. Can't stand the Tube, and sitting in a car in London I lose the will to live. And my dog Max, the most handsome Siberian husky on the planet.

What did you do for fun in 1991?
A club in Derby called Blue Note. I never drank, always drove.

What do you do for fun now?
YouTube. I start out looking for the Bay City Rollers and end up watching a nature documentary about jaguars. I get lost on it for hours.

What music were you listening to in 1991?
All the Manchester bands – the Charlatans, Happy Mondays, Stone Roses.

What music are you listening to now?
Everything from Mahler to Rihanna.

What did you look like in 1991?
I had a mid-length bob that made me look like an Eighties rent boy, and wore super-flared jeans with shirts with extraordinarily large collars.

What do you look like now?
I wear my hair cropped and have had it transplanted three times. Always painful, always worth it. And I have a uniform of a black, navy or charcoal jumper with black jeans, a Hermès belt and Church's brogues.

Who did you admire in 1991?
Vidal Sassoon and my mum. She tried to teach me what other people were thinking, to think about how to be fair and be a decent human being. She was the only person I was scared of in the world.

Who do you admire now?
1. Still my mum, even though she's dead. Still scared of her too – she'd be appalled at some of the things I do. (Sorry, Geraldine.)

2. Pat McGrath for the way she's built her brand.
3. Louise Wilson, the great St Martin's teacher who left such an incredible fashion legacy.
4. Zaha Hadid who was an iconoclast. She really changed the way we look at things.

What did you want to change about the world then and now?
Same thing: less fighting. There's no need for it.

Martha Lane Fox

Martha was born in 1973, the daughter of the academic Robin Lane Fox, and educated at Westminster School and Oxford University. 'I'm really lucky, I've had every opportunity.' But she didn't waste it: she co-founded lastminute.com, survived the dotcom crash, sold it, then shortly afterwards survived a car crash that broke 28 bones in her body. Now she chairs the government's digital skills charity Go On UK, sits in the House of Lords and runs the business Doteveryone. She also sits on the board of Marks & Spencer and Twitter, has a penchant for Topshop shoes and has just had twin boys with her partner Chris. 'All my friends thought I was nuts having anything to do with technology.'

What are your three favourite brands?
Hmmm – I'm not very good at brands but they range from massive, as in Mozilla (the maker of the Firefox browser that 'fights to keep the internet a global public resource open and accessible to all'), to small, as in Persephone Books (fiction and non-fiction by women, for women, about women).

What three objects can you not live without?
My smartphone, a novel and the custom insoles that balance out my fucked-up legs and help me walk!

What were you wearing in 1991?
I can hardly bear to think about it but red, 14-hole DMs, black jeans and (don't judge me) a frilly Adam Ant in 'Prince Charming' video-style white shirt.

What music were you listening to in 1991?
Groove Armada, Van Morrison and Jimi Hendrix.

What music are you listening to now?
Roberta Flack, Broken Bells, and Toots and the Maytals.

What did you do for fun in 1991?
Hard house parties in our really gross university student home.

What now?
Hard house parties in my awesome London home.

Who did you admire in 1991?
William Godwin, the father of philosophical anarchism.

Who do you admire now?
Ali Smith, the writer.

What did you learn in the recovery from the car crash?
When you've had a bad thing happen, one of the things people want you to say is 'the accident made me think about my life in a completely different way.' It didn't at all. It just reinforced the things I'd always thought were important, which is your friends and your family, and wanting to get on with every minute to try to make things as better as you can.

What did you want to change about the world in 1991?
The criminal justice system. I wrote to people in prison when I was at school and one of the people I wrote to killed themselves. I went to their funeral – it was one of the most surreal things I've ever done.

What do you want to change about the world now?
A fairer and better society because of more imaginative uses of the internet.

Define Generation X:
Lucky.

Ben Elliot

Ben went to Eton and Bristol University but his greatest influence was his uncle Mark Shand (brother of Camilla Parker Bowles), an environmentalist and traveller who inspired him to do good and be brave. He is CEO of the luxury concierge company Quintessentially, and has also produced films, run political campaigns and lobbied for social change. He puts most of his energy into the Quintessentially Foundation, a philanthropic venture. He is married with two young sons.

What did you want to change the most about the world in 1991?
Social injustice.

And now?
Social injustice.

How do you define us as a generation?
We're quite serious. Responsible. Even though we might enjoy partying, we wanted to do stuff. I think that we will be a thoughtful, caring, educated generation.

What are your favourite brands?
Adidas. Have loved them since I was a child and they seem to have grown as I've grown. The BBC. It educates me and indulges me in my great passion, cricket. And Badger Beer – it's the brewery from where I'm from.

What three objects are you never without?
The watch that was my grandfather's and the necklace that was my uncle's. And my iPhone.

What was fun for you in 1991?
I was 16, listening to late Chicago house, getting pissed with my mates.

Now?
My children would have to be involved. Family and friends, by the seaside or on a cricket pitch.

Who did you admire back in 1991?
Nelson Mandela. Ronald Reagan for being a marvellous leader.

Now?
The Prince of Wales, because he espouses so many things our generation cares about and talked about them way before anybody else did. What he says now is no different from what he was saying 30 years ago, but now people listen.

Are you still cool?
I'm married to a woman 13 years younger than I am and she occasionally hints I've still got it. I think I've still got some moves.

Thomasina Miers

Thomasina says she 'screwed up' her education and spent years drifting between modelling, running a market stall, financial PR and accountancy. She eventually met the chef Clarissa Dickson Wright, who told her that if she loved food then that is what she should do, and sent her off to Ireland on a cooking course. In 2005 she won *Masterchef*, shortly after she opened her first Mexican restaurant, Wahaca.

What music were you listening to in 1991?
Snoop Dogg, MC Solaar, hip hop, acid jazz – anything at Brixton Academy or Subterranea.

What music are you listening to now?
Pink Floyd, Fleetwood Mac, Vangelis – my parents' classics. My Spotify list also has Sufjan Stevens and Nick Mulvey.

What were you wearing in 1991?
Vintage. My grandmother was a model and I inherited all her wardrobe. I got really cross when vintage became cool as all the prices went up.

What do you like wearing now?
Matches is my weakness.

What was fun for you then?
I danced all the time, and cooked. I had a tiny flat – my flatmate was the head chef at the River Cafe – so we filled it with friends who sat around on boxes eating. And yoga; I did a lot of yoga.

And now?
I don't dance as much as I'd like to – I'll change that.

What is your favourite brand?
The Soil Association, because it really matters.

Who do you admire?
Alexander McQueen because he was an outsider, a rebel. And Amy Winehouse. Both of them were individuals who refused to be beaten down into the mass. The ones that won't fit in – they are the true heroes.

Your favourite objects?
My grandmother's Nina Ricci Fifties bikini. I have worn it so much the elastic is completely knackered. She's also got an amazing bowler hat I put flowers on. My pestle and mortar.

Who do you admire?
Women who did stuff and brought change – Prue Leith, she set up prison and school food revolutions. Rosie Boycott, a woman who goes out there and shouts for the things that matter. Deborah Curtis – her charity is entirely about creative learning for children.

Are you still cool?
When I go out with a six-month bump I still wear hot pants and mini-skirts. If I go out shopping for maternity clothes I invariably come out with sparkly pants, I can't help it.

Define Generation X:
Defiant, reckless and somewhat blind.

Kris Thykier

Kris started out in the film industry running for his hero, the director Jeremy Thomas. He was diverted during the Nineties by Matthew Freud when he worked for his PR business, representing everyone from Bono to Geri Halliwell. He eventually left and set up a film production company where he has produced such hits as *Kick-Ass* and *Harry Brown*. He is married to the TV presenter Claudia Winkleman, has three kids and is currently working on a TV series with Neil Jordan.

Three favourite brands?
Apple, for the relationship they have with their customers – I wouldn't know how to use a PC now. Disney, because it has bought all the great movie brands: Pixar, *Star Wars*, Marvel.

What was fun for you in 1991?
I like lunching. I've lunched professionally my whole career and I missed by a week the point where it was okay to drink at lunch. We may have partied hard as a generation – but I don't remember people drinking at lunchtime.

And fun now?
I've just discovered dancing. I was filming in Azerbaijan where it's customary to have big dinners and dance. As I was the film producer I would have to get up and start the dancing, otherwise it would be rude. It takes a lot to get me dancing – I have spent my entire life avoiding it. At 43 years old I've just discovered I enjoy dancing.

What did you wear in 1991?
I've always liked wearing suits. You can get dressed in three seconds. Easy.

Are you still cool?
It was my cool that stopped me from dancing. I suppose my cool is I really like people. I still get excited by meeting new people and hearing what they have to say. That's the bit I would hate to lose: a sense of wonder about the new.

Define Generation X:
Emotionally engaged and worryingly directionless.

Emma Gannon

Emma is my token Millennial: she aced her career by being the person at Unilever who built the Dove Facebook following up to 12 million. It was her first job out of uni, she was 21. She has been pretty much able to pick and choose since then, but reserves her passion for her blog girllostinthecity. She recently wrote a memoir, *Ctrl Alt Delete*, about a girl growing up online. She is always online, and says things like 'Work is life and life is work.'

Three favourite brands?
1. Facebook, because Mark Zuckerberg has pledged to give away all his money.
2. Apple, because my Mac makes me feel that's all I need to create something and be innovative. It fires me up for my day.
3. Airbnb, because it is an amazing, unique service and doesn't make too much noise. They are a quietly confident brand that don't have to spell it out.

What did you do for fun in 1991?
Poo in my nappy, probably.

What do you do for fun now?
Go on a city break.

What did you wear in 1991?
I seem to remember some brown cord dungarees.

What do you wear now?
Brown cord dungarees. Vintage.

What music did you listen to then?
Nursery rhymes.

What music do you listen to now?
Eighties – Toto, Fleetwood Mac, Phil Collins.

Who did you admire in 1991?
My little sister who had just been born.

And now?
Oprah. She's got money, she's spiritually happy, she's got a good squad around her and she has a family.

What did you want to change about the world in 1991?
More chocolate-flavoured baby food.

And now?
People to be more in control of their lives, and that goes across the board, from women facing oppression in third world countries to feeling good about yourself on a stressful day.

Acknowledgements

There are so many confidantes and a lifetime of friends and chance encounters that have fed into this book. But the biggest debt of all goes to the people who I got to work with at *Style*, such a creative, funny, fearless bunch that have an outstanding passion for life. To all of you: thank you, and YASSSS!

Then to all the fascinating people who allowed me to pin them down to talk about this book: Tom Aikens, Anton Bilton, Karen Blackett, Claudia Croft, Henry Dimbleby, Jamie East, Ben Elliot, Elaine Foran, Emma Gannon, Danny Goffey, William Higham, Tom Hodgkinson, Nicky Holloway, Alex James, Martha Lane Fox, Pearl Lowe, Thomasina Miers, Isabel Oakeshott, Richard O'Connor, Danny Rampling, Richard Reed, Serena Rees, Annabel Rivkin, Matt Roberts, Louis de Rohan, June Sarpong, Miranda Sawyer, Alice Temperley, Kris Thykier, Amelia Troubridge, Sue Unerman, John Vial, Ruby Warrington, Josh Wood and the man himself, Douglas Coupland. You were all so candid, every conversation was a joy.

To Jessie Brinton, Kate Spicer and Eleanor Mills, who are my sounding boards about most things. To Lindsay Baker for the read-through and excellent feedback.

To The Girls: we've lived it, and I wouldn't want to have done a second of it with anyone else.

To the HarperCollins team, who have provided me with an experience akin to taking a flight in first class, with Seat A1 on the ticket. In particular Kate Elton for getting it straight away, and Natalie Jerome for moulding it so cleverly.

Finally to my beloved parents. You are my greatest teachers, I owe you everything.

And Will. The best choice I ever made.